A Pilot's Memoir

Bob Kline

Blue Yonder Publishing ✪ Forest Hills, New York

Fasten Your Seatbelt: A Pilot's Memoir

Bob Kline

Blue Yonder Publishing
150 Greenway Terrace Suite 53W
Forest Hills, New York 11375

Reach the author by e-mail at BobKline9@aol.com

First edition

ISBN: 978-0-615-18835-5

LCCN: 2008921317

Manufactured in the United States of America

12   11   10   09   08   5   4   3   2   1

Design and composition: www.dmargulis.com

*T*HIS BOOK IS for Jovanna, Jacee, and Jeffrey. I never told them why I sometimes came home a little grumpy or preoccupied.

CONTENTS

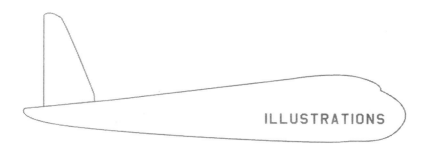

ILLUSTRATIONS

HEN I BEGAN flying to far away places, I often returned to the States with a pocketful of the unspent foreign coins I had collected during my trip. I decided to put them in a chest I'd carved that I named The Treasure Chest. When the bottom of the chest was covered with coins and it was truly becoming a treasure chest, I began actively accumulating the coins of the countries I visited. It was especially interesting to add coins from countries not on the typical tourist routes. After years of throwing the coins into the treasure chest, I eventually filled it up about three-quarters full. It probably weighed twenty pounds.

One day, when friends were visiting, their twelve-year-old son asked me if he could look at the closed chest. He had no idea of the treasure inside. When he saw the mass of coins, he immediately began asking questions, while he played with the francs, shekels, shillings, and marks. I was attempting to answer his questions about some of the coins and at the same time maintain an adult conversation with his parents. When I realized that his parents were also very much interested in the coins and the associated tales, the adult conversation ceased and I told pilot stories for the remainder of the afternoon. It also gave me a great idea. From then on, when children visited me, I showed them the treasure chest and let them run their hands through the coins. I explained to them that I was a pilot and flew all over the world—and that I had plenty of stories to tell. I then asked them to close their eyes and pick a coin out of the chest that would be theirs to keep. We looked at the coin and decided what country it came from; then I told them a story about why I flew to that country and a little about what had occurred there. I took out an atlas to show them where the coin came from and gave my visitors a short history or geography lesson.

Talking about my experiences was a treat for me: the kids loved it, and surprisingly enough, I realized that the parents liked the stories even better than the kids did. This was especially true if the father was about my age and, from the time he was a child himself, he thought he would like to become a pilot. This was not uncommon with men my age, because we grew up during the same time aviation was growing up; and we all drew pictures of World War II fighter planes instead of doing our grade school lessons. When I was a young child, passengers did not fly across the ocean; it was not until many years later that there were nonstop passenger flights across the Atlantic.

This book is the continuation of those afternoon sessions of telling stories. It contains some history and geography, but mainly it's a book about aviation. The stories are all true to the best of my recollection, and when taken as a whole they are a memoir of my lifetime in the cockpit.

ACKNOWLEDGMENTS

WANT TO THANK Helenmarie Hohman and Ellen Lemley for their proofreading and positive comments when the book was in its early stages. On a daily basis, I relied on my wife, Jovanna, to decide whether a sentence needed a comma or a semi-colon, or if it had a dangling modifier— whatever that is. I appreciate her command of the language and thank her for making my job much easier. I want to give a pat on the back to my editor, Dick Margulis, who was far more to me than just an editor. He performed the dozen or more steps required to turn my 118,000 words into a published book, and he did it with a smile. He probably learned a little bit about aviation, and I learned an enormous amount about turning words into a book. Kathy Rapp digitized the photos. Sharyn Mathews ably proofread the final pages.

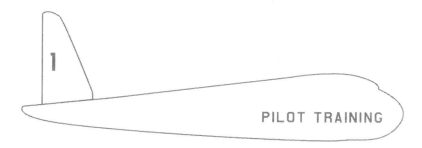

N 1960, IT cost the Air Force one million dollars to train a pilot. I was thrilled when I was accepted into the pilot training program; and I promised myself that I would overcome all obstacles, graduate, and get my wings. I was the poorest kid from a poor town, who was about to be given an enormous quantity of free education, and I was determined to take full advantage of it. Only in my early twenties, I had no inkling that I was taking my first step toward a lifelong career that would take me around the world. Pilot training was the beginning of my forty years in the cockpit, which ended when I landed a giant Boeing 747 with over four hundred passengers. This is the story of my hours of boredom and my moments of terror, from when I was a skinny kid who stuttered to my dual retirement as an Air Force colonel and a TWA pilot.

Hawk and Gator were the two sections, or flights, that made up Class 61E at Graham Air Base, near Marianna, Florida, an Air Force pilot training base. I was assigned to Hawk Flight. During my first day of training, the flight commander told us that at the end of six months, the midpoint of the training, only half of us would still be in the program; the remainder would wash out for various reasons. He got it wrong: there were fewer than half of us remaining. Clifford Berry, my first instructor, was assigned three students: Evanoff was Hawk 46, I was Hawk 47, and Barrickman was Hawk 48. After six months I was the only one of the three of us who was still in the program. Evanoff was killed in an accident, and Barrickman decided that pilot training was not for him; he quit voluntarily.

We flew five days a week and had the weekends off. One of the best sources of entertainment during a nice weekend was at the beach in Panama City, Florida, which was about an hour and a half from the base by car. The road was a typical two-lane country road through the small Florida scrub pine trees, a few very small towns, and what came to be called Evanoff's intersection by all of the student pilots. About halfway to Panama City, along the north–south road, there was an intersection with a local bar and grill on one corner, and, kitty-corner across the intersection, the scar in the trees where Hawk 46 was killed. We were flying the Cessna T-37 and were just a few months into the program. We had fewer than a hundred hours of flying time but were gaining confidence and feeling comfortable taking the small jet aircraft on a solo flight. It was a dangerous period for any student pilot who allowed a macho, cocky, I-can-do-anything attitude interfere with his common sense.

On a Sunday, Evanoff was on his way back from the beach at Panama City when he stopped at that bar, which was full of redneck beer drinkers. He was only about twenty years old and couldn't resist bragging that he was a jet pilot. It was only fifteen years after the end of the Second World War and about ten years after the jet engine began to replace the reciprocating engine; jets were the hottest thing in aviation. When he announced that he was a jet pilot, especially since he was just a kid, the beer drinkers taunted him, telling him to prove it. Evanoff told them he would be back the next day in a jet and would give them a show they would never forget.

We were just beginning to learn basic aerobatics, the precision maneuvers required of military pilots that teach a student to feel comfortable being inverted or pointed straight up or down. The easiest maneuver to learn was the aileron roll. All that was required was to push the stick fully to one side, which activated the ailerons on the wings and caused the plane to roll 360 degrees in about two seconds. When done correctly, which comes with experience, the plane loses very little altitude. It happens so rapidly that the most difficult part of the maneuver is stopping the roll when the wings are once again level with the horizon, right side up. Evanoff made a very low, high speed pass over the bar and attempted an aileron roll, just like you see in the movies. With so little flight time, he did not have the skill to accomplish the maneuver. He flew into the ground, inverted, within sight of any of the beer drinkers who were watching. He stuck to his promise: he returned the next day in a T-37. And they will never forget.

He was not the only pilot to do something really stupid during pilot training. It was the day after I'd flown my first solo flight, the initial hurdle for a beginning pilot; and I had only ten hours of flight time. Price was the only student in Hawk Flight who had any previous flying time. He had a private pilot's license, and he was the first in the class to solo. He did it with only seven hours of supervised flight time. We all gave him our congratulations, accompanied by the traditional cold shower. The next day, it was my turn to solo, which caught me completely by surprise.

We began our flight training in the single engine Beechcraft T-34, a propeller-driven, tandem-seat trainer. My seat was in the front and Cliff, my instructor, sat behind me. He flew with each of us every day for about an hour. On the day of my solo, I was the first student to fly. Usually, we flew to a few thousand feet and practiced some of the many maneuvers we were expected to learn; that day, however, Cliff and I just stayed in the traffic pattern while I shot touch-and-go landings. A touch-and-go is a practice landing; after touchdown, instead of stopping the aircraft, the pilot adds power and takes off again, which saves the time it takes to taxi back to the end of the runway for the next takeoff. When Cliff was confident that I was capable of flying the plane by myself, he told me to make a full-stop landing and then taxi back for another takeoff. When we reached the end of the runway, he opened the canopy, and before stepping out onto the wing and leaving me alone in the cockpit, he instructed me to make three landings. It was my turn to solo! I was going to fly an aircraft, by myself, for the first time.

The three landings were a piece of cake. I had cleared the first major hurdle toward becoming a pilot and had accomplished the task with only eight hours of flying time. The following day, I was assigned my own aircraft and was told to practice any of the maneuvers I had learned, gaining the confidence that comes with making all of the decisions by myself. Cliff briefed me to fly south about thirty miles to the vicinity of Round Lake, where he liked to take his new students. Flying to the same location every day made it easier for student pilots to find their way back to the base and enter the traffic pattern, a problem for all new pilots.

Round Lake was due south of Graham Air Base, and was easily identified from the air: it was a perfectly circular lake. New students could find it, do their air work, and then fly due north to return to the base. I had also been taught how to tune in a navigation radio at the field, called the VOR, and follow its signal (called flying the needle) back, if I thought I was lost.

For my first solo flight to the practice area, there was a cloud deck above me at about four thousand feet. This was not unusual when the wind was from the south, bringing the moist air up from the Gulf of Mexico. I could occasionally see a hole in the clouds and knew that it was clear above them. I flew around for a while under the clouds, practicing maneuvers called chandelles and lazy eights; because of the clouds, though, I didn't have the space available to practice everything I wanted to do.

When another small hole developed in the clouds and I could see the blue sky above, I decided to fly up through the hole to see what it was like on top of the clouds. I had never flown through a hole before, and I had never been on top of a cloud deck. This was a new experience for me. I added power and pulled the nose up, to fly through the light spot in the clouds; but soon I realized this simple maneuver required more speed. I had misjudged how much speed I would lose just in getting to the base of the clouds and had pulled the nose of the aircraft up too steeply for a sustained climb of a few thousand feet. I backed off my first attempt and started all over again, using my newfound knowledge. On my second attempt, I made it into the slight opening, but not all the way to the top of the clouds. I had, however, gotten close to the top, which was close to six thousand feet; and I could occasionally see enough blue sky to encourage me to fight my way above the clouds. Climbing through that hole scared me a little, but I soon forgot those feelings when I experienced the beauty and peace up there. The sun was bright and it was like being on top of a fluffy bed of cotton.

Twenty years later, flying for TWA, I had the opportunity to carry a passenger who had recently lost her teenage son to one of the childhood cancers. She was not flying anywhere in particular, but wanted to experience what it was like to "walk on the clouds with the angels," which was what her son had said about his feelings of facing death. A TWA flight manager introduced her and told us that she had been waiting for a few days for perfect cloud conditions; this was the day, and we were the crew. After takeoff, we were to fly through the overcast sky and then level off immediately after breaking through the clouds into the bright sun, skimming the tops of the clouds. I hope that our simple flight maneuver provided some comfort and closure for her.

But flying through the clouds and leveling off on top with a TWA passenger jet, for a crew with thousands of hours of flight time, the highest pilot's licenses and instrument ratings, plus the approval of Air Traffic Control, is different from doing it as a student pilot with only ten hours of flight time.

I hadn't the slightest clue as to what to do next. I practiced a sloppy chandelle and a lazy eight, but I soon realized that I needed—but didn't have—references on the ground to perform the maneuvers. After about five minutes above the clouds, I looked around at my flight conditions and, for the first time, recognized that I had no idea where I was or which way to turn to get back to Round Lake. From horizon to horizon, all I could see below me was the cloud deck. I tried looking for a thin spot in the clouds to fly down through, so I could return to familiar territory; but I could not find any part of the undercast that looked like a hole. I had no idea how I was going to descend through the clouds.

I still wanted to practice one more maneuver, the only one I had learned and had not yet tried—a spin. I had learned to enter a spin intentionally and to recover from the corkscrew flight path if I found myself in one inadvertently. So I combined my two dilemmas into one by deciding to spin the T-34 down through the clouds. I entered a practice spin above the clouds and recovered about two thousand feet lower, when I could see the ground below the clouds. This was the most dangerous and second dumbest thing I have ever done. The dumbest thing was to brag about it to my instructor and the other students. I was naïve enough to tell Cliff, and the other students at my table, about the thrilling day I'd had. Cliff let me know that if I ever pulled a stunt like that again it would be my last flight. I was too inexperienced even to know that I had done something that was a violation of the regulations, was a violation of common sense, and could have killed me. My career as a pilot might have ceased with only ten hours of flight time; I could either have been killed or washed out of the program.

Somehow, I lived through my six months of primary pilot training. Learning to become a pilot took thousands of unsure baby steps, but they all came together over the years.

I was newly married and lived in town, ten minutes from the base; I car-pooled to work with three other married students. Five days a week we would fly for half of the day and have academics the other half, alternating morning and afternoon every other week. We used to wear our flight suits to work when we were on the morning flight schedule. The flight suit was a green-gray, baggy, long-sleeved set of coveralls designed for fire protection. The material wouldn't melt into your skin during a fire as many types of clothing would. In later years, DuPont developed Nomex, which was a superior high temperature material; eventually, all flight suits were made of Nomex.

The coveralls had many pockets, which I filled with all of the equipment I needed for the flight. We didn't use a briefcase. The most interesting pocket was on the thigh of the right leg. It was designed to hold an open knife with a blade in the shape of the letter J; the knife was attached to the pocket with six feet of tough cord. The pilot was to use the open blade to cut certain parachute risers during the descent, in the event of an emergency that required ejection from the plane. I was instructed that if I was wildly swinging in the chute, I should cut the four red-dyed risers that went to the rear of the canopy. I always wondered if I would have the guts to reach over my head with the knife and actually cut four risers that were supporting me during my descent. Later parachutes were redesigned to eliminate the swinging problem and the cut was no longer required.

At one time in my military career I had the additional job of squadron safety officer. We were not allowed to wear rings when flying, even our wedding rings; and one of my duties was to ensure that no one working around the aircraft wore one. Wearing one around electrical equipment could cause a short circuit, and getting one caught somewhere could cause a more serious problem. I had some photographs that I showed to anyone I saw wearing a ring on the flight line. The photos were taken after a maintenance man fell out of the wheel well of an aircraft and his wedding ring hooked on a rivet on his way down. The photos showed his finger, with the ring still attached, hanging from the rivet; attached to the amputated finger was the eight inches of tendon that separated from his forearm. One picture is worth a thousand words, and it worked for me: I never wore a ring until I retired from aviation.

To protect my face and head, I wore a fitted helmet with a tinted visor that pulled down to cover the top half of my face and served as my sunglasses. During an ejection, the visor would serve as protection from the windblast, which could be a few hundred miles per hour. It would also protect my face from the debris in the cockpit when the canopy blew off and when I separated from the ejection seat. If a parachute landing were in trees or some place just as unpleasant, then, too, I would need the face and head protection.

Attached to the helmet was my high altitude best friend, my oxygen mask, which I wore all the time. My visor covered the top half of my face and mated with my oxygen mask, which covered the bottom half of my face. When I wore my helmet and oxygen mask and had my visor down, my head was completely enclosed within a protective bubble. I was required to wear high black boots and thin leather gloves anytime I flew. The only part of my body that was not covered with material that would protect me from a flash fire was the back of my neck, so I always kept the collar on my flying suit turned up.

Each of us was sized and fitted with our own parachute, which was stored in a special room in the flight shack, along with our helmets and oxygen masks. Depending on which type of aircraft I was flying, I had either a parachute that I sat on (a seat chute) or a back chute. The parachute replaced the bottom or back cushion of the ejection seat. As with the oxygen masks, the parachutes were inspected and repacked by specialists. The Air Force was providing us with the best safety equipment that was available in 1960.

Hawk Flight had a few foreign students from friendly countries. They were to receive their wings, as I was, upon completion of the training.

Ali sat at my table for about a month when the class began to shrink, because of students flunking out or quitting, so I knew him better than the other foreign students. His father was a general stationed in Washington, a member of the diplomatic corps from Iran. The Shah of Iran was in power and the United States and Iran had very good diplomatic relations; certainly not like today.

About a month into the program, everyone in the class had soloed, except Ali. He already had about twenty-five hours of flying time when they placed him at my table, with Cliff as his new instructor. He was moved because his father had made a phone call to the commander claiming that his son was not doing well because of the poor instructor to whom he had been assigned. A student had to exhibit a minimum skill level before flying without an instructor in the aircraft to correct his mistakes, and Ali had not reached that stage. A few more days passed without Cliff authorizing Ali to fly his initial solo. One morning, as soon as we completed our flight briefing, Ali announced to Cliff and everyone else in the area, "I am going to solo today." I could see that Cliff was as confused by the statement as I was, until Ali continued that he was embarrassed to be the only student in the entire class who had not soloed. He said, "If I do not solo today I am going to kill myself, but because it's the instructor's fault, not mine, I am going to shoot Mr. Berry before I shoot myself." I could not determine if he was serious about the threat, and I could tell that Cliff was also confused. The bottom line is that Ali soloed that day, way behind the rest of the class. Eventually, he progressed from the propeller-driven T-34 to the jet T-37.

The Cessna T-37, because it was a twin-engine jet aircraft, was safe for beginning pilots. The aircraft flew pretty well with only one operating engine. What the pilot had to do if an engine failed was to increase the power on the good engine and ensure that the landing gear and wing flaps were retracted, to reduce the drag. These procedures were in an emergency checklist that we had to memorize for immediate action. Frequently, Cliff would pull one of the throttles to idle power and say, "engine failure," to get us accustomed to performing the checklist items and flying with only one engine. I never had an engine failure during pilot training, but Ali did. His engine failure occurred on final approach, a minute or two from landing. Ali was incapable of analyzing his conditions; instead, he accomplished his memorized procedure for an engine failure, which included raising the landing gear and wing flaps. He was just seconds from landing, and any rational student pilot would have realized that raising the landing gear just before landing was a major mistake. With the landing gear

The author climbing into a Lockheed T-33 during pilot training. Note the parachute, which becomes his seat cushion and fits into the ejection seat, hanging from his back.

Cessna T-37

retracted, Ali landed on the belly of the aircraft and skidded off the side of the runway.

When the plane stopped, he was uninjured; he exited the plane by himself. Usually, in a situation like this, the emergency rescue crew finds the pilot either in the cockpit, injured and unable to get out, or a hundred yards away, on the chance the fuel might explode. Not Ali; he was sitting on the left wing, smoking a cigarette.

Ali ought to have been removed from the program after that accident; but once again he was rescued by his father, the Iranian general. Ali continued his training in the class behind mine.

Over the years I have trained pilots from Iran, Egypt, Turkey, and Saudi Arabia. I've found they did not have the technical mindset that US pilots have, and they did not analyze their problems the same way. We used to joke that while the American students were raised tinkering with old cars, the foreign students were riding their camels in the desert. Ali was a camel driver; he destroyed an airplane.

The initial screening process for pilot training was rigorous, both mentally and physically. The Air Force was looking for the cream of American youth and the screening was the first step in separating that cream. I had a degree in aeronautical engineering, which gave me a great technical background and trained me to effectively solve problems. I recall that the written exams placed great emphasis on analyzing spatial orientation problems, a way of evaluating a candidate's piloting aptitude. This was right up my alley; it seemed to me that I had been training for this type of exam all of my life; so I scored well. I also took an extensive physical exam, far more thorough than any I had taken before. Being a military pilot demands extreme physical fitness, and this was the time to start separating those with weak eyes, weak medical history, or weak anything else. And you had to be the right size to fit into a cramped military cockpit. Those who were not the correct height or who had the wrong belt size were eliminated.

Primary pilot training in 1960 was conducted by civilian contractors, using mostly civilian instructors. Cliff Berry, my only instructor during those six months, was a tall civilian, about forty years old. He owned his own airplane and had been in aviation his entire life. He was an excellent instructor and a gentleman, but there was no question who was in charge when we flew together.

Aerobatics training began early in the syllabus, to get us accustomed to pulling high g's and being in unusual positions relative to the ground. The g stands for the force gravity exerts on us at sea level, and we constantly pull one g. When we accelerate or decelerate, as in an elevator, we feel increased or decreased g's. In a maneuvering aircraft, accelerating in various directions, the increase in g's sometimes overstresses our fragile human bodies. Loops, Immelmans, and the split S are flown at four g's. I soon learned the effect that four g's had on me, and this eliminated my need to constantly monitor the g meter during the maneuver. I would start losing peripheral vision at four g's. When I could see straight ahead, but lost my side vision, I knew that I was performing the maneuver correctly: it was like looking down a gun barrel, and the effect is called gun barrel vision. If I continued to increase the g's, I would first totally lose my vision and then I would lose consciousness. I would regain both vision and consciousness almost instantly when the acceleration was reduced.

Most of my primary pilot training was in a small twin-engine jet built by Cessna, the T-37. I flew in the left seat and Cliff had the right seat; I could watch his actions. I could tell through his body language if he approved of my maneuvers even before he made a comment. We wore helmets and oxygen masks. We almost always had our visors down, so it was impossible to see his face. But after months of flying together, just the slump of his shoulders or how close his gloved hand was to the stick or throttle would indicate to me how I was doing.

I always relied on his judgment when we flew together and never questioned his decisions. The training was designed to teach me two things: first, how to control the aircraft; and second—and most important—how to make the best decisions, which is the most difficult part of a pilot's job. I was on a solo flight in a T-37 when I realized I was having a fuel problem. The fuel tanks were in the wings, and the fuel had to be burned equally from each wing to keep the aircraft balanced. I discovered that I could not get any fuel from my right wing tank and could not solve the problem. My only concern at the time was to land before I ran the left wing tank out of fuel, and that's what I did.

I was having such a great time flying solo that I didn't want to land early. I never considered that with my right wing full of fuel and the left wing almost empty, the T-37 was so unbalanced that I might be incapable of controlling the aircraft. At higher speeds the flight controls provide plenty of force to maneuver the aircraft, and I had no control problem. My problem occurred when I had to slow down to land. I realized on final approach, at my slowest speed, that the control stick was at the full left limit, touching my left knee. Another few minutes of solo flying, creating greater imbalance between the wings, and I would not have had enough aileron response to fly in a straight line. I would have been in a situation critical enough to cause me to eject. This time I was smart. I wrote up the malfunction in the aircraft logbook, to be repaired before the next flight, and never mentioned it to my instructor. I didn't consider the possible implications of my bad decision until years later.

Stalls and spins were taught right from the very beginning of the program and resulted in the most horrifying experience I had during the year I was in pilot training.

An airplane flies only if it has forward motion, which means airflow over the wings. An aircraft stays in the air because the wings produce the required amount of force, or lift, to keep it from falling. When the lift is not sufficient to support the weight of the aircraft, we say it stalls. That means it's in an aerodynamic stall condition; it doesn't mean the engine stops running, as it does when your car stalls. If the pilot doesn't take corrective action, the plane usually enters a spin, which means it follows a corkscrew path downward toward the ground. In pilot training, we learned to enter into and recover from a spin; and I performed this maneuver, under controlled conditions, until Cliff felt that I was proficient. Then, when by myself, if I inadvertently entered a spin, I would be able to recover. But even under the best of conditions, with my instructor in the right seat, things happened.

The T-37 was a wonderful pilot training aircraft, but the initial design had undesirable spin characteristics. The problem was supposedly corrected when the Cessna engineers placed a two-inch-wide strip of aluminum extending along each side of the nose of the plane. This changed the airflow around the forward section, thereby making it safe to have student pilots spin the plane. A practice spin began at approximately twenty thousand feet (about four miles) up. Normally you would lose a few thousand feet during the recovery. If you were unable to recover from the spin, our instructions were to eject at ten thousand feet.

When the jet engine was perfected, and speed and altitude increased, the old method of bailing out during an emergency was no longer adequate, so the ejection seat was developed. This allows the pilot to be shot away from the aircraft during an emergency and not be struck by the tail of the aircraft or pinned in the cockpit because of the g forces.

We each had our own parachute fitted to us, and this became part of our seat when we strapped in or, in pilot argot, "strapped on" the airplane. Once you pulled the safety pin with the long red streamer, you were sitting in a cannon capable of shooting you a hundred feet into the air. Ejection is an automatic process, once the pilot initiates it, and begins with raising the armrests and pulling the trigger in either of them. The shoulder harness locks you into position to minimize injury; the Plexiglas canopy blows off with a separation charge; and then the cannon shells shoot your seat, with you in it, out of the cockpit. If you are unconscious after the ejection, you automatically separate from your seat and your parachute opens at ten thousand feet, lowering you safely to the ground—if you're lucky.

We had certain maneuvers we performed at high altitude, and if the weather was clear, we would frequently spin back down to a lower altitude in order not to waste time flying a normal descent. One day we had just finished our high-altitude work, and Cliff said over the intercom the usual: "Okay, Kline, let's see if you still know how to recover from a spin." There was a series of steps that I had to accomplish. The first was to clear the area—look for other planes below me to ensure that we did not hit another aircraft on the way down. The cockpit was a bubble on the top of the aircraft, which means that I could not see anything directly below me—exactly where we were going to be after I entered the spin. To check for other planes under me, I rolled left to a nearly inverted position and searched for other planes, then rolled to the right side to search the sky again, before announcing through the intercom that the area was clear. I was at twenty-one thousand feet when I started to stall the aircraft by closing the throttles while maintaining my altitude. Without sufficient power from the now idle engines, the airspeed dropped. I was prepared for the buffeting and high control forces as we approached the stall. When I was deeply into the stall, just before losing control of my rudder, ailerons, and elevator, but still maintaining altitude, I applied full left rudder and pulled the stick full aft.

As soon as I applied left rudder and up elevator, we entered the spin. The nose pitched down and we began the corkscrew motion to the left. Because of the disorienting effect of spinning rapidly, it may be difficult for a pilot to determine the direction of the spin. An inadvertent spin can happen at night or in the clouds, with no visual references;

or you may be spinning inverted (flying upside down, with the ground spiraling up to meet the top of your head), which would be extremely confusing. I confirmed to Cliff that we were spinning left, which is exactly what I intended to do by applying left rudder during the entry. It was difficult to speak through the intercom because of the g forces and the disorientation, but I had experienced the sensation before and was expecting it.

Once we were established in the spin, I neutralized the controls and let the spin stabilize for a few rapid turns before I applied full right rudder against the spin to begin the recovery. We were probably still at about eighteen or nineteen thousand feet, but descending rapidly. A few seconds after applying the right rudder, the rotation slowed and the aircraft started to buffet, exactly what I was looking for. This was my clue to push the stick full forward to get the aircraft to recover to a steep nose-down attitude and stop spinning. I pushed the stick all the way to the forward stop—but nothing happened. We were still spinning.

This was the first time that I had been in a spin and had not recovered on the first attempt; rapidly, I reviewed my procedures to make sure that I hadn't skipped a step. Cliff was all business now. He began to talk me through the maneuver in a calm but firm tone of voice to ensure that we recovered the second time. He ordered, "Full left rudder and up elevator," to go through the entire spin procedure once again. What began as a routine maneuver was rapidly transitioning toward an ejection and loss of the aircraft. Plus our own lives were at stake. I pushed that rudder pedal as hard as I could, all the way to the end of its travel; simultaneously, I yanked back on the stick. I checked our altitude: we were passing seventeen thousand feet; we had lost four thousand feet and were just beginning our second attempt at recovering.

A few weeks before, in the flight shack, Cliff had talked about ejecting. He made the comment that he didn't think that he could eject without his kneecaps hitting something on the way out of the cockpit, either the instrument panel or the top of the windscreen where it mated with the overhead canopy. He was the tallest of all the instructors and had just met the limit for height, but he thought that he was too large. There were two fifty-caliber shells that fired the pilot and the seat out of the aircraft during the ejection process, and if his knees hit something on the way out of the aircraft he would incur a serious injury. I am sure that this was going through his mind as we began our second attempt to recover.

Failing to recover from a spin during the first attempt, for no known reason, is what aviation experts call an anomaly. I did everything correctly, but we were still spinning, and we were starting to follow the only guidance we had on this anomaly, which was to do it again. Cliff let me continue to manipulate the controls while he gave firm orders as to when to accomplish each task, just as he had done the first time we ever did a spin. He never demonstrated a maneuver the first time; instead, he would allow me to stumble through, with him also on the controls, to keep me out of serious trouble. I remember the first time I had ever been at the controls for takeoff. I had only been in an aircraft a few times before in my life, certainly never in the pilot seat. We were at the end of the runway and he said, "Let's go!" I hesitated, not knowing what to do, he said: "Come on, Kline, there are other planes waiting; push the throttle up and let's get out of here."

I trusted him then, things somehow worked out, and we made it off the ground. Now was not the time to lose my faith in his piloting ability.

I went through the entire spin procedure for the second time, with his guidance, but still we did not recover. I was thinking that this couldn't be happening to me. We were at thirteen thousand feet, still spinning, and I was very concerned that his next order would be for me to eject. He then said, "I got it," which was a great relief because he was taking control of the aircraft and relieving me of the responsibility for recovering.

When my hands were free of the controls, I began to prepare for ejecting. We had been spinning for a mile and a half and I knew that we only had one more attempt at recovering. Immediately, I pulled down my visor completely to ensure that it was locked down, sat back into the seat cushion to protect my back, and placed my head firmly against the headrest; then I placed my hands on the ejection seat handles. I was uncomfortable from the continuous spiraling but I was still thinking clearly and was fully capable of functioning. With Cliff now in control, I had time to review my ejection procedures. I had been in an ejection seat training device where an instructor had watched all of my actions and I now felt confident that I remembered enough of what I had been taught to have a successful ejection.

Cliff began one final attempt at recovering the aircraft. This was it: now or never. I'm positive that he was preparing for an ejection, just as I was, and I wonder if it crossed his mind for a split second that if he survived that he might never walk again if his knees did not clear the aircraft, as he had predicted. In my forty years in the cockpit, I never saw anyone move the controls more rapidly; I would even call it violently. The result was just as violent. When he slammed the stick full forward after going through the rudder maneuvers, thereby applying immediate full down elevator, I think we tumbled tail over nose, and found ourselves inverted, heading nose down. At least we were no longer spinning, and the altitude was eight thousand feet; ample altitude to recover to level flight. We had gone right through our ten thousand foot mandatory eject altitude, but I hadn't even noticed.

All Cliff Berry ever said about the incident was, "I've had enough fun for one day, Kline. You have the aircraft. Take us home." That evening and a number of times afterward, I mentally reviewed what had occurred. It was like I had taped the entire spin and was now able to replay the tape. I'm convinced that we recovered on the third attempt because the atmosphere at lower altitudes has a greater density than at high altitudes, which translates to a more effective response from the flight controls. The second thing that I considered was how close I had come—inadvertently—to ejecting myself. When we passed thirteen thousand feet and Cliff took control of the plane, I had placed my hands on the ejection handles, preparing to begin the ejection process. When we recovered, with that violent swapping of ends, we pulled strong negative g forces. The force yanked my hands off the ejection handles and slammed them into the cockpit Plexiglas over my head. If I had a firm grip on the ejection controls, instead of a loose grip, I would have accomplished step one of triggering the cannon shells, which was raising the armrests. I could also visualize that I might have squeezed one of the triggers at the same time, as my hands flew, uncontrollably, over my head. To this day, I feel that I was very close to ejecting myself inadvertently, because of the unexpected negative g force encountered during the spin recovery.

For weeks after the two-and-a-half mile straight-down ride, I would wake up at night and replay the spin, in real time. Then I would lie awake and wonder if I was doing the right thing by continuing to stay in the pilot training program. All I had to do was march into the commander's office and tell him that I wanted to quit; that I didn't want to become a pilot; and then I would revert to my old, safe position as an officer in aircraft maintenance. Students were getting out of the program all the time and it would have been the easiest thing for me to do. After a great deal of soul searching, I decided that I would not quit, that I had promised myself that I would get my wings if I was able to do so, and that I would put the spin behind me and move on. Over the next decades there were dozens of times that I had to put something behind me and move on. I guess that comes with being a professional pilot.

Training lasted a year—six months each for primary and basic. I had my pilot's wings. Then I attended advanced training, which prepared me to fly an operational aircraft and to be assigned to a squadron. I was still an inexperienced kid, a long way from being a real pilot.

The Air Force has three levels of pilots. When I was awarded my wings, I was called a pilot. When I had seven years in the cockpit, I became a senior pilot, analogous to a master's degree. When I had fifteen years as a pilot and three thousand hours of flight time, I received my command pilot's wings, the rough equivalent of a PhD. All of those years and thousands of hours in the air gave me an inner sense of what it really means to be an experienced pilot. I now look back on some of the incredibly stupid things I did as a new pilot and am thankful I survived. As the saying goes, there are old pilots, and there are bold pilots, but there are no old, bold pilots. I had dozens of friends and acquaintances who never lived to be old pilots.

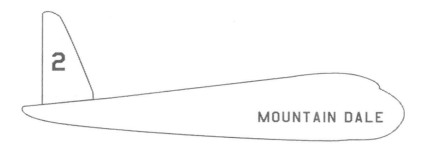

PILOTS GROW UP in every part of the country, from isolated rural farms to the centers of the largest cities. I'm the only professional pilot my hometown ever produced: my town was different.

When I was born, my father, William, went through the village of Mountain Dale, New York, proudly telling everyone, "It's a man-child!" It was Columbus Day, October 12, 1937. He called all of the three hundred people who lived in town by their first name, and he considered everyone his friend. There were no house numbers and street names; our address was Post Office Box 143. If you wanted to know where we lived, you parked at the only traffic light and asked the first person you saw. They didn't give you directions, they pointed at my house.

My father was born to Orthodox Jewish parents who immigrated to the United States from Lithuania over a hundred years ago. They bought a farm in the eastern part of Brooklyn, somewhere in the vicinity of what is now John F. Kennedy International Airport. When my dad was seven years old, they sold the farm and decided to try their fortune in the new

Jewish area that was forming in the southern foothills of the Catskill Mountains. They traveled the hundred or so miles from the farm in Brooklyn to Mountain Dale in a wagon pulled by two horses. My grandfather, Abraham, originally bought a farm but soon sold it and moved his family into town, where he opened a butcher shop.

The population of the town was increasing rapidly with the influx of Jews from New York City; at the same time, it was developing into a summer resort with hotels and bungalows for working class city families. My grandfather passed away when he was about sixty-five. He lived in New York State all of his adult life, ran the butcher shop, and never spoke a word of English; his language was Yiddish. I grew up next door to my grandparents, but because we spoke different languages, I never spoke one word to them. I would get a pat on the head or a few pennies as a present, and sometimes a two-line poem that rhymed in Yiddish—Roite hunt / A fennig a funt—and translated to Little red dog / A penny a pound. It referred to my curly, bright auburn hair—my trademark. The town was probably eighty percent Jewish in the mid-twentieth century, when I was growing up. There were no black families living in town (or Negroes, as we'd have called them then); and there weren't any other racial minorities, such as Asians or Hispanics. It's only in looking back on my childhood that I realize how unusual it was to grow up Jewish in a small town and not be in a minority.

I started first grade a month before I was five years old. The school required a minimum number of students to remain open, and the year I began first grade was the year the town ran out of kids. To keep all twelve grades from being bused to the next town, I was placed in the first grade. They were short one student, and I was "it": the oldest child in town not already enrolled in school.

The school was eventually closed, and twelve years later, I was graduated from the combined school for the area, Fallsburgh Central. I had completed all of my formal education one or two years younger than my classmates. That head start also resulted in my commissioning as a second lieutenant in the Air Force, and having one hundred people working for me before I was twenty-one. I was the "Old Man" then, but I was too young to have a beer in the State of Florida, where I was stationed.

Growing up in this small, remote town, I did what most kids did during those years. We played basketball and baseball; and we spent many hours playing stoop ball, a game that New York City kids of that era played. I owe the agility and hand-eye coordination I still have to playing ball as a kid, especially stoop ball.

I fished in the brook behind my house every day when the weather was nice. During the winter months, I trapped fur-bearing animals and sold the pelts. My father had a trap line when he was a kid, and I inherited a dozen of his No. 1 jump traps.

Every day after school I would check the traps; and on the rare occasion that I caught something of value, I would spend weeks preparing the pelt for sale. The next step was to mail the dried muskrat or raccoon pelt to the Taylor Fur Company in St. Louis, Missouri; they would grade the pelt and mail a check to me for my efforts. My earnings were usually about $2.50 a pelt, which worked out to about ten cents an hour.

About fifteen years ago, I was walking in downtown St. Louis when I noticed the name of the original establishment above the door of a restored building: Taylor Fur Company. That transported me back forty-five years to the Mountain Dale post office. I was waiting there for the mail to be sorted, constantly checking my family's box for the envelope from the St. Louis Company that contained my earnings.

Mountain Dale has severe winters for that part of the country. Its elevation, just under two thousand feet, combined with its location in relation to the higher mountains to the north, causes a lot of snow. The winter of 1953 was so bad that the skunks that normally lived in the surrounding woods moved into town to feed on garbage. We were overrun with skunks. You couldn't take a walk in the evening without seeing one; and of course, if they felt threatened, they defended themselves with their spray. For weeks, the town had a persistent, pungent, skunk odor. I can testify that all of the remedies for removing the smell, if you've been the victim of a direct spray, are nothing more than old wives' tales. The odor stays with you for days and then gradually fades away, but the memory fades more slowly.

That year, Fallsburgh Central High School had a good basketball team, in spite of being one of the smaller schools in the league. I attended as many of the Friday night basketball games as I could, and was a regular on the school bus that transported the fans to the away games. The game at Kingston occurred when the skunk invasion was at its worst. It was not only the town that smelled of the skunks; the odor had permeated my skin, hair, and clothing; it was impossible to remove. I sat in the back of the bus all by myself, and no one was within ten feet of me in the bleachers of the crowded gymnasium. The odor was not only persistent but also offensive. It was recently tested as a crowd control agent, but I could have saved them the cost of the test.

I didn't get the eau de skunk just by walking around town in the evening. Patty Michaels was the only policeman and also the unofficial mayor and elder statesman in town. He approached me to see what I could do about trapping the skunks, and he told me that I would be a hero if I saved the town. I hesitated until he mentioned that I would get paid three dollars for every skunk I trapped. I trapped twenty-two skunks in a few days, never got paid my money (shame on you, Patty), and to this day will not even drive over a dead skunk on the road for fear of getting the smell on my tires. The entire episode was worth all the humiliation, however, because I, Bob Kline, saved the town; at least in my eyes.

In the early 1950s, when I was a young teenager, Mountain Dale was a thriving summer resort for New York City middle class Jews. The winter population was a few hundred; the summer population was about ten thousand. The town had maybe fifty bungalow colonies, rooming houses, and small hotels. The southern Catskills, home to several large summer resorts, was nicknamed the Borscht Belt. The resorts provided entertainment of all sorts for their guests and they were thus the venues where many young comedians, singers, and musicians honed their craft on the way to becoming nationally known performers. The area developed into a resort because of its cool summer climate. It was a way to beat the city heat for the summer, not spend a fortune, and still be within a few hours' drive of Brooklyn or the Lower East Side. The normal routine was for a city family to rent, depending on their economic status, a bungalow, a room at a resort, or a bedroom in a rooming house that had cooking privileges in a community kitchen, from the fourth of July until Labor Day. The wife and children would stay the entire summer. The husband would work during the week in New York City and travel to the mountains on Friday nights, returning to the city—and the work week—on Sunday nights. The commuting husbands took the Short Line bus service or the Ontario & Western passenger train; or he drove the old Route 17, which was a hundred-mile drive and went through the main street of every town. Driving was only for those who were brave enough and had the stamina for a five-hour, one-way trip. These husbands worked all week in the hot city (this was before the days when everyone had air conditioning) and had not seen their wives since the previous Sunday. They were ready to play as soon as they reached their weekend getaways, and they responded to the same primitive instinct that a bull in a pasture responds to when a cow is in heat. My dad used to call the train from the city that arrived on Friday evenings, full of working husbands, the bull train.

The entire Catskill resort industry started declining during the second half of the twentieth century. The spread of air conditioning and cheap airfare killed the Borscht Belt. It's largely gone now, although the area remains a rare pocket of rural Judaism in this country.

By the 1950s, some of the original hotels and rooming houses were in a state of disrepair and required complete remodeling, which was not economically practical. Some of the resorts just closed and decayed, although a few were modified for other uses. The majority of the places burned to the ground. It was understandable that a large wooden building, with old electrical wiring, no sprinkling system, and no city water supply for fire hydrants would burn to the ground. What always puzzled me was why they started burning past midnight, when no one was around, soon after Labor Day, when the building was vacant and would not be profitable until the next summer; and all four corners of the building started burning at the same time. I guess, when the insurance companies wrote the check to the owner for the value of the policy, they listed the cause as "fire of unknown origin." Locally, we attributed the fires to "Jewish lightning."

The town had two prominent organizations that a large majority of the population either belonged to or supported. The men belonged to the Mountain Dale Volunteer Fire Department; both my father and my older brother, Bert, have held the position of Fire Chief; the most respected position in town. Dad was always proud that, in the 1930s, he went to the American LaFrance company near, Elmira, New York, to pick up the first fire engine for the town. Years later, when I was in junior high, the town bought a new fire truck, same brand, which was the pride of the county. They also built a beautiful new firehouse with a large meeting hall, the only place in town large enough for a majority of the population to assemble. The truck and building were paid for, partially, with a regular fire department–sponsored bingo game. Bingo put Mountain Dale on the map, attracting a full house not only from the town, but also from the surrounding area. Bingo paid the bills.

The women's organization was Hadassah. This is a Jewish service organization that now builds hospitals and other medical and educational institutions, mostly in Israel; in the late Forties, the local chapter devoted its time and energy exclusively to more basic support of the fledgling Israel.

Israel was desperately in need of financial support, and American Jews collectively felt guilty if they did not support this new country; Hadassah was the medium for this fundraising in town. The fire department had been so successful in raising money with their bingo games that the women of Hadassah petitioned the men to rent the large hall in the firehouse, together with the bingo equipment, so that they could conduct their own bingo fundraising event. The men refused to allow this infringement into their fundraising territory. The women of Hadassah felt that the firehouse was the only meeting place in town; therefore, it was not the exclusive territory of the men and the fire department. Both sides felt their cause was just, and the small town divided into male and female camps; they went to war. The men won the first battle, with signs in the store windows that read "NO BINGO," with an explanation of their position. The Hadassah women won the war with a persuasive campaign that featured a battle cry that would have made Madison Avenue proud. Their slogan was "NO BINGO—NO BANGO," and they withheld their sexual favors from their fire department husbands. The women stuck to their plan: they didn't let their guard down, and they kept their knickers up. They got their bingo; the men of the fire department got their bango; a thousand dollars was donated to Israel; and everybody had smiles on their faces.

We got a lot of snow in Mountain Dale, and the roads were covered with a mixture of sand and snow for the entire winter. Spring was a welcome relief, but when the snow melted the streets were covered in mud. The solution was for the fire department to exercise the pumps on the fire truck and wash the sand into the storm drains that went beneath the town. This was a rite of passage every year, signaling the end of winter. Every spring, the streets were the cleanest they would be all year.

The storm drains emptied into a three-foot-diameter pipe that collected the water from the entire town and became an open stream that ran through my back yard before draining into the brook. This open stream and brook were one of my playgrounds when I was growing up. It was the place where I fished, trapped, shot my BB gun, and spent most of my time, when I was not playing ball. The number of times I fell into the brook—sometimes just to my ankles, but many times at the cost of a thorough drenching—are too numerous to recall. The brook was also the water supply for the town in case of a fire; so the fire department had deepened some areas for water storage, to ensure they would not pump the brook dry. These deep areas became the best fishing holes along the entire brook, and when I got lucky I would provide dinner for my family. It sounds like a wonderful place for a child to grow healthy and strong, doesn't it? But guess what. The storm drains not only collected the runoff from the streets but also were the collection system for the sewer lines that that ran from each house in town. My playground was the town sanitary sewer.

The water supply for the house I grew up in was a shallow, hand dug well about a hundred feet from the intersection of the open sewer and the brook. I'm confident that not only did I play in the open sewer, but I also drank from it through seepage into our six-foot-deep well. Somehow we all survived, though; and as far as I know, no one ever had any serious illness that could be traced to the water supply.

Our house was one of the shabbiest in the town. It consisted of two separate structures that had been placed side by side. The seam was never correct, and there was a two-inch step to get from one side to the other. On the outside, there was an obvious mismatch of the siding. The front third of the building had been a small store, although I remember it only as a vacant room. It had been a pool hall operated by my dad and was later converted to a beauty parlor operated by my mother, all before I was born. The only leftovers of the failed businesses that I can remember were the scoring beads for keeping the score during pool games and a beautician's chair, which was sold when I was a child. My mother, Helen, was a good hair stylist and continued to have one or two customers a day all through my childhood. She moved her small business to our kitchen and a large commercial hair dryer was one of the features of our very small home.

The vacant store in front of the living quarters was the collection area for our junk and empty milk and soda bottles. You had to navigate an S-shaped path through junk in the store to get into the house. There was no light, it was lined with our empty bottles, and over time became an imposing challenge for anyone to visit at night. Each milk bottle had a three-cent deposit, but we didn't return them until the path became non-navigable.

I was normally very respectful during my extra-curricular studies at Hebrew School, but one time I was out of line. Rabbi Feldman followed through on his threat to talk to my parents about my conduct, and he showed up that night, as we were eating supper. He made so much noise knocking over and trying to replace the milk bottles in the dark that we all went to see what was causing such a commotion. He stammered, at last, that he hadn't realized that we were eating and would return another time; he never did, and I was saved the humiliation. God works in mysterious ways.

The most remarkable thing about that house was not the roar of the rain on the rusted tin roof nor the fact that the exterior was bare wood that had never been painted nor that that it was uninsulated but that we lived over the live chicken market, which was in our basement. My grandfather not only sold beef, veal, and lamb but the butcher shop also featured freshly killed kosher chickens. When Abraham passed away, the butcher shop was closed and the building was sold; however, my father kept the live chicken market in our basement as his own. It was never a thriving business, but it did bring in some desperately needed money.

The chicken coop was the old and dilapidated blacksmith shop, which was immediately behind our house. The only thing that remained of the village smithy's shop was the forge along one wall, built of brick and covered with the droppings of many generations of chickens. The chickens roosted in the open rafters, and the droppings, which were never cleaned out, were inches deep on top of all of the horizontal surfaces. I assume that the floor was made of wooden planks, but it was covered so deep with chicken manure that I never saw it.

The chicken market was most active on Wednesdays and Thursdays, so the Jewish housewives could make their traditional Friday night Sabbath dinner: in my house the first course was always chicken soup, the entrée was always boiled chicken. During the summer months, when the resorts were in high gear and business was booming, I often had to assist my father in the market. We had freshly killed, still warm chickens available for the housewives to select from. There were, however, some women who wanted to choose their own live chicken and wait to have it processed, no matter how long it took. The market was a one-man operation, so it usually fell to me to help the customer select a chicken. The two of us would go to the old blacksmith shop where the house-wife invariably spent a minute or so eyeballing the dozens of Rhode Island Reds available to her. Years of experience, coupled, perhaps, with a genetically inherited ability to select the best chicken, made experts of these women. The price was sixty cents a pound, live weight. This weight was with feathers, entrails, and any droppings that were not deposited on me. I guess that would be equivalent to paying about ten dollars a pound in today's dollars, and she was going to get her money's worth.

I quickly learned that the housewife would never accept the first chicken I caught, but would hold it with its wings twisted together to keep it quiet, while I caught the second and third. The first to be snatched, with the chicken hook snagging the foot, was easy, but the squawking and the ruckus stirred up the entire coop. The remaining chickens would then fly out of easy reach, mostly into the rafters, which made catching numbers two and three more difficult. I had to be careful not to injure or bruise the chicken while bringing it down from the high rafters because she was paying for a perfect chicken; an injured one usually became my family's dinner. By the time the number three chicken had its wings twisted for inspection, the coop was a nasty place, with the feathers, dust, and squawking all around. The dust was not what you're probably visualizing; it was thick and composed exclusively of dried and powered chicken droppings, which became airborne when the chickens flew into the rafters. If there were a hundred chickens in the coop, the ammonia-laden dust would be overpowering, requiring that the inspection and selection process be done outdoors. There is nothing like the good, healthy life of a country boy!

The chicken selection process invariably was the same, and I assume it was passed down through generations of Jewish women of European heritage. With wings twisted, she would first feel the six-pound bird's breast for fullness. Second, she would blow away the fine feathers on the underside to check the color: yellow meant a lot of fat. I was raised on chicken fat, a staple of European Jewish cooking. Finally, she would inspect for any minor defect. After making the most demanding decision of the entire week, she would take the bird to the market, while I would look for Rabbi Goldstein, who would slaughter the chicken. In Mountain Dale, the ritual Jewish slaughter was performed by the rabbi to bolster his income. Larger towns would have both a rabbi and a shochet, who would slaughter the animals. There were three live chicken markets in town; the other two were on the opposite side of the village. I had to search for the rabbi in one of the other markets and bring him to our shop, where he would earn his ten cents a chicken. For those few non-Jewish women who wanted a freshly killed bird but did not want to spend the ten cents, we had an old chopping block and meat cleaver so she could do the nasty job herself. Invariably, the non-kosher housewife tried to get me to behead the bird. Invariably, I refused.

The shochet used a knife with a rectangular blade about six inches long and an inch wide, which he would hone once or twice on a stone. Occasionally, he would carefully glide the knife over the end of his left thumbnail, checking for burrs. Next, he would inspect the exterior of the bird for obvious defects. Then, holding the chicken wedged between his left forearm and ribs, he would expose the neck by pulling the head back with his thumb and forefinger and pluck a few feathers off the neck. One forward and aft stroke of the knife, which was in his right hand, would complete the five-second process, and the bird would bleed out, into a collection barrel. After a short time, my father would remove the feathers with a machine, and open the chicken for inspection by the rabbi. He was trained to inspect for indications of disease, and if he did not certify the chicken kosher, we would throw it away and start all over. Very few chickens were diseased and discarded, because my father would inspect for sickly looking birds when he purchased them every week. And of course there was the thousands of years' worth of genetically passed down instinct of the pure-bred Jewish housewife who selected the bird.

The shop had two feather-plucking machines. One removed the majority of the feathers, the large ones; then my father would remove the small, fine feathers with the second machine. The final step was to remove the smallest feathers and hairs by burning them off with the flame of a two-burner propane stove. The entire process took less than a minute. Before they got the machines, my grandparents plucked the chickens by hand. I can remember seeing them sitting in chicken feathers up to their necks. It was the family business, and everyone worked to make it a success.

A description of the property would not be complete without a feel for the most interesting building, the abattoir. To supply beef and sometimes lamb to the butcher shop, we had a slaughterhouse, a large walk-in cooler, and a holding pen for the animals: this was the barn. Before electric refrigeration, ice was used to keep the beef from spoiling; so there was an icehouse near the barn. Ice was hand-cut on Silver Lake during the winter and stored under sawdust, in the icehouse, to be used during the summer. The slaughterhouse was the biggest show in town when it was in operation, drawing dozens of onlookers. If you enjoy going to a hanging, or watching movies rated R for violence, you would probably get a kick out of seeing a three-quarter-ton animal slaughtered and quartered. My recommendation is to continue eating your occasional hamburger and forget the seamy side of how the beef got between the buns.

I hated birthdays. My mother always tried to have a birthday party for me and I always refused to allow it. The last party I had was when I was thirteen and had a Bar Mitzvah celebration. Everyone had a grand time except me; in my eyes, it was a disaster. I had a disagreement with Rabbi Feldman, the Hebrew School teacher, concerning who to invite to the shul. He placed a notice inviting all of the students, and I objected on the grounds that he didn't have to right to do it: inviting the students and friends was my responsibility. He removed the notice, and then I proceeded to invite all of the kids, anyway. I was angry, and I wanted to exert my authority. I won the battle, which was extremely difficult for me, but I lost the war. I needed Rabbi Feldman's support at that difficult time in my life, and I destroyed our excellent relationship, for no logical reason. This tactical error on my part is my predominant memory of what should have been an enjoyable experience.

With my sixteenth birthday approaching, and knowing my feelings about parties in my honor, my mother decided that she would make a surprise party for me. Boy, was I surprised! I was upstairs in the bedroom that I shared with my brother when all the kids in town came storming into the house. When I realized the reason for all of the commotion downstairs, I refused to attend the celebration. There were about fifteen kids in the tiny house; everyone was downstairs and I was refusing to come down. The downstairs living area could not comfortably hold our family, which at the time was four of us, much less all the kids in town. My refusal to march down the stairs ended when the boys came up and dragged me down. They were not to be refused the pleasure of giving me my coming-of-age birthday gift.

Each of the kids had bought me a standard birthday present of a shirt or something else of minimal value or use; however, the boys had an additional gift. I knew something more than the routine party was about to unfold because there was an undercurrent of excitement among the boys. The gift they had planned for me could not be given in the open when the rest of the gifts were unwrapped; they had collectively purchased one condom and gift-wrapped it.

A condom, a rubber as we called it, was not an easy thing for kids to buy in Mountain Dale, New York, in 1953. Condoms were not publicly displayed in the stores as they are now; they were hidden behind the pharmacist's counter, so he could control their distribution. There was only one kind: white latex rubber. No choice of color, no choice of material, no reservoir ends, and certainly no ribs to increase the sensation. I knew very little about condoms and had only a vague idea of why they were needed. Later in life, I did learn a little more; however, at the party I learned a wonderful lesson about human nature when I was handed this special present, in the corner of the room with only the boys around to view the unwrapping.

Mountain Dale had one drug store. The owner, Mr. Joffee, was the pharmacist; and his wife and two daughters all worked in the family business, which consisted of a marble soda fountain in the front of the store and the pharmacist's counter in the rear. I don't remember Mr. Joffee's first name and I cannot remember ever having had a conversation with him other than during a request for an item that he sold; however, I do know that he had a sense of humor and went to great pains to pull off a wonderful practical joke.

A few years ago, I saw a movie that had a scene where a teenage boy goes into the local drug store to buy a condom and has to wait for the counter to clear so no one will hear or witness the event. As soon as he makes his request to the pharmacist, the situation spirals downhill, out of the control of the teenager. All I could think about while watching this episode was Charlie Weiner, the ringleader at my party, waiting for the right time to ask Mr. Joffee for a rubber. I expect that Mr. Joffee had been waiting years for this moment, because normally, a youngster from town would never buy a condom in Mountain Dale; he would travel to the other side of the county where he wasn't known. Mr. Joffee produced a single wrapped package and gave Charlie oral instructions not to open it until it's to be used, because the latex is very thin and it is vacuum packed to keep it from degrading and getting holes. The packaged condom was then gift-wrapped by the boys and presented to me with great fanfare.

I hesitated before opening the gift. When I realized that all of the females, including my mother, were occupied elsewhere, I finally had to see what was causing all of the excitement. I had seen used condoms previously in the open town sewer that flowed behind my house, but the look of this one confused all of us. It looked like a very large, white, unrolled latex condom; however, attached to each side of the open end was a four-foot piece of string. We all guessed that the string was to tie around your waist to prevent it from slipping off. It was years later, when I finally had a little sexual experience, that I figured out what Mr. Joffee had sold to Charlie Weiner. I now know that Mr. Joffee bought this item from a veterinary supply store and may have had it for years, to be used for just this occasion. What I received for my sixteenth birthday gift, from the boys of Mountain Dale, was a device that a dairy farmer would place over a milk cow's teat to keep it clean. We were correct about the use of the string: it was to tie over the back of the milk cow to keep the "condom" from sliding off.

Fast forward to 1967. I'm an Air Force captain, an aircraft commander on the C-130 Hercules. My crew has recently returned to our base in Tennessee from two weeks in Vietnam. After a few days off, we are assigned an eight-hour flight to accomplish a number of requirements to maintain our proficiency. My navigator, Harvey Manekofsky, has a requirement to plan a route to an imaginary drop zone and arrive within

seconds of the scheduled time. This training simulates dropping Army paratroopers behind enemy lines, but without the
complication of the actual drop. Harvey and I are looking at
a chart, deciding on a location for the simulated drop, when
he suggests a small town about fifteen minutes by air from
Mountain Dale.

I convince Harvey to change our destination to Mountain
Dale, and we plan to arrive over the simulated drop area at
five in the afternoon. I phone my mother and tell her that I
will fly over the town at exactly five o'clock and she and dad
are to go outside about ten minutes to five just in case I get
there early. She asks me how will they know what to look for?
I tell her that she will know when she sees my plane. I hadn't
seen my parents for about a year, and I knew that this would
give them a big thrill.

The weather was beautiful: clear sky all the way from Tennessee to our destination close to the New York-Pennsylvania
border. When I was about twenty minutes from the simulated
drop area, I cancelled my instrument clearance with the New
York Air Traffic Control Center; I informed them that I was
going to fly "visual" at low altitude for about thirty minutes
and would contact them later. We were too far away from
Mountain Dale to see it from the air, but we knew exactly
where we were, and Harvey confirmed that we were right
on schedule. I hoped that my parents were just putting on
their jackets and were preparing to go outside. My mother
had difficulty walking, and I knew it would take her a minute
or two to make her way out of the house.

The best landmark in the area was Route 17, a four-lane
divided highway, the major road in the area, which runs
east–west just above the state border. It was easy to find the

horseshoe bend near Wurtsboro, where the road carved its way down one side of the mountain and up the other side. Once I was able to locate something on the ground that was familiar, I told the other crewmembers that I knew where I was and that Keith, the copilot, could stop map reading and devote all of his attention to pointing out obstructions. Harvey continued to direct the aircraft to the village of Woodridge, one minute from our destination, and lined up with our make-believe drop zone: Main Street in Mountain Dale. I had the crew conduct all of the necessary checklists for dropping the simulated paratroopers, with the exception of opening the aircraft jump doors.

We arrived at our initial point, and the one-minute point, right on schedule, just as I expected. Harvey was an Air Force Academy graduate and an outstanding navigator. We were at our simulated drop altitude of one thousand feet above the ground and flying very slowly, 125 knots, when we passed right down the quarter-mile-long Main Street of my hometown. I could see my mother in the middle of the road, waving her arms over her head, and I could almost hear her shouting, "That's my son, that's my Bobby!" She was almost incapable of walking, but I swear that I saw her jumping off the ground in her excitement.

Mountain Dale had high hills immediately north and south of the Main Street, so I decided that I would make another pass at high speed in the opposite direction, to avoid a north–south pass. I climbed about a thousand feet and made a large turn around for a second pass. The turn back took me about five miles from town and I had a little difficulty locating the town a second time because it was hidden in the valley. Once I again located the road leading to the village, I increased speed and flew over Main Street at low altitude and high speed. This was the technique we used to avoid being detected by enemy radar when flying in high-threat areas, and we practiced it all the time.

I was well below the tops of the hills and had briefed the crew to point out any very high television antennas that were still located in town. Cable television was newly available, but many people were still using antennas perched on top of one-hundred-foot high towers to receive the New York City channels, which were transmitted from the top of the Empire State Building, over a hundred miles away. On this pass, I could see the backs of dozens of my old friends and neighbors in the street, all looking for me to fly over again from the same direction as the previous pass. My mother had phoned all of her friends to watch for me and my first pass alerted every-one else that something unusual was occurring. The entire population of the village was in the middle of street.

The low-altitude, high-speed second pass caught them all by surprise and scared a number of people into believing that I was about to crash. It has been forty years since that low-speed pass and it is still the first item of conversation when-ever I see anyone who was in the street that day. The C-130 had four extremely loud, turboprop engines, and I guess I'm lucky that there were no heart attacks among the onlookers from the excitement caused by the loud noise and vibration of the massive piece of machinery, running at high power, only a few hundred feet above them.

After the second pass, and remembering the minor prob-lem I'd had in locating the village after the first pass, I decided to reverse my course, using a precision reversal of direction called a ninety, two-seventy. I had learned this maneuver when flying a search and rescue mission out of the Azores. I was looking for a small aircraft that was crossing the Atlantic, got lost, ran out of fuel, and ditched in the ocean. We never found any trace of the aircraft or the pilot, but I did learn how difficult it was, when we saw something floating in the ocean, to reverse course and locate it a second time for a better look. That was when I learned the precision maneuver used to turn around and fly over the same place.

I climbed up to about one-thousand feet, made the ninety-degree left turn, and was halfway through my two hundred-seventy-degree right turn, searching for some familiar land-mark to guide me back for my third pass, when I glanced straight down and immediately knew exactly where I was. My maneuver had placed me directly above the Monticello Racetrack, and a race was in progress: I saw about eight trotters pulling their sulkies on the backstretch.

The overflight didn't bother the horses, but I did disrupt the small grade school in Mountain Dale, which was right on Main Street. The school principal rang the fire alarm and evacuated all of the students when I flew over. She was sure that I was looking for a place to land, because of an emergency, and was going to use the school playground as my landing area. Little did she know that I would have required fifteen playgrounds placed end to end to even consider it for an emergency landing.

I lived in Mountain Dale until I was almost seventeen, when I left to attend New York University and live in the dormitories on the Bronx campus during the school year. During the summer months, I worked as a busboy or a waiter at one of the numerous resort hotels in the Catskills, where I lived in the quarters for the help. My parents and older brother, Bert, continued to live in town; my younger brother, Harold, like me, left the area. Although I haven't lived there since my teenage years, Mountain Dale, New York, has always been home.

3

MY LIFE AS A TANKER PILOT

AT THE COMPLETION of pilot training, when all of the grades are tallied, each student pilot picks their next assignment in order of class standing. Amid much fanfare, the top student in the class chooses his assignment first, and the bottom man doesn't get a choice: he gets what no one else wants. I was near the top of the class and was the first person to select a multi-engine airplane; the single-engine fighter aircraft were highly sought after, since they were hot and sexy, but they were not for me. I had two criteria: first, I wanted a multi-engine aircraft; and second, I wanted to be stationed somewhere in the Northeast. I had worked very hard to get what I wanted, and it paid off. My assignment, after completion of pilot training, was to fly a KC-97 for SAC, the Strategic Air Command.

The aircraft, developed by Boeing, was used by Pan American World Airways as the first aircraft to fly scheduled passenger service across the Pacific Ocean and was later converted to perform the air-to-air refueling mission: we called it a tanker. It could be immediately identified as a tanker because of the large refueling boom under the rear of the plane, used to transfer fuel, in flight, to another aircraft. My first airplane after pilot training had four of the largest reciprocating engines ever developed and was the end of the propeller-driven large aircraft. When I began my training, the KC-97 was already being replaced by a new jet tanker. The aircraft was old and new engines were no longer manufactured; this led to numerous engine failures and other unusual emergencies. I had as many serious emergencies in my first five years after pilot training, flying the tanker, as I had in the next twenty years.

I was only on my second training flight in the KC-97 when we had a serious problem while refueling a bomber; I began to wonder if my decision to fly an old tanker was really the best choice I could have made. It didn't take me long to realize that the Air Force was paying me hazardous duty pay for a reason. I was on an eight-hour training flight with another pilot who had also just received his wings. Our instructor stayed in the left pilot's seat and I rotated in and out of the right seat. I had just finished my turn flying during the air-to-air refueling of a B-47 bomber, and now it was the other student's turn to do the same thing. Instead of staying in the cockpit, I decided to go to the rear and watch the actual refueling.

The real action takes place when the bomber comes into position below the tanker. The tanker pilot flies the aircraft as smoothly as he can and the bomber pilot slowly moves forward until he is about thirty feet away. When the bomber is in the correct position, the tanker boom operator uses a set of wings on the boom and flies it, side to side and up and down, until it's in position and locked into the receptacle on the bomber. When there is a solid connection between the two planes, both flying at the same speed, a few hundred miles per hour, the fuel is pumped from the tanker to the bomber.

I was watching the refueling by looking over the back of the boom operator, who was lying on his stomach, looking downward, with all of his controls at his finger tips. His station is in the pod that extends below the bottom aft portion of the tanker. Through the Plexiglas windows I could clearly see the student bomber pilot struggling to remain in formation with us and not get out of position, which would break the connection and stop the fuel transfer. The jet fuel we were pumping into the bomber flowed through a four inch fuel line, under high pressure, to transfer the fuel in the shortest possible time.

I smelled the fuel before I saw it. The stress of hundreds of refuelings was too much for one of our old fuel line couplings, and it developed a crack. Under the high pressure, similar to a fire hose that ruptures and sprays water out of the break; in a few seconds we had a large amount of jet fuel flooding the upper deck of the tanker. I think the boom operator recognized that we had a major malfunction before the cockpit did; and he called, "breakaway, breakaway, breakaway" the code words for stopping the refueling and separating the two aircraft. Otherwise, an electrical spark would probably destroy both aircraft. We had to get separated.

I didn't see the breakaway but I know that within a few seconds the bomber was hundreds of feet below us. I was running to the cockpit to tell them about the leak and get them to stop the fuel pumps, but by the time I got there they had already completed the emergency checklist: the fuel pumps were off, stopping the leak; and they had about ninety-nine percent of the electrical power on the aircraft shut off. There

The photo was taken over the left shoulder of a KC-97 boom operator, looking out of the boom pod on the lower aft of the tanker. A Boeing B-47 medium bomber was seconds from having the tanker's refueling boom lock into the refueling receptacle on the nose of the bomber.

Boeing KC-97 Stratotanker

were a few critical electrical items that were left on, but they were designed not to cause a spark, specifically for the situation we were in.

On my way to the cockpit, and in my panic, I ran through the fuel, which had formed a large puddle and was spilling down into the lower deck. Once the initial panic had subsided and the electrical power was shut off, greatly diminishing the chance of an explosion, we opened all of the hatches, sucked out all of the fuel fumes; and then we made an emergency landing and had the mess cleaned up. When I got home that evening, hours late, my wife was upset that her dinner was ruined. Her ranting ended with, "You stink, go take a shower." I had gotten quite a lot of jet fuel all over me, which had since evaporated, but I can imagine how bad I smelled. I never told her what had happened.

The KC-97 had monstrous Pratt & Whitney R-4360 engines. The R-4360 was an air-cooled radial engine with twenty-eight huge cylinders arranged in four banks of seven. For additional efficiency, each cylinder had two spark plugs, for a total of 56 plugs per engine. The four engines had a total of 224 spark plugs.

SAC was known for squeezing the utmost out of their aircraft, and because of the heavy weight that we used for takeoff, the spark plugs had to operate at full efficiency. To assist in determining the efficiency of the plugs, the flight engineer had an ignition analyzer and could determine their condition in flight. If the plugs were fouled or burned, the engine would not produce the power required for a heavy takeoff, and the bad plugs would have to be changed before the next flight.

One time, on three flights in a row, we had to make emergency landings because of engine failures. Many of the engine failures were caused by the spark plugs failing, but one very scary takeoff was a little different.

I was at the civilian airport at Birmingham, Alabama. We ferried our aircraft from Massachusetts to Alabama, where a civilian company, performing contract maintenance for the Air Force, would overhaul the engines. I was the copilot on John Garrison's crew when we flew to Birmingham to return a recently overhauled plane back to Westover Air Force Base. This was an easy mission; a commercial airline flight down to Alabama with a lightweight, short, flight back. When the engine overhaul was done, John signed the paperwork giving the plane back to the Air Force and we were on our way back to Massachusetts.

Joe Robinson, "Robbie," was an outstanding engineer, and he performed a thorough check of the newly overhauled engines during our high-power engine run, before takeoff. Everything looked good, so we completed our checklists, taxied onto the active runway, and made a normal takeoff. Immediately after getting airborne, we could hear backfiring from one of the four engines. It took a few seconds to positively identify which engine was faulty. We were facing an engine shutdown; if we shut down a good engine instead of the bad one in error, we would not have had the power to continue flying. We then realized that we had a problem far more critical than the possible failure of one engine: all of the engines were backfiring. We learned later that the

civilian contractor had installed the wrong spark plugs by
mistake—all two-hundred and twenty-four of them. Under
the maximum power of the takeoff, they had started failing
within thirty seconds. We managed to keep the airplane in
the air, limp back to the runway, and land without incident. If
this had been the usual, heavyweight, takeoff, we would not
have had the power to keep the airplane flying, and we would
have become just another SAC statistic.

The refueling missions were brutal on these old reciprocating
engines, causing them to fail at about five hundred hours of
flying time; therefore, engine failures were common. To put
the five-hundred-hour failure time in perspective, in later years
when I flew for TWA, the jet engines lasted about twenty-five
thousand hours. The TWA engines were monitored constantly
for indications of failure and were removed and overhauled
before they stopped on their own. On Air Force aircraft, there
were a few dozen times that I made an emergency landing because of engine problems. In contrast, during all of my years
with TWA, I never had an engine failure. The main problem
with the R-4360 engine on the tanker was that we continuously
operated it at maximum power for about four hours during
every refueling mission, destroying the engines.

We carried two types of fuel on the aircraft, aviation gasoline for our reciprocating engines, and jet fuel for the bombers
we refueled. A jet engine can burn either type of fuel, but we
could burn only the aviation gas; therefore, we had separate
tanks for the two different fuels. On a few occasions, when
we had to fly a very long flight, we flushed the jet fuel out of
the tanks and filled all of our tanks with aviation gas. On one

occasion, I had the privilege of flying a flight of twenty-two hours and forty-five minutes. That was the longest flight I have ever flown. We only had two pilots; it was torture. At the end of the flight we had fuel left over, but we were out of oil for the engines—a common occurrence on those long flights.

Like everything else on that engine, the oil system was massive; low oil quantity, not low fuel, was usually the limiting factor that determined the maximum range of the aircraft. There were hundreds of moving parts on the extremely complex engine, and the failure of any one part due to the lack of lubrication would result in an engine failure. The aircraft carried 220 gallons of oil for lubricating the engines—almost 200 times more oil than the five quarts of oil in an automobile engine.

There is an aviation saying that a pilot's life is hours of boredom punctuated with moments of terror. The oil system on the KC-97 caused one of my moments of terror.

I was in SAC for four and a half years, and during about one-third of that time, I was on alert, at a remote location, waiting for a war to begin and waiting to perform my mission to refuel a bomber that was probably headed for the Soviet Union. This was the era of the cold war, and one of the reasons it remained cold was the overwhelming nuclear capability of the Strategic Air Command.

Only once, to my knowledge, was the alert force launched, and that was for a massive exercise. This was an announced mission to test the war plan, and it was probably a show of force to intimidate the Soviet Union. I was on alert at Sondrestrom Air Base, Greenland, and in preparation for the publicized launch, an additional force of six tankers was placed on alert. We were informed that at noon the secondary force would become the primary alert force, and anytime after that we could be called on to fly our wartime mission. It was a relatively straightforward flight; we were to refuel a B-47 bomber on an easterly heading just north of the Arctic Circle, over the water between Baffin Island and Greenland.

Sondrestrom was on a fjord, with high terrain to the north and east, so all takeoffs and landings were over the fjord, regardless of wind conditions. This would be a maximum weight takeoff, which was always hazardous, but the wind was favorable and the weather was good. If we did have an engine failure on takeoff we could fly down the narrow fjord until we were high enough to clear the hills on either side. I was looking forward to an interesting day, a once-in-a-lifetime opportunity.

Exactly at noon, the Klaxon horn sounded and caught me by surprise; I was not expecting it so soon. I'd had my lunch before noontime in preparation for the mission and was fully prepared for the flight, but I felt uneasy because it was a highly unusual mission. I had never refueled this far north, even though I had many flights through the area. I'd always been concerned about having to survive in the frigid ocean if I were forced to ditch or bail out. We had the best survival gear available—life rafts and rubber suits plus radios, flares, food, and drinking water; the problem was the water temperature. At the warmest, in the middle of the summer, I could survive only for a short time in the water, if I was wearing a survival suit. Without the rubber suit on, survival time would be only a few minutes in the cold waters of the Davis Strait. Our entire mission was over water except for the takeoff and landing.

Everything went as planned for the first hour. We were climbing out on a westerly heading; I was number five in the six-ship formation. All six of the aircraft were in a straight line, with numbers two through six stacked higher than the aircraft in front, to stay out of the turbulence. I could see the four tankers in front of me, and Tom Dominguez in number six could see the entire formation.

We were flying to the air refueling control point, where we would reverse course and take up the side-by-side refueling formation. The bombers would take up the same formation so that all of us could refuel simultaneously. The navigator in the lead aircraft, using a radar beacon and the radio, was responsible for contact with the bombers. My crew didn't even have to worry about controlling the rendezvous with our bomber, a tricky task for the navigator, because it was taken care of for us. This was turning into an easy, beautiful, picture-perfect mission.

At sixteen thousand feet and about two hundred miles from land, I could feel the aircraft yaw to the left, because of a loss of power. Immediately, we got a fire bell and red light warning, indicating an engine fire. The bell and light are designed to get the crew's attention, and they worked. I could feel the adrenaline pumping; my entire body was in survival mode. An engine fire in flight, over water, with no place to land, is nothing to take lightly. We identified the number two engine as the problem; the fire was on the inboard engine on the left side. Occasionally, the fire warning system malfunctioned, indicating a fire when none existed; so we had to confirm that it was not a false warning. In this case, even though we could feel the loss of power on the left side, we still went through the procedure of asking the boom operator, Bob Hunt, to scan the engine for fire. Bob confirmed our worst fears, and we immediately began working through the emergency "fire in flight" checklist.

We shut off the gasoline, oil, and hydraulic fluid lines to the engine with a gang-bar that flipped the three valve switches, thus cutting off the sources of fuel for the fire; and we feathered the prop, reducing the drag.

Bob was watching the number two engine from a window in the rear on the left side of the upper deck. He reported that he no longer saw any flame, but there was still a lot of smoke trailing behind the engine. The smoke indicated that we continued to have a problem, and John Garrison, the aircraft commander, decided to discharge the fire extinguishing agent to combat the still smoldering fire.

We had only two attempts to put out the fire. When Robbie moved the switch, the engine was engulfed with half of our supply of fire extinguishing agent, cutting off all oxygen to the fire.

Shortly, Bob reported that the smoke had stopped, and I started breathing again.

Fighting the fire had taken only about a minute, but it was a stressful minute for me. We were loaded with thousands of gallons of fuel and we were all aware of the possible consequences of a fire in flight.

With the fire out and everything under control, I began planning ahead for our return to Sondrestrom with three engines. First, we would have to descend a few thousand feet because we were too heavy to remain at altitude with only three engines. Next, we would have to jettison fuel: we were well above our maximum landing weight and the fuel we were going to give to the bomber would have to be dumped, to evaporate into the air.

John had just started to turn left and descend out of the formation. I was getting ready to inform the formation leader of our engine problem and that we were returning to Sondrestrom. I remember sitting back and taking a deep breath to get my emotions under control, when a radio call made me freeze. It didn't come from my airplane but from the aircraft behind us. Tom Dominguez made the radio call: "This is number six; number five just exploded. I'm going to follow him down." Just when I thought that everything was okay, Tom was telling the rest of the formation that my crew and I had been killed or would be in a few moments.

I was confused, and didn't understand why Tom would transmit the message that the tens of thousands of pounds of fuel in my airplane had just exploded. My next thought was, Dying is easy. It was like watching a scene in a movie; I was detached from my own imminent death. Next, real confusion set in, and I was jarred from my movie scene. Tom couldn't be correct. I began to reason that there had been no explosion, the cockpit was intact, we were in a left-hand turn to leave the formation and descending because we were too heavy for the altitude. No one on my crew said a word; there was only a stunned silence.

The radio chatter started; everyone in the formation was requesting information. I was the one on the radio, informing the rest of the aircraft that we had shut down the number two engine, we were under control and going back to Sondrestrom, and I didn't know what Tom was talking about.

The flight back was routine under the circumstances. The emergency equipment was waiting for us when we landed and followed us down the runway; this was normal procedure for landing with a failed engine. When the maintenance crew examined the engine they determined that the large Gyrotor oil pump that lubricates the entire engine had disintegrated.

As a result of the pump failure, the thirty gallons of hot oil in the engine oil tank was pumped as an aerosol into the exhaust system, where it started to burn—not in the engine but behind the aircraft. From inside, we had no idea that we had a huge fireball of burning oil behind us; but Tom said it was so large that all he could see was our right wingtip. From Tom's position behind us, it looked as if we had exploded and were engulfed within the fireball.

Prior to this incident Tom was the copilot for Jack Larabee when they had a mid-air collision with a B-52 bomber during an air-to-air refueling. The bomber crashed, but Tom and his crew managed to get the tanker to a runway and land. Under the stress of the refueling, the new B-52 pilot, instead of keying his radio, moved the wrong switch, changing the elevator trim to Up, which caused the bomber to climb into the tanker. The upward motion forced the refueling boom up, breaking through the rear of the tanker, coming to rest in, and jamming, the elevator and rudder. The Boeing engineers who looked at the severely damaged KC-97 said it was impossible to fly an aircraft in that condition, but Jack and Tom flew it.

The only reason the United States spent a million dollars training me to be a pilot was to fly one mission during the first minutes of a nuclear war. My job, along with the other four crewmembers, was to get the KC-97 SAC tanker off the ground, thereby protecting it from a nuclear explosion. Once airborne and relatively safe, we would transfer almost all of our fuel to a B-47 bomber whose mission was, most probably,

The Bob Hope USO Christmas show. Sondrestrom Air Force Base Officers' Club, 1962. Standing, left to right: Terry Williams, Anita Bryant, the author, Rosemary Franklin, Bob Hope, Roger Dyer, Dorothy Provine, John Hill. Kneeling: Dick Bryant, Ted Newcommer, Charlie Hill, Ray Heinrich

to drop its nuclear weapons somewhere within the Soviet Union. The bomber would most likely take off from a base in the northeastern part of the United States; by the time it reached the refueling area, it could take all the fuel from two tankers. If the mission required, we would transfer our total fuel load, keeping only enough for a controlled crash landing or ditching. This was probably a one-way flight for the bomber crew; my chances of living until day two of the war were much better.

SAC crews called their alert facility the mole hole. I was on a SAC combat crew, flying a tanker, from 1961 until 1965, which meant that I was on alert every third week. Some units pulled alert at their home station; I had my alert duty under the code name Operation Reflex, which meant that I had to fly to a forward location to pull alert. I had dozens of tours of SAC alert, reflexing to Harmon Air Force Base on the western shore of Newfoundland, near Stephenville. At Harmon I lived in a mole hole.

The mole hole was a standard SAC design consisting of a steel and concrete blast-proof building, which was mostly underground. Entry to the building was through two ramps. One led to the upper level, which had offices and the mess hall; the second led to the living quarters, deep underground. Each ramp was enclosed in a steel tube about ten feet in diameter, with a blast-resistant door for the entry. The entire building was a restricted area, surrounded by a high chain-link fence topped with concertina wire. There was only one entrance in the fence and there was always a guard at the gate. SAC took security seriously. The crews were high-value assets, which meant that we lived in the restricted area and access was permitted only with a restricted area badge.

Pulling alert meant one thing to me: boredom. One of my favorite ways to kill time was to sit in the mess hall, drinking coffee and listening to stories from the few World War II veterans who were still around. These folks were at the end of their military careers, and they kept us entertained for hours with their stories—some true, some probably just a bunch of bull, but all entertaining.

Lieutenant Colonel Bob Alexander, whom I later crewed with, had been shot down on a bombing raid on the oil refineries at Ploiesti, Romania, and had spent the remainder of the war as a POW. When Bob was telling stories, I listened. I remember two things about him that were a result of having been a prisoner of the Germans for a few years. First, every time we had a flight, he had a bag full of sandwiches with him; usually, he ate just one, but he said he never wanted to be hungry again. Second, he always shaved with an old razor, the double-edged-blade type, which was common at the time. That razor, an inexpensive one, had been given to him by the Red Cross when he was a POW; it was the only thing he had from that miserable time of his life.

A few times a week, the sound of the Klaxon horn reminded us of why we were on alert. There were horns throughout the alert facility as well as at any other location on base where we were allowed to go. In other words, we were never in a location where we would be out of Klaxon communication with the SAC command post. The Klaxon horn was loud enough to wake up the soundest sleeper instantly. If the sound didn't give you a heart attack, the adrenaline that was pumped into your system got you moving at top speed. The sound of that horn was our indication to go to the aircraft immediately and start engines. Practice alerts were mostly in the daytime, so I would take my shower late at night. The last thing I wanted was to have to get out of the shower and dry off, then get into my flight suit and boots (including quilted long underwear and a parka in the winter), then meet my crew at the station wagon for the high-speed drive to the aircraft. We had six minutes to get all engines started from the time the horn went off, and there was not a moment to waste.

Every crew had their own vehicle for responding to an alert. Usually, they were standard, dark blue Air Force station wagons with flashing lights on top that we turned on when racing to the airplane. We always parked our vehicle at a hitching post, a parking area with electrical outlets. An alert vehicle had a pigtail electrical connection in the rear that was plugged in, to power the engine heater. Without an engine heater, we would not have been able to get the cold vehicle started. The vehicles also had snow chains on the rear tires for the entire winter, because all of the roads were snow covered.

Everyone had a specific job during an alert. The first person who got to the assigned station wagon was the driver, and everyone else just piled in. We had the right-of-way during an alert and any vehicle not responding to the alert was required to pull to the side and stop. When we arrived at the aircraft, we parked the vehicle under the left wing. It was always a mad scramble outside the aircraft: dust covers had to be removed from the engines; various covers and plugs were removed and stored; and last, the wheel chocks and static wires were pulled. If the temperature was extremely cold, we couldn't run and overexert ourselves, because the cold air would injure our lungs. My job as copilot was to immediately get in the cockpit, put on the headset, which was freezing cold in winter, and copy the message from the command post informing us whether this was a practice alert or the real thing.

The message from the command post was encoded in a specific format and had to be copied and decoded by two individuals, the navigator and me, working separately to ensure accuracy. While we were decoding, the pilot and engineer were starting engines, and the boom operator was outside with the crew chief, assisting in the engine start. The security guard on the aircraft was removing the signs, ropes, and stanchions indicating that this was a restricted area and deadly force would be used if the area was entered without authority. Usually, the message I copied from the command post directed us to shut down our engines; and the practice was over. Occasionally, though, we would have a more elaborate exercise: we would taxi to the end of the runway and perform a high-speed taxi down the runway, simulating a formation takeoff. We knew these alerts, which occurred a few times a week, were practice runs.

A few times during my four and a half years in SAC, I decoded messages that were not practice but were meant to increase the readiness of the entire SAC alert force. These were deadly serious; and each time they occurred, my heart beat so fast I thought it was going to pop out of my chest. These alerts usually occurred when there was a breakdown in communications among the worldwide SAC outposts and the commander was unsure of the cause. He would then place the entire force on a higher state of readiness, meaning we would hold at the end of the runway, with engines running. In case of a real international crisis, he could quickly launch the entire alert force, have them airborne and starting their wartime mission but waiting for further coded instructions before proceeding past a certain point. As far as I know, this never happened outside of Hollywood movies. The risk of going that far was that the Soviet Union, thinking that we were initiating a nuclear attack, would take similar counter-measures, and the situation might spiral out of control.

Every crewmember knew exactly what his duties were when he was on alert, and it was highly unusual when some-thing didn't work exactly as planned. We routinely had to attend a certification session. I would face a board of senior officers, who would question me about any portion of my mis-sion. When they were confident I was capable of doing my job, they would certify that I was authorized to be on alert.

For me, the worst part of being on alert so far north was the
severe weather. Once I had to work outside for eight hours
to prepare my aircraft for alert, a job that took less than an
hour in normal weather; but the temperature in Greenland
that day was forty-three degrees below zero and the wind
was blowing at forty knots. The wind chill index was minus
125 degrees. I nearly got frostbite even though we had our
alert vehicle running, with the heater going full blast, to take
a break from the cold and wind. It was the coldest weather I
have ever experienced.

Occasionally, during a blizzard, the alert force would be
"degraded," because it was impossible to fly in the heavy snow
and wind. When the planes were cleaned off, the ramp, taxiways and runway plowed, and our vehicles dug out, we would
go back on alert. During one blizzard, I was in the Officers'
Club, having dinner, when we were notified that everyone
was to remain where they were; no one was to go out of the
building they were in. I spent two days in the Officers' Club
and another day digging out, before going back on alert.

Winters were brutal; summers, however, were beautiful in
the arctic. One summer day when the temperature was in the
seventies, we all decided to play a little softball on the field
alongside the mole hole, outside of the restricted area. We
had just enough people who wanted to play to make up two
full teams, and we had a great time. Most of us were playing in
flight suits and flying boots, which made it pretty uncomfortable, but we were always cognizant that we were profession-
als, and were always prepared for an alert. I'd played a lot of
softball and baseball in the schoolyard in Mountain Dale, and

I was a pretty good ball player. I had not played for a number of years, but it all came back as soon as I picked up the glove and bat. We all had such a great time that we decided to play again the next day. When the testosterone took over, a simple game of softball was no longer adequate. The enlisted men decided to challenge the officers; and to make it even more interesting, there was a small wager on the outcome. Finally, there was something to relieve the boredom.

The officers' coach, Roger Dyer, picked me to play left field and he also gave me the honor of batting fourth. I was having the time of my life, and like most of the other players, I showed up in shorts, tee shirt, and sneakers. This was now serious business! We all hung our flight suits on the chain-link fence separating the ball field from the restricted area and placed each crew's clothing together, so we would not waste time looking for our own gear, in case of an alert. We put our boots under each flight suit; and all we had to do was pull on our coveralls, run to the alert vehicle, then put on our boots while driving to the aircraft. Everyone who didn't have to work inside the alert facility was outside, either cheering or playing. Even the young guard at the gate to the restricted area, who had the most boring job on the base, showed an interest. He could not leave his post, but he was close to my position in left field, and he was watching the game while guarding the entrance.

Foul balls on the third base side hit the chain link fence and bounced back onto the playing field, but an occasional fly ball would go over the fence into the restricted area. Since my position in left field was closest to the entrance, I became the player who would retrieve the foul balls. I had to get my restricted area badge from my flight suit and pin it on my tee shirt for inspection by the gate guard before retrieving the ball inside the fence. Then I would put the badge back on my flying suit, to be prepared for the dreaded Klaxon horn going off. The gate guard, like everyone else in SAC, had a set of orders, and they were never to be violated. It had been drilled into him that he was never to let anyone enter the alert facility without proper authorization; disobeying that order would result in severe disciplinary action. I retrieved a few foul balls, going through the same tedious procedure of pinning and re-pinning my badge each time; and the guard performed his tedious procedure of inspecting my badge each time before permitting my reentry. I would then continue playing, and he would continue watching the game.

Since it was a nice warm day, some of us decided to remove our shirts to take advantage of the summer sun. I placed my tee shirt with my flight suit, to be put on before donning the coveralls. The next high foul ball over the fence hit the mole hole, bounced around a few times, rolled a little, and finally came to rest just behind and to the side of the gate guard, but still inside of the restricted area. I thought the ball was going to roll out of the entrance, and I was now standing face-to-face with the nineteen-year-old SAC security guard, not saying anything, but indicating with my body language that he was expected to pick up the ball, which was just behind him, and toss it to me.

No words were spoken between us, but any red-blooded American kid who has a baseball a few feet from him picks it up and throws it back to the nearest player. This is the American way, until you understand that this was not your usual nineteen-year-old. This young man had been conditioned to follow orders, and his orders were that he was not to leave his post and that no one was to enter the restricted area without proper authorization: a restricted area badge. I thought the ball was going to roll out of the fenced area, therefore, I hadn't bothered to get my restricted area badge from my flight suit; also, I didn't have a tee shirt on to pin the badge onto for inspection. I continued standing about eight feet away from the guard, considering my options for retrieving the ball and getting the ball game underway again. Should I get my badge, or would he allow me to take a few steps into the restricted area to pick up the ball?

The standoff continued. I rationalized that he knew who I was because he was watching the game and we had done this a few times previously, the ball was right behind him, and everyone was shouting for me to pick up the ball and keep the game moving. I took two steps into the restricted area and picked up the ball.

I had challenged him. He responded by following his orders, and I lost. He pointed his black automatic M-16 at me, probably removed the safety, and ordered me on the ground, spread eagle. He then rang the security alarm, which would bring him assistance. I knew I had a big problem, and I was smart enough to follow his orders and keep my mouth shut. His orders were to use deadly force to prevent entry into the restricted area, and he had followed his orders precisely to this point. There was always the chance that if I tried to get up or argue with him, he may have considered me a threat, and the confrontation would have escalated further. I remained silent, face down with my bare chest on the pavement, arms spread out, waiting for someone to get me out of this predicament.

Roger Dyer was an imposing man. He was about six-feet-two, two hundred and fifty pounds, all muscle, with a shaved head. He had been a college football player, and then played semipro ball, before becoming an Air Force pilot; also, he was well spoken. Everyone gathered around outside the gate, having a great time, shouting and whooping it up as if they were in a strip club, except Roger. He was our self-appointed leader, and he realized that this incident could get nasty. He put on his flight suit, which prominently showed his major's leaves, got everyone to shut up, and tried to reason with this young enlisted man. The guard ordered him to remove himself from the area, just as his security backup arrived.

There was a security breach, and they responded in a very short time with about a dozen guards riding in a tracked vehicle with four fifty-caliber machine guns mounted on top. The vehicle parked about twenty feet from me, and I could see that the quad fifties were manned and pointed directly at me. The security team quickly backed everyone away from the gate, and now there was complete silence; there was no doubt about who was in charge. It was quite unnerving to be lying face down on the pavement and have this heavy artillery pointed right at me. Now, I was totally submissive, as were the rest of the jeering ballplayers. The operating procedures manual described the method of frisking me for concealed weapons, and that is exactly what they did, even though I was wearing only shorts and sneakers. Some youngster's hands moved over my bare arms and armpits and over my back; then he turned me over to search my hairy chest and stomach area. Next, my bare legs were searched, and I didn't move a muscle when he searched my crotch.

The on-scene security chief was a major who then negotiated with a few of the senior officers, led by my buddy, Roger. After vouching for me, then giving me the required tongue-lashing, he released me—only to be further humiliated by my good buddies, the rest of the ball players, for being so stupid. These were the same guys who'd been egging me on to get the ball and continue the game.

Between the humiliation of lying almost naked on the dirty pavement and the continued taunting from my friends, my day was ruined. I don't even remember who won the game.

4

A NIGHT ON THE GREENLAND ICE CAP

SONDRESTROM AIR FORCE Base was bleak and desolate. It was located on the western side of Greenland, ninety miles from the coastline, on a fjord. The town of Holsteinsborg was on the coast to the west, and the Greenland ice cap began about ten miles to the east of the base. The only way in or out of Sondrestrom was by air. This was my first forward base for pulling SAC alert when I was a new copilot on the KC-97 tanker. The US Air Force's facilities were to the south of the runway, and Scandinavian Airlines, SAS, had a small installation on the north of the runway that they used as a refueling stop on their over-the-pole flights to New York. The SAS passengers were permitted to exit the aircraft to stretch their legs and buy some craft items handmade by the local indigenous population. Greenland was almost entirely covered by the ice cap, but there were large grassland areas near the southwest coast, where the Eskimos lived. We were not permitted to have any contact with the Eskimos, because we were told that they had no immunity to measles; what was a minor illness for us was a fatal disease for them.

If I managed to have some time off during my nine-day tour of alert duty, and if the weather was okay, I would walk on one of the many trails, exploring the area surrounding the base. It was summertime and the weather was unusually warm and sunny. I had an entire day off and had planned a long walk—until I met the commander of a C-130 during dinner at the Officers' Club. His aircraft was equipped with skis for landing on ice or snow, and his mission was to fly supplies to a radar site on the Greenland ice cap. He invited me to fly with him the next day, instead of taking my planned walk with Dick Adams and Bob Hunt. It was to be a flight of less than an hour each way and was probably the only opportunity I would ever have to actually stand on the mile-thick ice cap; I instantly accepted. I told him about my plans for spending my day off with the navigator and boom operator, so he also invited them.

He let me ride in the cockpit, with a headset on. I was amazed at the capability of the C-130. I had never flown in a turboprop aircraft, but I was aware that they were designed for high performance during takeoff and landing. Landing at the radar site was a thrill. There was no formal runway, merely some red flags in a straight line indicting where we should land. The pilot first made a low pass over the area to see if everything looked okay for landing; then we flew a standard traffic pattern and landed on the skis. Sondrestrom, where we made our takeoff, was close to sea level. When we landed on the ice, the aircraft altimeter indicated 7,800 feet. At the radar site, the ice cap was almost a mile and a half thick.

The Distant Early Warning Line (DEW Line) stretched across northern Canada. It was a line of radar stations built to give an early warning in the event that the Soviet Union launched nuclear bombers at the United States. These radars would give the Strategic Air Command enough warning to launch a retaliatory strike before the Soviet warheads detonated, presumably destroying a major portion of the United States. There was a cold war between the two countries, a nuclear standoff, for about forty years; the Soviets never launched anything against us, nor did we, against them; so far, nuclear war has been averted.

When the technology became available, the Canada DEW Line was extended to include Greenland, with three radars: DYE 1, 2 and 3. I thought Sondrestrom was the end of the earth, but DYE 2 was one of the most isolated places on the planet. The nineteen workers who manned DYE 2 used Sondrestrom for rest and recuperation (R&R). We had just landed at DYE 2 with supplies, mail, and two of the Danish workers who had been at Sondrestrom for R&R. We were told that it was impossible to walk off the ice cap because of the enormous crevasses along the edges of the ice sheet;

C-130 on the Greenland ice cap at Dye II. Notice that the aircraft is on skis.

however, an all-white arctic fox made it over the ice and found the site. This was the DYE 2 mascot, probably the best fed fox in all of Greenland.

We were invited into the site, the largest installation of this type I had ever been in. It had the overall look of the oil drilling platforms used for drilling in deep water, but without the drilling equipment. It was a large black building built on eight pillars sunk into the ice, four on each side. On top of the building was an enormous radar antenna in a spherical enclosure that looked like a huge golf ball. On the side facing the United States were communications antennas; the side facing the Soviet Union had additional radar equipment. The station generated its own electrical power with fuel flown in on the C-130s, and their water supply was melted snow, which they scooped in with a dragline and bucket. The scenery was like the view one might get from a small boat in the ocean, out of sight of land. There was nothing to see except the ice and the horizon meeting the sky, for 360 degrees. We were given a tour of the facility and a delicious lunch in the mess hall. The workers were so isolated from normal life that high-quality food was important. Greenland belongs to Denmark, and all of the workers were Danish civilians; all spoke English. A visit by the supply aircraft was a source of great excitement for them, and they treated us royally.

The maximum thickness of the Greenland ice cap is eleven thousand feet, or over two miles. It is not ice, technically, but hard packed snow. The weight of the ice cap is so great that the land mass under it has been depressed, forming a bowl which is lower than sea level. The ice cap covers all of Greenland except for the coastline. It was receding at the edges; but it was getting thicker, because of the annual

DYE II radar installation

snowfall. This had caused a problem for the designers of the radar site, because the radar antenna had to be maintained at a constant height above the ice. In the 1960s, the depth of the ice was increasing at thirty inches a year, requiring the radar antenna to be raised thirty inches every year. The process of raising the height of the antenna was designed into the site by building it on the eight columns embedded in the ice. Each of the columns was a huge hydraulic jack, and the antenna was raised by jacking up the entire site. After a few years, when the building reached the top of the existing columns, they extended the top of each column by adding more structure.

After the cargo was unloaded, it was time to fly back to Sondrestrom, which would have been routine except that it was sixty-two degrees Fahrenheit, which may have been the warmest day of the year. The warm air caused the surface of the snow to begin to melt, making it soft and sticky, which caused a problem for the takeoff. The skis would sink into the snow, causing a great amount of resistance. If the four large turboprop engines did not have sufficient power for the takeoff, there was the assisted takeoff system, or ATO, for backup. The ATO consisted of rocket bottles attached to each side of the airframe, near the rear. During takeoff, at the appropriate speed, the rockets would fire, for that extra kick in the pants to get us airborne. The combination of the warm temperature and the eight-thousand-foot altitude reduced the power produced by the aircraft engines; hence, the crew calculated that the rockets would have to be used.

Once again, I was in the cockpit sitting on the lower bunk, seatbelt fastened, listening intently to the crew discussing their takeoff conditions. The aircraft charts indicated that we needed to reach sixty-seven knots to lift the nose ski off the snow. From another set of charts, it appeared that this was also the maximum speed we would be able to attain, using full engine power and the rocket assist. Getting off the ice cap would be marginal because of the temperature and altitude.

We headed directly into the wind, which gave us the greatest advantage for getting airborne, and then started our takeoff with maximum engine power. When we reached the calculated speed, we fired the rockets. The copilot was calling off the airspeed, and at sixty-seven knots the pilot pulled back on the yoke, causing the nose ski to lift off the soft snow. We stayed in this attitude for about ten seconds, then the rockets burned out and nose ski slowly settled back onto the snow—we never got off the ground. The combination of the friction of the wet snow on the two main skis, the increased aerodynamic drag produced by raising the nose, plus the ATO burning out was greater than the lift produced by the wings. We didn't have enough airspeed to get airborne, and the C-130 was transformed into a huge sled with turboprop engines.

The pilot made the decision to continue the takeoff moving straight ahead with maximum power on the four engines. All of the rocket bottles had been used and were now useless. If the snow conditions improved, he could possibly get enough speed to lift off. There was no formal runway; we could have attempted a takeoff in any direction and proceeded until we reached a crevasse, hundreds of miles from our location. We continued at about sixty knots with maximum power on the engines, hoping to attain flying speed. Skiing across the surface of the ice cap felt like being on the ocean in a high speed boat when there are almost no waves, just small ripples slapping the bottom. There were low ridges in the snow caused by the wind, and the skis hitting these snow waves made it feel like we were airborne and in light turbulence. We continued straight ahead; and every few minutes, when our airspeed would increase slightly, the pilot would lift the nose off the snow, only to have it fall back down. We continued over the ice cap for about twenty minutes, maintaining our sixty knots and lifting the nose every now and then, only to have it settle back down each time.

My other two crewmembers were in the rear cargo bay without a window to view the outside conditions. Thinking we had taken off twenty minutes earlier, Bob Hunt came up to the cockpit to get a cup of coffee and see what the ice cap looked like from the air. He was stunned to see that we were still on the ground. The motion of the aircraft, the noise level, along with the elapsed time, had led him to believe we were airborne and at altitude. This was the mother of all takeoffs.

The longest paved runways are less than three miles long, and we had already traveled for about twenty miles over the ice cap with no success at finding better snow. On the last at-

tempt at lifting the huge aircraft off the sticky snow, the conditions had changed. This time the nose came down faster and
the nose ski caught a large snow ridge at the wrong angle. The
ski probably twisted when it touched down, and a hydraulic
line, used for steering or lifting the nose gear, broke. Almost
immediately, all of the hydraulic fluid from that system was
pumped out of the broken line and onto the snow.

When I exited, it looked like the C-130 was bleeding to
death. Hydraulic fluid is bright red, and a large puddle had
collected on the nose ski, spilling off onto the snow. I knew
we were stuck until we could get some help. The tracks left
by the skis were prominent, but when I followed the tracks
back to the horizon, there was no radar site in view. We were
over the horizon from the site, so it was not visible. The sun
was bright, and it was warm enough so that a jacket was not
needed, but I was still concerned about getting back to the
site. I was envisioning walking the twenty miles back and was
concerned that the warm temperature would not persist; I
had seen the temperature drop forty degrees in a few hours
at Sondrestrom. My worries were needless: the radar station
had a large vehicle, designed for travel on snow, which they
sent to the aircraft to drive all of us back to the security of
the permanent installation.

A maintenance team was assembled at Sondrestrom, and
the required hydraulic line was located in supply, to be flown
in the next day. This meant that I would have to spend the
night on the Greenland ice cap. We ate another great meal,
saw a movie, and talked a lot with the off-duty Danish workers,
who were glad for the company. They put up with the isolated
duty because of the huge increase in salary that it brought,
even though there was no place to spend their earnings. At

bedtime, we were told that they had no quarters for visitors, so it was a case of finding a place to sleep that suited you. The site operated twenty-four hours a day, so there were always a few people using the sofas in the common areas and they were not available for sleeping. I searched for a quiet place and finally found one. My one night on the Greenland ice cap was not exactly glamorous: I slept in a storage room next to the cartons of toilet paper and I used a large sack of donut mix as a pillow.

The next morning after breakfast, Dick Adams and I decided to take a look around the exterior of the site. The living quarters had few windows, to conserve heat; and the day before, with all of the excitement, we hadn't had a chance to explore outside. We put on our parkas and went outside, where the temperature was back to normal. We guessed it was slightly below freezing, because there was something like ice, or snow crystals, in the air. It was not like they were falling, really; they were so fine that they were floating in the air. Greenland is a semi-desert, with very little precipitation; just a few inches of water forms the thirty inches of snow received every year. In addition to the ice crystals, it appeared to be foggy. I guess that was from all of the moisture created by the melting snow of the day before. The conditions were unusual for this location: the combination of ice crystals and fog created a complete whiteout. Visibility was about ten feet, and we were concerned about losing our sense of direction and getting lost when we were only a few yards from the only structure in this part of Greenland. I have been in dense fog where the visibility was only about one foot, but this was different. In normal fog, you can see contrasting color when you look down at the ground. On the ice cap, the ground

*The author on the ice cap during a whiteout. There
is no visible sky, ground, or shadow.*

was white and invisible. Every place we looked was white
and devoid of shadows. It was like being totally enclosed in
a white, fluffy, cotton ball.

We took a picture of each other in the whiteout. In the
photos there is no shadow and it appears that all of the background and snow we were standing on had been digitally
removed. When we realized that the visibility was improving,
we decided to stay out for a while longer and continue our ex-
ploration. Within a short time, the visibility increased enough

for us to see that we were standing in front of an enormous radar antenna. The area was enclosed with a rope fence and "Danger—Keep Out" signs, but the rope had fallen from a few of the poles, and it was at that precise location that we had wandered into the danger area during the whiteout.

We didn't waste any time getting away from in front of the antenna. A small radar unit on an aircraft has warnings about turning the equipment on with personnel in the area. Radar emits an energy pulse that bounces off an object and is returned to the radar antenna. The energy pulse from an aircraft is powerful enough to injure a person; the radar pulse from the site may have been a thousand times as strong. We were fortunate: we must have been underneath the pulse that emanated from the center of the huge radar dish. Had we been in the line of the radar energy, we would have been cooked. We were both concerned about the future effect the radar may have had on our bodies, but when we developed the film in our cameras and realized that the film was not damaged, we figured we probably weren't either.

The three of us flew off the ice cap on the C-130 that brought in the maintenance crew and the replacement hydraulic line. Because of the much colder temperature, the takeoff went smoothly, and we landed at Sondrestrom a short time later. After spending the night at DYE 2, returning to Sondrestrom made me feel that I was back in civilization. Everything is relative.

5

THE CUBAN MISSILE CRISIS

WHERE WERE YOU during the Cuban Missile Crisis? We relate the most important news events in our lives with where we were when we learned of the event. For me, the two events that stand out from the early 1960s were the Cuban Missile Crisis and the death of President Kennedy.

I was at Dover Air Force Base in Delaware, attending my annual simulator training, when I first heard of the Cuban Missile Crisis during a report to the nation from President Kennedy. From October 18 through October 29, 1962, the world came as close to a nuclear war as it has ever been. Recently, I watched an old TV interview with the secretary of defense at the time of the crisis, Robert S. McNamara. He made the chilling comment that the situation with the Soviet Union was so out of control that after a Saturday night meeting he stood on the steps of the White House and looked at the full moon with tears in his eyes. He placed his thumb and forefinger about an inch apart and said we were this far from having a nuclear confrontation with our cold war enemy and he thought he would never see another full moon. The results of a nuclear war were predictable: total annihilation of both countries and an end to civilization as we know it.

The Soviet Union, under the leadership of Nikita Khrushchev, was installing nuclear-tipped missiles, in secret, on the island of Cuba. At its closest point, Cuba is only ninety miles from Florida. The missiles had the capability of reaching as far north as Washington, D.C. This was a situation that the United States could not allow to continue, and President Kennedy took the stand that the missiles would be removed or we would take whatever action was necessary to remove them. Premier Khrushchev had met John F. Kennedy and is reported to have perceived him weak, young, and inexperienced; he decided to test our president's resolve.

The first time the American people heard of the crisis was during a prime time TV address by the president, from the Oval Office. President Kennedy showed aerial photographs of the missiles as well as the launch sites under construction, and he explained why we could not allow this threat to our nation. I was eating dinner with John Garrison and Joe Robinson, in the bar of the Officers' Club. We wanted to see the president's speech; it had been publicized very well, and we could watch TV in the bar while eating dinner. As the pilot, copilot, and flight engineer of a SAC tanker crew, we had to attend simulator training annually in order to practice all of the emergencies that were too dangerous to do in an actual aircraft. There were only a few KC-97 simulators, and the crews traveled to the location of a simulator to take the three-day training course. Sometimes we took the training in Texas; this time, we drove to Delaware.

As soon as the president was finished speaking, there was a phone call from the command post at Westover AFB in Massachusetts for John, the aircraft commander of our crew, with specific instructions. We were to drive the few hundred miles back to Westover immediately for a takeoff at six o'clock the next morning, to go on SAC alert. I was to drive through the night, and John and Robbie were to sleep in the car; that way they would be rested to fly to Newfoundland, and I would sleep during the flight. One pilot and the engineer were sufficient to operate the aircraft if it was a routine flight. We were on alert at our forward base, at Harmon, in Newfoundland, the next day, as were hundreds of airplanes and thousands of crew members at all of the SAC bases around the world. I was part of the strategic nuclear force that would attack the Soviet Union, but this was only a portion of the mobilization that was occurring within the United States military. Tactical Air Command moved a large force of fighter aircraft to the southeast US, should an attack on Cuba become necessary; and, of course, the Army and the Marines were preparing for this operation, too. The Navy set up a blockade of Cuba and was not going to permit any more missiles to be shipped from Russia. The military forces of the US were preparing for war.

I was married with two children, both in diapers. We lived within walking distance of a base that contained two SAC bomb wings; each wing had three B-52 bomb squadrons and a tanker squadron. Within a few miles of where we lived, there were probably hundreds of nuclear weapons; this made Westover a prime target for the Soviets. In the basement of our house, I had stored food, water, and other survival gear; but this was not sufficient for the severity of the threat we now faced. This was during the years when more affluent families were building underground bomb shelters instead of swimming pools, in an attempt to ensure their survival. The entire country was on the verge of hysteria because of the possibility of a nuclear war, and now our president stated that we were going to have a showdown with the other super-power. Before leaving for my six o'clock flight to go on alert, I instructed my wife to take the kids and stay with my older brother in Mountain Dale. My thought was that if the war was somewhat limited, they might survive in that relatively remote area. I spent the entire crisis on alert at Harmon AFB in Newfoundland, and my family stayed with my brother Bert and his family.

The first few days at Harmon were pretty bleak, with ter-rible living conditions. Because there were so many crews on alert, there were neither enough quarters nor enough vehicles; so the majority of the crews, including mine, lived on the airplanes. We slept in sleeping bags inside of the air-craft, ate canned rations, and used the latrine facilities on the plane. We could not leave the immediate area of the aircraft, and had to keep one person on a headset at all times, listen-ing to the command post frequency. In order to have heat and electricity in the aircraft, we kept our auxiliary power unit, or APU, running continuously. Since we faced the pos-sibility of having a carbon monoxide (CO) buildup within the aircraft, due to the continuous running of the APU, each crew was issued a CO detector. For twenty-four hours a day, we kept two crewmembers on duty in the cockpit, listening for a message from the command post and monitoring the CO detector. In a few days, our conditions got slightly better: we were provided with a hot meal for breakfast and dinner, served from the back of a pick-up truck that drove through the rows of airplanes. They loaded a nice shiny thirty-gallon garbage can with scrambled eggs and ladled it into our mess kits for breakfast; for dinner, the garbage can was filled with stew. We did have a choice: we could either eat or not eat. Another improvement was that portable latrine facilities were installed near the aircraft, along with an outside area where we could wash and shave. Shaving in cold water, in the late fall mornings in Newfoundland, was not pleasant.

Harmon Air Force Base became the tanker capital of the world. When all of the Strategic Air Command went on alert, maybe one quarter of the tankers were having maintenance performed on them. When these additional aircraft were brought into commission, they were also placed on alert, and the huge ramp at Harmon was filled with tankers, row after row, wingtip to wingtip. I would guess there were well over a hundred of the large, four-engine aircraft filling the entire ramp, leaving just enough room to taxi and take off. Every tanker was filled, and then topped off, with fuel. Scattered and dispersed throughout the United States, the bombers were doing the same thing we were: waiting for the message from the command post, telling us that it was time to fly our one mission. We did have plans for a follow-on mission, but I never thought that a second mission would be possible after a nuclear engagement.

The first mini-crisis evolved when the world learned that a Russian ship, the Voltava, was headed for Cuba with additional missiles loaded on the deck. The US Navy, enforcing the president's mandated blockade, would not allow it to pass beyond a certain point on the open ocean. This was critical, because seizing or sinking a ship outside of our territorial waters is an act of war, technically, and this was a Soviet ship. All of the crews were in their cockpits, listening to the low-frequency navigation radio, which could receive the local civilian radio station. The radio station was our only source of news; the Air Force did not provide us with any information about the crisis we were so deeply involved in. It was an enormous relief when the Canadian radio station reported that the Russian cargo ship had turned around without confronting the US Navy. All 500-plus crewmembers on alert at Harmon, including me, felt like dancing in the street; loud cheering could be heard from all of the surrounding aircraft.

After the first few days of the crisis my crew moved to an open-bay barracks. It was much better than the aircraft, but it was still pretty nasty. I had an upper bunk in a room that held six crews—thirty people. After that, my crew got lucky: because this was my squadron's advanced base and it was our turn to pull regular alert, we were transferred to the mole hole, the best of the three locations to pull alert. Now we had an alert station wagon and the freedom to move around the base, which meant that we could go to the Base Exchange or to the base movie theater. We had been through a lot, so this was pure luxury.

When we left the States, some crews requested, and received approval for, permission to carry civilian weapons with them, which would aid in a survival situation. We thought that our one mission would probably end with us ditching or crash landing because of lack of fuel, and the military did not supply us with weapons; therefore, John Garrison brought his 30-30 deer hunting rifle and a forty-pound wooden box full of ammunition. For some reason I do not recall, we were not permitted to leave this civilian rifle on the aircraft, so we had to drag it—and the ammunition—with us every place we went on the base. This included to the movie theater, which we visited the first night we had the vehicle. We saw the movie Strategic Air Command, with Jimmy Stewart playing the lead role. He was a colonel, a bomber pilot, doing precisely the same task that we were doing. When we left the theater at the end of the movie, the other patrons were waiting outside for us and began clapping as we walked past. This was their way of saying thank you for our part in defending the nation during the crisis. I wonder what they thought about the hunting rifle and the large box of ammunition that sat on a seat between us in the movie theater, and was in full view as we walked out.

During the entire Cuban crisis, we were informed that there would be no practice alerts. If the Klaxon horn sounded, it would be the real thing. Having this information made pulling alert much easier, but it also gave me the biggest scare of my entire life. It was either late at night or early in the morning, just the time that I am in my deepest sleep, when the alert horn sounded. I was in a room with Dick Adams, the navigator, and both of us said the same thing simultaneously as we jumped out of bed: "They said no practice alerts!" Then the realization set in: this was no practice. We did not say another word, but in record time, we were dressed in our winter flight clothing and out the door, running at full speed to the alert vehicle. I was firmly convinced that it was the beginning of a nuclear war, and I was very scared.

There was one part of the hallway in the mole hole that had a dip in it, and was full of raw sewage because the septic system had overflowed; it was about six inches deep, and blocked the entire hallway. Everyone whose room was in the area used another exit to get around the puddle, even though it was a slightly longer distance to the alert vehicles. In our fear and excitement, thinking that we would have to fly our wartime mission, all five of us on my crew ran into the sewage. Four of us got the bottoms of our flight suits and our boots wet; the navigator slipped, though, and fell into the sewage. He was drenched! This was small stuff compared to what we thought we were in for. We learned later that almost all of the crewmembers living in that part of the mole hole had run through the sewage, but Dick was the only one who fell in it. There was even some good-natured banter the next day among the supervisors who were not on alert and so had not been awakened from a deep sleep thinking that they were going to war: they suggested the sewage in the hallway was not from the septic system; rather, it had been deposited there by the crews, as they ran for their vehicles.

The alert ramp was about a mile in length, and my KC-97 was parked near one end, in the middle of the next-to-last row. When I got to my airplane, I could see a big fire on the far end of the ramp, about a mile away. Harmon Air Force Base was built on the western side of Newfoundland; the asphalt of the ramp and runway ends only a few feet from the Gulf of Saint Lawrence. One of the big concerns we all had during this crisis was that a Russian submarine would get close enough to the base, through the Gulf of Saint Lawrence, to lob one shell onto the ramp. There was over a million gallons of fuel in the close-packed planes on the ramp, and it would probably explode if a shell from a submarine landed anywhere on the ramp. This scenario was discussed among the crews during our bull sessions in the mess hall. Someone started the rumor that a submarine had been sighted, but I didn't really believe it. The seed, however, was planted in the back of my mind. If we'd thought of a submarine attack, why couldn't the Russians?

When I climbed into the right seat, I was sure that the worst had occurred: the submarine story was true! It looked like a fuel fire, because of the black smoke. I reasoned that because of the location, it had to be a tanker on fire; and I was in grave danger, even though I was so far away. I put on my headset to copy a message from the command post, but all I received was the gibberish of dozens of copilots, who, just like me, were looking for the standard SAC coded message with instructions on what action to take. It had been beaten into our brains that the only method of moving the alert force was by copying a formal radio message, which had to be decoded and authenticated before the message could be acted upon. We'd been coached, too, that it was possible for this same mythical Russian submarine to transmit a phony message in an attempt confuse the SAC forces, and we were not to take any action without a perfect message. I listened to the confusion and panic of the crews who were close enough to the fire to know that they had to take some action, but they were fearful of violating the regulations that our entire existence was based upon. At last, the command post transmitted a message, but it did not authenticate. This was exactly what we were previously briefed would happen if the enemy were transmitting the message: they would not have the classified codes to make the message authenticate.

The fire was so far away, and the confusion on the radio so enormous, that by the time John and Robbie had engines started, we still didn't know what to do—we just sat and listened. We listened to the confusion that was coming over the radio, and we listened to our hearts pounding in our chests. I was trying to figure out a course of action to take if all of the aircraft in front of us started exploding, but was unable to come up with an acceptable solution; there was no place to go. I still thought that this was the beginning of the war that I'd dreaded, and I wondered how I had gotten myself into a situation where I might be only seconds away from dying, with absolutely no options.

Of course, this was not the beginning of the war that might have ended civilization on earth. The fuel for all of the aircraft came from a tank farm located in a remote area on this huge military installation, with an underground pipe system to the ramp to enable rapid refueling of the aircraft. The fuel pumping station, which was at the end of this underground fuel system, at the far end of the ramp, had caught fire. None of the airplanes were burning, as it had appeared from my position, a mile away. The crews on the tankers nearest the fire, recognizing the extremely critical situation and their proximity to the burning fuel, moved their aircraft out of the danger area. Technically, they violated our regulations; however, they were praised for taking the action necessary to prevent a catastrophe. No one was injured, and nothing was damaged, other than the pumping station. The message from the command post was slow in arriving and did not authenticate because of errors by the controller on duty under these tense and very unusual conditions.

Dick Adams washed his flying clothes, but had to put up with an enormous amount of ribbing from the other crewmembers. I added to his misery by saying that I was right behind him running down the hallway and didn't see him fall in the sewage, so he must have pooped in his pants. We all needed something to relieve the tension, and the stink of Dick's clothing and the humor of it all (to everyone but Dick) provided that release.

The Cuban crisis was defused when Khrushchev agreed to remove the missiles from Cuba and, in exchange, Kennedy agreed to remove our intermediate range ballistic missiles from Turkey. The system worked for both sides, but to prevent the possibility of a breakdown of communications during another possible showdown, a red telephone, the original hotline, was installed between the White House and the Kremlin. Then, our president was only seconds away from talking directly, and immediately, to the Soviet premier, through a translator.

Where were you when you learned that President Kennedy was assassinated? I had been in Spain on SAC alert; and my crew, along with a few other crews, was given a couple of days off for R&R. My unit had arranged for an old C-47 to fly to Rome, with a stop in Mallorca to give us a real mini-vacation. There were about two dozen SAC crewmembers on the plane, but only four of us went to Rome. We rented one hotel room and immediately went to the number one tourist destination, the Vatican. On the steps leading up to St. Peter's Basilica, we began speaking to an American priest who was working in this city within a city. He informed us that the pope was holding a special mass the next day for members of the American military and that we were invited. My three friends jumped at this once-in-a-lifetime invitation. I accepted, too, but was not excited about spending the major part of another day in the Vatican. Also, because I was Jewish and young, I had never attended a Catholic mass; so I felt uncomfortable. That evening, we had an early meal in a restaurant recommended by the priest and went to bed early; we were exhausted from the flight and the tour of St. Peter's. It was November 22, 1963.

The next morning I was not feeling well, and I told the other three that I was not going to the Vatican with them but would see them back in the room before dinner. I had a croissant and cappuccino for breakfast and then went to buy a pair of white leather gloves for my two-and-a-half-year-old daughter. The two sales girls in the shop did not speak any English, and I didn't speak Italian. At first, I thought that they were excited to have an American customer in their small glove shop, because I was getting a lot of attention, but without real communication. They kept saying: "Kennedy!" which was the only thing I understood. After a few minutes of their attempting to tell me something and my not understanding, they took me to a nearby newspaper stand and showed me the headline: "Kennedy Assassinated." Although the newspaper was in Italian, the meaning was clear. My first knowledge of the death of my president was on a street in Rome, from a newspaper, the day after he was shot.

I was stunned and needed more information, which I could not get from the sales girls. I had to know who, what, when, where, and most importantly, how it affected me. Did I have to get back to my base in Spain because of a military emergency? Was the country having another military crisis? Was all of SAC going back on alert as had happened with the Cuban crisis? Did the Soviets assassinate President Kennedy? All of this went through my head, and I couldn't find anyone who spoke enough English to answer my questions.

I remembered that the United States Embassy was walking distance from where I was, so I headed there. A large crowd was surrounding the entrance, held back by the Rome police on the outside of the gate and the US Marines on the inside of the gate. It was difficult to work my way to the front of the sympathetic crowd, only to get pushed away and ignored by the police. When I was insistent, and they realized that I was a member of the United States military, they allowed me to approach a young Marine whose post was just inside the gate. When I identified myself as an Air Force captain, he allowed me to enter the embassy, where I found someone who explained to me what had occurred and assured me that it was not necessary to report back to my base. It was then about eighteen hours after Walter Cronkite had announced to the nation that President John F. Kennedy was dead. I was probably in the last one percent of all Americans to hear the terrible news.

Amid all of the turmoil and sorrow, the Vatican did have a religious service for the assassinated American president in St. Peter's Basilica. It was hosted by the pope, one of the two most famous Catholics in the world, for the other one, who had just been killed. It was my choice not to attend, and I've been kicking myself ever since.

MAYDAY, MAYDAY, MAYDAY!

LMOST ALL OF my adult life was spent in the cockpit; and like all professional pilots, I had my share of emergencies. Some of the problems were serious, but by far the greatest number were routine. I have had dozens of engine failures and a few fires, as well as numerous emergency landings; but only once, forty-five years ago, did I make an emergency Mayday! radio call.

It was early November, 1962. The Cuban crisis was just over, and it was time to get back to the normal routine of flying to maintain proficiency and pulling SAC alert. We had to take care of one important piece of business first: everyone who had not logged four hours of flying time in the past month had to do so, to receive their flight pay. There wasn't any exception to the rule: no flying—no flight pay; and that was about a quarter of my total income. My crew, with John Garrison as the aircraft commander, was the first crew scheduled to fly. We had two crews on board the aircraft for this simple mission, and each crew would log four hours of flight time. Since I was the primary copilot, the right seat was mine for the first few hours.

The weather at Westover Air Force Base was beautiful: there were a few fair weather clouds, the sun was bright, and the temperature in the cockpit was comfortable (in summer, the cockpit could be miserably hot).

Five crewmembers made up Garrison's crew. I was the copilot; Joe Robinson, "Robbie," was the flight engineer; the navigator was Dick Adams; and Bob Hunt worked in the back of the KC-97 tanker as the boom operator. The pilot, copilot, and navigator were commissioned officers; Robbie and Bob were sergeants. We flew together, ate together, socialized with our wives and kids together, and tried to keep each other going when things got tough. That day, we tried to keep each other alive.

Getting an aircraft off the ground, for an experienced crew, is about as hard as backing your car out of your driveway. You have done it hundreds of times, and it becomes routine. You can do it with your eyes closed.

Like us, the aircraft we were flying had not flown for a few weeks; sitting idle like this is bad for a large, complicated piece of machinery. Planes seem to have a much better maintenance record when they fly more often. We went through the pages of checklists—mostly challenge and response. One of the pilots reads the checklist and the appropriate crewmember answers, while double-checking to ensure that the hundred or so switches, and all of the systems on the aircraft, are ready for takeoff.

John was flying, which meant that my job was to read the checklists, use the radios, follow his directions, and, of course, double-check each of his actions. The takeoff was normal until he called for "gear up," which occurred just a few seconds after the aircraft lifted off the ground. On this aircraft, electric motors raised and lowered the landing gear. Every other air-craft I have flown had hydraulic motors for the gear, but on the KC-97, we used most of out hydraulic power to operate the refueling equipment. I placed the gear switch in the up position; and at about that time, I heard a commotion from the six crewmembers in the rear of the aircraft. My assumption was that they were cheering because we were getting back to normal after the very stressful two weeks of being on constant alert during the Cuban crisis. I glanced over my left shoulder to view the rear of the aircraft through the open cockpit door and saw a boiling black cloud of smoke forcing its way toward the cockpit. What I heard were not shouts of joy; they were shouts of terror. This was not the friendly smoke you see coming from burning wood at a campfire; this was the thick, black, angry smoke that comes from an oil fire, and it was starting to engulf the cockpit.

My mind went into what I call my survival mode, which happens when I am seriously threatened. Some people shut down and cannot function, but I go into a state in which I think clearly and react immediately. My first thought was what I had learned during my simulator training: when faced with an emergency situation, first protect yourself; then fly the airplane. To protect myself, I had to get my oxygen mask on and ensure that I was breathing pure, one-hundred-percent, oxygen. One breath of that thick smoke could incapacitate me. I shouted a warning to the other crewmembers, and im-mediately started putting on my oxygen mask as rapidly as I could. John was still flying the aircraft, and I would have to take control, with my mask in place, to allow John to get his mask on. It was only ten second after taking off, so we were still very close to the ground. I knew that if I panicked and stopped functioning, we might not survive.

When my mask was on, I took control of the airplane and started concentrating on getting some altitude so that we would be able to think about how to handle the situation we found ourselves in.

We had no idea what was happening, other than the fact that our airplane was full of vicious smoke, but we knew that we were in a life or death situation. The smoke was so thick that I had very little visibility; by leaning far to my right, though, I was able to get my head in a place with much less smoke and pretty good visibility out of the side windows. I was having trouble seeing the instruments, but with my side vision, as well as being so close to the ground, I didn't need them. I was still on the Westover Control Tower radio frequency, and for the only time in my life, I made the traditional emergency call: "Mayday, Mayday, Mayday!" All I said was that we had a fire in the rear and the cockpit was full of smoke. I never established two-way contact with the tower; I just keyed the mic and transmitted. The tower never said a thing. I felt embarrassed that my voice cracked during the five-second transmission.

Once we had our oxygen masks on, we started to get over the initial shock of having the cockpit full of smoke, but we still had a severe problem. We were breathing one-hundred-percent oxygen, but the smoke was affecting our eyes and we didn't have smoke goggles to protect us. In later years, all aircraft carried an inexpensive pair of specialized smoke goggles for each crew member; smoke goggles use oxygen to clear the smoke from around the eyes, preventing the irritation which we experienced. If we had had smoke goggles available to us, our crisis would have been a little less desperate.

John started turning left to fly around the traffic pattern and land on the same runway we had used for takeoff. Robbie said he was going to start dumping fuel so we could reduce weight. Just when I thought things were going to be okay, everything began to fall apart. John didn't have the power available to climb, and he leveled off in an attempt to increase our airspeed a few knots. We were only a few hundred feet in the air and getting close to our stall speed. I was confused that we didn't have more engine power available and was concerned about our lack of airspeed and altitude. I pulled my mask away from my face and shouted to Robbie over my left shoulder that he had to dump fuel. This was our only way to reduce the weight of the aircraft and the first step to combat the condition that we were in, if we were going to keep flying. Robbie, in his frustration, angrily shouted back at me that he was trying to dump but he couldn't. He then realized for the first time that we did not have electrical power. The pumps that permitted us to dump fuel had electrical controls and were now unusable. We were so concerned with the smoke filling the cockpit and our inability to see the instruments and gauges that we did not initially notice the loss of our main power supply—the electrical system.

John needed more engine power, to increase our airspeed, and called for RPM 2550. If we could increase the RPM, that is, have the propellers turn faster, we could have more power from the engines. Robbie moved the RPM lever forward; it was a reflex on his part when one of the pilots asked for an RPM change. He told us that the RPM was stuck at 1900: we needed electrical power to change it. I couldn't understand why we had such a low RPM setting, but this wasn't the time to try to figure it out. I was beginning to realize the full impact of what the loss of electrical power meant. We had lost about ninety percent of our capability to control the aircraft; almost everything was electrical. We were in a terrible situation; we had a fire on board, with a cockpit full of smoke; we couldn't dump our fuel to reduce weight; and we had four engines operating but producing only about half the power they were capable of.

It is normal, in this type of crisis to gain information and process it slowly. I was starting to realize that we had numerous problems to overcome if we were going to get the plane back on the ground in one piece, and I was thinking that a controlled crash landing may be in my immediate future. We depended on a report from Bob, in the rear of the aircraft, to inform us of the nature of the fire, but we had no contact with Bob. Without electrical power, we did not have an intercom system; so we'd lost contact with the rear of the plane. We still had no idea what was burning and the condition of the six people in the rear. They were in the worst of the smoke and there was no oxygen available for the extra crew.

Bob came running into the cockpit wearing a portable oxygen mask and reported that the smoke was coming from the lower deck, but he had no idea what was burning. He also told us that the spare crew was crawling on the floor, where the smoke was lighter, trying to breathe, and that they were putting on their parachutes. This last statement, that they were possibly going to bail out, scared me. We were only a few hundred feet above the ground, which was not sufficient altitude to allow their parachutes to open: a bailout from this altitude would have been fatal. I shouted to Bob not to allow them to bail out, that we were too low. He could tell by the urgency in my voice that I meant for him to stop them immediately. He ran out of the cockpit without saying anything.

I seemed to be the only crewmember that was not having severe smoke problems, so I took on the task of removing whatever smoke I could. That seemed to be our most critical, immediate problem. Our procedure for removing smoke at low altitude was to open a hatch in the rear of the aircraft. The outside airflow in that location would suck out some of the smoke, which would then be replaced with fresh air. But I was afraid to let Bob open a hatch in the rear, to reduce the smoke, because of the possibility of someone jumping. My decision not to use the hatch required an alternate method of bringing fresh air into the aircraft. Our flight manual stated specifically not to open a cockpit window during smoke removal. With a rear hatch open, the airflow would be into the rear hatch and out of the cockpit window, thereby bringing all of the smoke up to the cockpit. I was desperate: I knew that the rear hatch had not been opened and decided to crack open my sliding window, in violation of the manual. If things got worse, I could always close it. As soon as I opened the window a crack, there was a blast of fresh outside air into the cockpit. The book hadn't covered this situation, but most of the smoke cleared from the cockpit quickly. When the smoke began to dissipate, the desperation I was feeling also dissipated; and I began to think maybe we could get back on the ground. John was continuing to turn slowly back toward the runway, but we were still only at very low altitude and just above our stall speed. He was doing the best he could to get us on the ground in the shortest time, and Robbie was adjusting the throttles trying to squeeze all of the horsepower he could from our RPM-restricted engines.

With the reduction of the smoke, the second crew was able to begin to function and assist us. The second flight engineer donned a fire fighting mask, attached to a portable oxygen bottle, and went downstairs with a flashlight, crash ax, and fire extinguisher, in an attempt to find out what was burning.

It took a lot of guts to open the hatch and go into the smoke-filled lower deck by himself. When he finished his inspection, he came to the cockpit and stunned me with the information that the main electrical panel on the aircraft was the cause of the fire, and there was a large electrical flare shooting from the panel that looked like the flame from a welder's torch. It was about an inch in diameter and a foot long; and it was pointed between two fuel lines.

The lower deck was filled with fuel tanks for our air-to-air refueling missions and large fuel lines connecting the tanks with the refueling pumps. The enormous quantity of smoke had come from the electrical flare. It burned through thick copper cables covered in heavy insulation, through automatic switches, circuit breakers, and insulating components of the main power panel. All were vaporized. Finally it destroyed the metal box covering the equipment, leaving the flare itself exposed. That panel was where power from four generators, each turned by an engine, joined, supplying the aircraft with electricity. There was normally enough electricity flowing through that panel to supply a small town. Now the panel was gone and the electrical torch from the generators was inches from our fuel lines.

We had no way to shut down the generators. The only way to stop the electricity was to shut down the engines, which we couldn't do and still continue flying. We decided to ignore the electrical flare, pray that it would not change direction and hit one of the fuel lines, and concentrate on landing the aircraft as soon as possible. We were only a few minutes from landing and seemed to have the situation under control. If the flare did not contact the fuel lines, we would probably land successfully. Things were looking up!

We had no radio contact with the control tower, but on final approach we received a green light, from a light gun in the tower, indicating that we were cleared to land. They were watching us with binoculars because of our very low altitude and they could see us trailing smoke. Our flaps were still in the takeoff position, which was okay for landing, and I was feeling greatly relieved when John called, "Gear down." I placed the gear switch in the "down" position, and for the first time we all remembered, almost simultaneously, that we could not put the landing gear down without electrical power. We had been so involved with handling the massive smoke problem that we forgot that we needed electric motors to lower the landing gear. We were about two minutes from landing and had two options: we could crash land on the belly without the landing gear down, or we could attempt a go-around with our limited amount of power available, while we lowered the gear manually. It was John's decision to make, but we all agreed. We decided on the go-around, even though we had very low engine power and no way of getting any more.

Now we entered a difficult and unexpected phase of the emergency. The main landing gear would have to be lowered with a hand crank, which required 650 turns to lower each side: a total of 1,300 turns of the hand crank. The nose landing gear was no problem. It would free-fall, and be blown into the down and locked position by airflow.

The lowering mechanism for the main gear was located on the bottom deck, attached to the same bulkhead as the electrical power panel, which was still smoking. The lower deck was still full of smoke, because we had no method of ventilating it and bringing in fresh air. Cranking the main gear down had to be done in the smoke, only a few feet from the exposed electrical flare, which had to be avoided.

We had a total of ten people on board the aircraft and three of us—John, Robbie, and I—had to remain in the cockpit to keep the airplane flying. We positioned the aircraft so that as soon as the landing gear was down, we would fly only a short final approach and land immediately. This also gave the three of us our first chance to discuss what equipment we still had operating and to talk about landing with so many systems inoperative. The aircraft commander of the second crew had seven crewmembers at his disposal, and was assigned the responsibility of getting the main landing gear down and locked as fast as possible.

The first person to turn the crank was the flight engineer on the spare crew. He returned to the cramped area on the lower deck, wearing the fire fighter's mask with a portable oxygen bottle attached. He had the large fuel tanks for our air refueling mission on both sides of him, from floor to ceiling, and on the forward bulkhead he had the still smoldering main power panel and the exposed flare coming out of it. The physical strain of cranking the gear down, combined with the stressful conditions, caused the flight engineer to breathe rapidly and deeply; he sucked the portable oxygen bottle dry in less than a minute. When there was no oxygen remaining, he sucked the acrid smoke into his lungs. He nearly lost consciousness and had to be dragged through the small hatch, back up to the upper deck, where better conditions existed.

To remove as much smoke as possible from the lower deck, all of the hatches were opened on the upper deck and the two floor hatches to the lower deck were opened. This greatly alleviated the smoke, and conditions improved. Two people at a time then went to the lower deck, protected with the only two portable oxygen masks we had on the aircraft. They cranked the main landing gear emergency extension system until they were tired or out of oxygen and then returned to the upper deck for rest and recuperation, to be replaced by someone else. Everyone in the rear took a turn at the crank, wearing a mask and changing the oxygen bottle with a fresh one when the old one was empty. They ran out of portable oxygen while working on extending the second landing gear. But by this time most of the smoke had dissipated, and the task was completed without oxygen.

In the cockpit, we had no indication whether the landing gear was down and locked because the indicators were electrical, so we waited for a verbal report from the rear. As soon we were told that they had completed cranking and they confirmed that the gear was locked in the down position, we turned onto the final approach for the second time. This time, we were prepared for the landing because we'd had a chance to talk about the equipment that was not operating. The airspeed indicator, the only instrument that was required to fly the approach in visual conditions, did not require electricity and was working; and we had our hydraulic wheel brakes to stop the aircraft after landing. We had everything we needed to land; we just wanted to get on the ground and shut the engines down to stop the electrical flare that caused our initial problem and could still cause us to explode.

I could see all of the emergency equipment waiting for us near the runway. Westover was a large Air Force Base, with numerous pieces of specialized aircraft fire fighting equipment. I knew that if we could make it to the ground, my survival was almost guaranteed. I put everything else out of my mind except the approach and landing, which required nothing out of the ordinary. We had come full circle; all that was required to complete the short flight, which had never left the traffic pattern and never even reached traffic pattern altitude, was a visual landing.

John made the landing, and as soon as we stopped, still on the runway, we shut down the engines and evacuated the aircraft. Shutting down the engines finally stopped the electrical flare. Normally, each piece of electrical equipment on an aircraft is protected with an aircraft-style circuit breaker that pops out when there is an overload on the circuit, protecting the equipment from damage. In our case, though, the initial surge of power from the generators fused all of the circuit breakers shut. In other words, instead of breaking the circuit as they were designed to do, all of the circuit breakers were welded shut, allowing the huge surge of electrical power to go directly to the hundreds of pieces of equipment and instruments. The high power surge destroyed every electrical component on the aircraft. Normally, when an aircraft has an electrical failure, some of the most important equipment continues to operate from the aircraft battery. In our case we had a total failure of the electrical system, including the emergency battery equipment. The damage was so severe that it was not economical to repair, and the aircraft never flew again.

Newer aircraft designs have differential fault—or feeder fault—protection, an automatic system that isolates the faulty generator from the aircraft electrical system when a similar malfunction occurs. On a modern plane, the flight engineer can shut off the electrical output of a generator at the engine, instead of allowing the surge of electrical energy to enter the fuselage, as happened to us. The problem we encountered cannot occur on more modern aircraft.

Later aircraft that I flew had smoke goggles, which supplied oxygen to the eyes; thereby alleviating one of the major smoke problems we encountered that day. Newer oxygen masks are "quick donning," meaning a pilot can put one on, with one hand, in seconds. In 1962, the mask I had required two hands to put on, which meant that I could not manipulate the flight controls and put my mask on at the same time.

When we were safely on the ground, we began to try to figure out what had really occurred. I did not know how we got stuck with a propeller RPM so low that we were just barely able to remain airborne. For takeoff we had maximum power on all of the engines, and after the electrical failure the RPM mysteriously dropped to 1900, restricting our power output. The most logical explanation that I could come up with, after hearing everyone's story, was that we had the electrical failure at the exact instant that John was adjusting the power. When I initially shouted to everyone that we had a fire, I immediately put my mask on. John, however, was flying; and he performed the first step of the emergency procedure for a fire. He set the engine power, or at least he thought he was setting the power. The takeoff RPM was too high, so he immediately grabbed the RPM lever and pulled it back about an inch an a half, to reduce the speed of the propeller. Realizing he reduced it too much, he immediately pushed it forward about half an inch. This was a normal occurrence; I always had difficulty setting the RPM, the same as John did that morning, because the lever was tight and did not operate smoothly. I would usually ask the engineer to set the RPM for me. I assume that we lost our electrical power at the instant the RPM was at the lowest point, just before John pushed the lever forward again. He said that when he was setting the power he took his first breath of smoke and probably became so distracted that he never glanced back at the propeller RPM gauge. This is an outstanding example of Murphy's Law—if something can go wrong, it will. It did go wrong, at the worst possible time, and almost caused us to crash because of lack of power.

We had a great deal of luck on our side, though. First, if we hadn't had the additional crew on board, cranking the landing gear down may very well have been beyond the physical capability of our five-man crew. I don't think the five of us would have had the stamina, under the conditions, to complete the gear extension; and we would have probably landed with only partial landing gear. The next bit of good luck was the position of the power panel that burned in relation to the two fuel lines that the electrical flare was passing between. If either had been designed a little bit differently or positioned a few inches higher or lower, the flare would have hit one of the fuel lines. Most probably, it would have burned through in a few seconds, causing the aircraft to explode. The next condition that allowed us to walk away from the aircraft was that the weather was good, so we did not have to use instruments and radios to fly the aircraft. It would have placed us in an impossible situation if we had been in the clouds when we had the electrical failure. The combination of low engine power and our proximity to the ground, with none of our electrical flight instruments operating, probably would have resulted in our losing control of the aircraft and flying into the ground. Finally, the power setting we were stuck with was low, but it was enough to allow us to continue flying.

During our debriefing, I mentioned that I made that desperate mayday radio call to the control tower to let them know we had a fire and the cockpit was full of smoke. The tower said that they never received the transmission and they realized we had a problem only because of our very low altitude and the visible smoke behind the aircraft. I then realized that I made the radio call after putting on my oxygen mask, which was after John had attempted to set the propeller RPM. I made the emergency radio transmission after the power failure. With no electrical power, we had no radios and the only mayday call I ever made never left the aircraft.

I survived partly because I was a competent pilot, but I was also a lucky pilot. I was also the only one on the plane that day who did not spend time in the base hospital for smoke-related injuries.

GOODBYE TANKER, HELLO TRANSPORT

MY SQUADRON WAS on a three-month rotation to Lajes AFB on Terceira Island, in the Azores. I had been flying the KC-97 for three years as a copilot when I convinced Dick Bryant, a flight examiner, to give me an aircraft commander's check ride. I requested the opportunity, without having the formal training normally required, and he consented with the caveat that if I did not pass I would continue in order of rank, with the other copilots, and would not be given another chance to upgrade to the left seat for many years. I accepted the challenge. For my check ride, I had to fly as the pilot of the lead tanker, in a six-ship formation that refueled six B-47 bombers returning to the United States from their alert duty in Spain. I passed the check ride, and became a brand new aircraft commander. For the first time, I was qualified to fly in the left seat of a large, four-engine aircraft and make all of the decisions.

I was the youngest aircraft commander in the squadron, and there was some discussion that I might be the youngest aircraft commander in SAC; without computers to check the ages of all the left seat qualified pilots, though, there was no easy way to confirm the supposition. I was able to get the required experience in the left seat, and thereby be bold enough to request the flight check, only because I was lucky. I had been crewed with John Garrison for several years and he had recently become an instructor pilot. His new job required that he maintain proficiency in both pilot seats. He needed right seat practice, so I began flying alternate missions in the left seat; we both became comfortable in either seat.

My first flight in the left seat was due to a shattered outer layer of the windscreen on the left side. That problem reduced the forward visibility from the pilot's seat to zero. John decided that the mission would be safe if he made the takeoff and landing from the right seat. That was the opening I needed; I agreed to fly the mission from the left seat, behind the shattered windscreen. Only the outer layer of the windscreen was shattered, it looked like the inner layer was okay and would not cause a further problem. After that first flight in the left seat, on future missions we rotated seats about every other flight.

The windscreen of an aircraft has to be strong enough to keep a bird from entering the cockpit and incapacitating the pilot. The usual standard is that it must be capable of withstanding the energy of a five-pound bird, traveling at the maximum speed of the aircraft. There is a facility that checks the strength of windscreens by shooting dead chickens (chicken crash dummies are used nowadays, rather than real birds) into them with a specially constructed air cannon. If the chicken penetrates the windscreen during the test, it's back to the drawing board for the design engineers.

To have the required strength and visibility, the windows are built in two layers with a clear, electrical heating element between the layers. Both layers are heated. The acrylic inner layer is the structural member and the heat allows it to deflect when struck by a bird. The heated thin, outer layer is non-structural and prevents ice and snow from building up and obstructing the pilot's vision. When a windscreen shatters, the sound is like a rifle shot; it may shatter into thousands of little shards, making it almost impossible to see through. But I have never had one that did not remain in place, even with both layers shattered.

I was flying in the right seat late one night, between Hopedale and Cape Dyer, in northeastern Canada. The heating element for the windows drew a lot of current, and there were heavy wires and other electrical equipment fastened to the window frame about a foot from my right side. It was dark out; we had been flying for hours and were bored. No one in the cockpit was talking or telling jokes; we all were fighting to stay awake. Then I heard a crackling sound coming from the electrical fittings at the base of the side window nearest my seat, so I glanced to my right to see what was causing the unusual noise. Almost immediately, there was a loud crack, like a large dry tree limb breaking, and an electrical flare, just like the flame of a blow torch, that extended almost to my right arm.

I could feel the heat from the flare, and I could smell the burnt wires and insulation; I wanted to get away from it, but I was trapped. My normal exit from the seat was to my right, but that was just where I didn't want to be. If the flame hit me I would probably get burned instantly. I realized that my only escape was to climb over the radios, on my left, and into the flight engineer's lap. I was lying in Robbie's lap before he had a chance to realize what was going on. It always takes a few seconds to determine what is causing the problem, and then another few seconds to find the switch or circuit breaker to correct it; however, Robbie was able to get the power shut off to the windows, which stopped the dangerous arcing, before I had time to get off of his lap. Not only did I almost wet my pants, but I also had to take a good-natured ribbing from the rest of the crew. It was all part of the job.

After I became an aircraft commander, I remained on Garrison's crew as the copilot, but occasionally I would fill a vacant left seat on other crews. Having two fully qualified pilots on one crew eventually led to some friendly competition between John and me. Routine missions usually lasted eight hours and almost always included a four-hour refueling. Then we had four hours remaining to fly practice approaches and landings or maybe allow the navigator time to get his specialized practice.

One night we were flying practice instrument approaches and touch-and-go landings. To add a little interest to the four-hour session, John and I took turns flying an approach and landing, with the crew deciding who had made the better landing of each pair. Of course, there was a little wager involved. At the end of the four hours, I was losing by one; but since I had the last landing, it was possible that we could finish the long night in a tie.

In my attempt to make the smoothest landing, I held the aircraft off the ground as long as I could by pulling up the nose as the aircraft slowed down; I was looking for a "grease job." I thought that the main wheels were about one foot above the runway. As later became evident, the aircraft was actually on the ground; but no one had felt the touchdown. Because I didn't realize that the aircraft was on the runway already, I continued to pull the nose up until the boom pod, which is in the rear and is the lowest part of the aircraft, struck the runway. The friction of the bottom of the boom pod with the pavement burned a hole about the size of a quarter through the aluminum. There was a shower of sparks into the boom pod, making us think that we had some sort of fire; but as soon as I lowered the nose for the final landing, the sparks ceased. The hole needed only a small patch, and the repair took about one man-hour. That was the only damage I ever did to an aircraft.

But who won the bet? John claimed I owed him a beer because I had damaged the aircraft on the landing; my claim was that since no one knew that the aircraft was on the ground, it was obviously the best landing, and the incident had occurred after the landing. We called it a tie, and everyone, except me, lived happily forever after.

The Boeing manual for the aircraft stated that the pod cannot possibly be scraped during a landing, so I was not held responsible for the minor incident. For the next few weeks, though, every time I had a flight, there was a cardboard roller skate taped to the bottom of the boom pod. I don't know who the keeper of the roller skate was, but it did serve its purpose: it reminded me that I was not perfect.

Later jet aircraft that I flew for TWA did have a serious problem with striking the lower aft portion of the fuselage on the runway during over-rotation on takeoff. The aircraft that it was possible to damage in this manner, such as the Boeing 727 and Lockheed 1011, had tail skids that extended for takeoff and landing to prevent the same type of incident that I'd had. Instead of hitting the aircraft structure on the runway, as I did, the skid was designed to strike the runway and prevent structural damage. Whoever designed the cardboard roller skate was ahead of his time.

I did have a serious landing incident in the KC-97; fortunately, though, I did not damage the aircraft or injure anyone. I was flying the third aircraft in a flight of three, with a ten minute separation, going to Harmon AFB in Newfoundland to go on alert. The weather from Massachusetts to Newfoundland was great, but the runway at Harmon probably had the worst conditions I have ever landed in. They had an ice storm that had stopped only recently, and they were reporting the braking action on the runway as "nil." This is the term used to convey to the pilot that the ice is too slick to get a reading on the amount of braking I could expect after landing. To measure how slippery the ice is, an automatic measuring device is pulled behind a car driven down the runway; the reading is then transmitted to the pilot, who looks it up in the aircraft landing charts to determine whether the runway is suitable for landing. That day, the ice was so slick that they could not get a reading. The ice was not the only problem; the runway had a crosswind from the right at twenty-five knots. Either of these conditions would have resulted in a difficult landing, but the combination of the ice plus the crosswind made for conditions that were too dangerous to land the aircraft.

I should have proceeded to my alternate airport, but there were extenuating circumstances. I was carrying two extra crews, who were needed, along with my crew, to go on alert.

And the two airplanes in front of me had landed about ten minutes before ours, without difficulty. I was being pressured by the SAC command post to try the landing. I was not comfortable with the decision, but I decided to land.

The runway at Harmon was over a mile and a half long, which, under normal conditions, was suitable for any aircraft. When I made the decision to try the landing I had no idea that I would need a few thousand feet more in length and few hundred feet greater width. The approach to the runway was over high terrain, requiring an extremely steep approach—the steepest I have ever flown, other than combat approaches in Vietnam. The steep approach, plus preparing for the crosswind landing, made stabilizing the aircraft in the seconds before touchdown even more difficult. The far end of the runway, where the pavement stopped, was about a hundred feet from the Gulf of Saint Lawrence. The buffer between the water and the runway consisted of huge boulders placed there when the runway was built. If I could not get the aircraft stopped on the runway, I would hit the boulders first, then probably continue into the freezing water.

Everything was normal during the approach, considering the strong crosswind and the resulting turbulence from the terrain. I landed as close as possible to the end of the runway, so that I would have plenty of room to slow to taxi speed before reaching the far end of the runway—and the rocks. As soon as I was firmly on the runway, I put all propellers into reverse thrust. This is the best method the pilot has of slowing down from the high landing speed to a slower speed, where the brakes can be used to continue the slowdown. As soon as I applied reverse thrust, the aircraft turned about sixty degrees to the right, and we were in a full skid, sliding sideways down the runway. Ned, who was in the other seat, summed up our situation with two words: "Holy shit!"

I don't know what caused us to the turn to the right. It could have been one of the propellers hanging up when going into reverse, or maybe a gust of wind hit our large vertical stabilizer, causing the tail to weather-vane to the left. The bottom line is that I was in serious trouble immediately after touchdown, and the probability of having an accident was increasing. We were still near the center of the runway, with over a mile of runway remaining, so I took engines three and four out of reverse, and kept numbers one and two in reverse. This succeeded in bringing the nose to the left, which I was trying to do, but it also pulled us to the right side of the runway, placing the nose gear outside of the runway edge lights. The lights marked the side of the runway and were about fifty feet inside the edge of the pavement; they were raised about a foot above the surface so that they could be seen when the runway had a light snow cover. I now had my nose gear outside the lights, with the main gear inside the lights, and I was still skidding down the runway at about eighty knots.

A pilot has a number of ways to steer an airplane on the ground. First, during normal taxi, the pilot uses nose-wheel steering. There is a steering wheel that is connected hydraulically to the nose wheel, and the pilot steers the plane the same way you steer your car. Just like your car, nose-wheel steering is useless on slick ice. The second way to steer is with differential braking. Unlike your car, the pilot has a brake for each side of the aircraft, independently operated with his right or left foot. On slick ice, this method of steering is also useless. The third way of steering is by using the rudder of the airplane, to aerodynamically move the nose of the airplane to the left or right. This method can be used effectively only at the higher speeds: as the speed decreases it becomes less effective, and at about sixty knots, it is almost useless. That leaves one way to steer the airplane on slick ice at low speed: the engines. The KC-97 had four reciprocating engines and reversible propellers; two on each wing. If I wanted to make the airplane turn to the left, I could reverse the propellers on the left side of the airplane, or I could add forward power to the engines on the right side of the aircraft, or use combinations of the two methods. In my situation, sliding sideways down the ice covered runway at Harmon, the only effective method I had of straightening out the aircraft was differential power.

I had to find a way to get the airplane stopped before reaching the end of the runway. Sliding into the rocks and the water off the end of the pavement would cause a major accident, with the possibility of fire and fatalities. At the same time, I had to keep the airplane from going off the side of the runway, which would probably collapse the landing gear.

My only way of controlling the aircraft was reduced to the four throttles in my right hand. If I pushed a throttle forward, I added forward thrust, and if pulled a throttle back, past a certain point, I reversed the propeller, providing backward thrust. I continued to manipulate the throttles in an attempt to get the airplane pointed straight down the runway. I could get the nose to swing to the left, but could never keep it there during this balancing act between engine power and weather-vaning into the crosswind. I was still straddling the runway edge lights, and was concerned about hitting them; breaking one off could damage the tires.

I continued for about a mile in this condition, and it seemed to take forever. I was out of control, on the far right side of the runway, still moving at about sixty knots; I wasn't slowing down. When the tower had informed me that the braking action was nil, they were not exaggerating: there was no friction at all between the ice and the tires.

This runway had markers to inform the pilot of the distance remaining to the end of the runway; they were spaced every thousand feet. When I saw the number two marker, which was two thousand feet from the end of the runway, I decided to concern myself only with not going off the end into the rocks, and nothing else. At this point, I didn't care about damaged runway lights or tires or even structural damage to the aircraft; I was trying to save my life, plus the lives of my crew and passengers. I had almost run out of options. Nothing that I attempted to this point had been successful, and I had been fighting this situation for about sixty seconds. Sixty seconds doesn't sound like a long time, but it was an eternity for me.

With two thousand feet remaining, I placed all four engines in maximum reverse and clamped down on both brakes, this was all I could do to stop the airplane. At one thousand feet remaining, we were still going pretty fast. Ned, in the right seat, said that we were going to go off the end. I thought, too, that we were going to slide into the rocks and maybe into the frigid water. I could see the large concrete pad at the end of the runway, which was used for engine run-up when taking off in the opposite direction, and the large, black, moss-covered rocks immediately beyond the run-up pad. All I was doing at this point was going along for the ride; I had run out of runway and options.

I reached the run-up pad going very slowly, about twenty knots, but I was sure that we would still slide into the rocks, which were the size of a car. Then, unbelievably, I could feel the tires grab, and we stopped. The nose of the aircraft was in the run-up area, the main tires were still on the runway, and the plane was exactly ninety degrees to the runway. Ned once again said, "Holy shit!" and I just sat there like a wet noodle. I couldn't believe that we were stopped. I couldn't believe the position of the aircraft at ninety degrees to the runway, and I couldn't believe that we'd slid for over a mile and stopped, finally, at the very end of the runway, right next to the boulders.

No one in the cockpit said a word; we were all stunned. I was sitting there, attempting to regain my composure when the airplane started backing up! I was so relieved to be stopped that I'd forgotten that I had maximum reverse power on the engines and was pointed directly into a twenty-five knot wind; together, they were pushing me backwards. I regained control of the airplane, and all I had to do was to taxi straight ahead to get the tail of the plane off the runway. The tower informed me that they were closing the field because of the ice, and the taxiways were to too slippery to use. I was instructed to shut down my engines in place, and they would send a bus for us.

Somehow, I did not hit any of the runway edge lights, so there was no damage to the aircraft. I was told that the field was closed before my landing, but that the commander directed it to open just long enough to allow my aircraft to land. I learned a valuable lesson during that landing and made a promise to myself which I vowed never to violate; in the next thirty-five years, I never did. The promise was that I would never allow someone on the ground to make a decision concerning the safety of an aircraft for which I was responsible or pressure me into doing something in violation of regulations. Occasionally, I have refused missions or proceeded to alternate airports, for example, when the conditions were not acceptable to me, and I have never been criticized. I was the pilot in command; I had the responsibility for the safety of the airplane, crew, and passengers. If I was the one responsible, I would be the one to make all of the decisions.

I was the last one off the aircraft when the bus came; everyone had gotten on the bus, and they were waiting for me as I took my time loading everything back into my briefcase. I was really trying to calm down before getting on the bus; both mentally and physically, I was a wreck. Finally, I was ready to exit. I had my briefcase in one hand and my military suitcase in the other. I stepped off the aircraft steps, onto the ice and my feet slipped out from under me. When I fell, I slammed the back of my head on the ice. What an appropriate ending to my worst landing ever!

I don't know if it was luck or divine intervention that stopped the aircraft just a few yards from the end of the runway, but we slid into a small area where there was no ice, and the main gear found that small hole. The ice-free patch could have formed because the ground was a degree or two warmer than the surrounding area; we were only a few yards from the water, which was probably warmer than the ground. Or maybe salt spray from the waves had formed a puddle in that location that had evaporated, leaving a salt residue, which melted the ice. I don't know the reason for that patch of unfrozen pavement; but I'm glad it was there.

During my five years of flying tankers, I was assigned to the 384th Air Refueling Squadron. Every Monday morning at eight o'clock, everyone at the squadron's home station attended a briefing. I was climbing the steps one Monday morning in October of 1965 to attend this mandatory briefing when I was almost knocked over by crewmembers rushing in the opposite direction. The squadron had been disbanded! No briefing, no more alert, no more KC-97 tanker, no more living in Chicopee Falls, Massachusetts. But what went through my mind first was: no more lobsters. My entire life had been changed in an instant. I had exactly one week to report to Sewart AFB near Nashville, Tennessee, to fly the Lockheed C-130. The war in Vietnam was getting bigger every day, and the Pentagon had decided to increase the size of the C-130 force to support the war. Goodbye, Strategic Air Command. Hello, Tactical Air Command and the C-130 Hercules.

One of the best fringe benefits ever had to be returning from alert in Newfoundland carrying a load of live lobsters. We would place our order for the number of lobsters we wanted, and they would be delivered by the local lobstermen, packed in wet seaweed, about a dozen to a crate, just before we flew back to the States. We also carried five hundred lobsters each for the Officers' Club and the Non-Commissioned Officers' Club back at Westover, where they could offer a lobster dinner for less than the cost of a hamburger dinner. I used to bring back half a dozen for my family and take orders from my neighbors before I left home. My neighbors even chipped in and bought a huge pot, which we would bring to a boil over an open campfire in the backyard. My return from SAC alert was celebrated in grand style with a neighborhood lobster boil. The size of the lobsters varied, but the price was consistent for years: forty cents a lobster. In early 1965, the price increased a nickel to forty-five cents apiece, and everyone grumbled, but it was still cheaper than hamburgers.

8

THE HERCULES

IFLEW THE C-130 Hercules for the Air Force for fifteen years, both on active duty and as a member of the Air Force Reserve, traveling all over the world and accumulating numerous stories. I worked my way up through the ranks from aircraft commander to instructor pilot to evaluator, and was even selected to be a member of the committee to rewrite the Air Force manual on operating the aircraft. The most rewarding military job I had was as the commander of a C-130 squadron.

Lockheed designed the C-130 as a combat aircraft capable of delivering troops and supplies to the battlefield. It could airdrop paratroopers and their equipment for an operation hundreds of miles inside enemy controlled territory. It could land on what the Air Force called unprepared runways to resupply the combat zone with vehicles, artillery, and other heavy equipment necessary for a sustained engagement. An unprepared runway could be anything from a cow pasture to a clearing in a jungle, scraped clean with bulldozers; a paved runway was not required. And it had the speed and agility to penetrate enemy controlled territory without getting shot down by radar controlled missiles or guns.

When I was transferred from tankers, I moved my family to Nashville and began my new job as an aircraft commander: I did not have to fly as a copilot, as I had at my last job. My first mission after coming out of C-130 school was a flight to the Dominican Republic. The newspapers had daily headlines about military and diplomatic efforts to stabilize this small Caribbean country, which shares the island of Hispaniola with Haiti. If there was something newsworthy involving the United States military, there was a good chance my squadron would be involved, and that usually meant me.

The information I had received was limited. I was to fly to an army installation near Savannah, Georgia, where I would pick up my load and deliver it to San Isidro Airfield, near Santo Domingo, the capital. I was an Air Force captain at the time, and my copilot was a major who had been one of my classmates in school but was trained as a copilot; this was also his first mission. It was during the buildup of the C-130 fleet for the war in Vietnam, and the Air Force was bringing back into the cockpit many of the pilots who had previously held office jobs. My copilot had not flown for a few years and was still getting the feel of his new job. I was grateful to have an experienced pilot in the right seat for my first mission in a new aircraft.

We arrived in the Savannah area to find that the weather was bad. The only instrument approach was the primitive ADF, a system that had been developed in the Thirties but was still in use. It would have been my last choice for an instrument approach in bad weather; there were much newer and safer approach options available, but not at this airfield.

I had no other choice, and for my first mission, I flew this archaic instrument approach, in terrible weather conditions, and landed. This was my introduction to the C-130 mission: I would be flying into some of the most primitive conditions on the earth and had nothing to assist me besides my knowledge and skill.

After landing, I was briefed that my load was to be an air-transportable bridge, used to span a small river, which had been designed to fit into a C-130. The mission had been approved to fly at the wartime emergency weight of 175 thousand pounds (twenty-two thousand pounds heavier than the normal maximum weight) because the bridge was so heavy. There was only one other time in my fifteen years of flying the C-130 that I operated an aircraft at that weight; the second time, both the weather and runway conditions were infinitely better, and I had a lot more experience.

The runway was just long enough for this very heavy takeoff, and there was a small hill near the end of the runway that I would have to clear. Using the takeoff and climb charts I determined that we would be able to get airborne and clear the hill, but by only the slimmest margin. I completed the paperwork and filed my flight plan in Base Operations, then got a quick bite to eat and took back hamburgers for my two loadmasters, who were supervising the Army troops loading the bridge. The aluminum looked like a large Erector Set waiting to be built, and it took up every inch of space within the cargo compartment. I was assured by the chief loadmaster that it was tied down properly. If it were to shift in flight, it could damage the aircraft or possibly relocate the center of gravity enough to cause me to lose control of the aircraft. It was now close to midnight; we were all getting sleepy and definitely not looking forward to the hazardous takeoff and the night flight to the Dominican Republic.

I wanted to have every foot of pavement available for takeoff, so I turned onto the active runway and then taxied backwards until the main wheels were right at the edge of the pavement. By pulling that trick, which few aircraft other than the C-130 are capable of, I captured the few hundred feet of runway that would otherwise have been lost behind the aircraft.

I completed the before-takeoff checklist, received takeoff clearance from the tower, and silently reviewed in my mind what I would have to do if we had an engine failure during the takeoff. I pushed the throttles up with my right hand; my left hand was used to steer down the runway, using the nose wheel steering. The copilot held the yoke for the initial portion of the takeoff. When I had enough speed to steer by using my feet on the rudder pedals, I switched my left hand from the steering to the yoke. With my hand on the yoke, I could move the flight controls, talk to the crew through the intercom or talk to the tower through a radio, and trim the elevator by using my left thumb. With my feet, I controlled the rudder and brakes with two pedals on the floor. My right hand controlled the four throttles.

For a normal takeoff, I would release the brakes and advance the throttles slowly; for this takeoff, though, I wanted all the power I could get right from the start of my takeoff roll. I pushed the throttles up to the firewall, checked the engine temperatures to ensure that I was not overheating the turbines, and then released the brakes. With maximum power, a light aircraft would leap forward and you would feel the acceleration instantly. Instead, we just began moving

forward slowly. I knew it was going to be a looong takeoff
roll. We were getting near the end of the runway when we
finally reached takeoff speed, and I lifted the nose wheel off
the runway by pulling back on the yoke. I could feel that the
aircraft was very sluggish and did not have the performance
that I was accustomed to. I called for the copilot to raise the
gear, and established my maximum performance climb speed,
which would give me the best angle of climb to clear the hill
immediately in front of me. On a normal takeoff, I would not
even pay attention to this small hill; I would probably clear it
by a thousand feet.

It was dark out, but the hill was silhouetted by the clouds
behind it, which reflected light from the nearby Army post.
I could clearly see the small knoll right in front of me, and I
was very much concerned about not having the power to get
over the top. At this time, there was no turning back. I was
committed to clearing the top, and all I could do was maintain
my speed and pray that the climb charts were correct, that
the hill was measured at the correct height, and that a tree
had not grown up into my flight path. I expected to clear the
hill by only fifty feet, not realizing how close fifty feet really
was. When the hill was in front of me I could see it; when it
went below the aircraft, because it was night time, I could no
longer see it. I have no idea how close we came to flying into
the top of that small hill except that it was very, very close.

There were dozens of C-130s flying to San Isidro that night,
and air traffic control gave me radar vectors so that I would
enter into the stream of traffic with ten minute spacing to the
planes in front of and behind me. Everyone was flying at the
same altitude and speed, so we were in a very large formation,
one behind the other, all vectored and controlled by radar

until we were south of United States radar coverage. I had the problem of being too heavy to climb to the same altitude as the rest of the aircraft, so I flew a few thousand feet lower, which didn't make any difference.

We were to fly to a Tactical Air Navigation (TACAN) station, which was aboard a US Navy destroyer about ten miles south of Santo Domingo. Using the TACAN, I was to fly a jet penetration (a high-speed descent), and I had instructions and charts for locating the San Isidro Airfield once I was over the Navy destroyer. The runway was only about twenty miles from the ship, so I didn't expect any problem.

Sometimes the operation works according to plan, and sometimes "shit happens"; the mission to the Dominican Republic was somewhere in between. I had no problem flying the jet penetration to get under the clouds or finding the destroyer. The first thing that I realized when I was under the clouds, which were at three thousand feet, was that there were a number of airplanes in the area, and mine ought to have been the only one.

One of the reasons for the numerous aircraft was the difficulty some of the pilots had in locating the runway. Our information placed the destroyer due south of Santo Domingo. Unknown to the Air Force, the ship didn't remain in one place but cruised back and forth parallel to the shoreline. It could have been twenty miles or more from the location we were expecting to find it. Many aircraft had difficulty finding the airfield and either went back to the ship for a second try or began circling to search for the field. This resulted in many airplanes under the low clouds, all doing their own thing without any air traffic control to separate us.

A second reason for the chaotic situation was that offloading at the airfield was going slower than expected; so the aircraft in front of me were not permitted to land and offload. I also had to wait my turn, so I became one of the planes flying around trying to not have a midair collision in the crowded sky beneath the clouds.

The reason the planes were at ten-minute intervals was to provide the time to unload the cargo using an unloading system that was unique to the C-130. If everything worked perfectly, there would only be one aircraft on the ground at any time. When I landed and turned off the runway, we opened the ramp and door at the rear of the airplane and prepared to offload the bridge. When I was on the taxiway parallel to the runway the two loadmasters pushed the aft pallet, which was on rollers, out the rear of the plane, and it fell onto the taxiway. After doing this five times the bridge was unloaded. I never stopped taxiing the aircraft.

By the time all the pallets were unloaded, I was getting near the takeoff end of the runway. The ideal situation was to have only one aircraft at a time on the ground. The pallets I dropped on the taxiway were picked up by a forklift and moved to the side, clearing the taxiway for that the next pilot. My takeoff made room for the next airplane, ten minutes behind me, to land and offload using the same method.

This rapid offload was a common method used in Vietnam, when the aircraft were vulnerable to a mortar attack when they were on the ground, and getting them airborne as quickly as possible was a priority.

It was just getting light by the time I landed and off-loaded the bridge. I knew there was no fuel available at San Isidro, except for emergency use; and I had to make the decision to fly to a large Air Force base on the west coast of Puerto Rico for fuel or head for the States, where I would have numerous options to land and refuel. We were all tired, so I decided to head for the States and see if I could make it home without another stop.

I arrived back in Tennessee totally exhausted, after being gone for almost twenty-four hours but without having had to make an additional stop for fuel. I was now in what we called the trash hauling business. My new job in the Tactical Air Command was very different from my previous five years in SAC, where all of my flying was rigidly controlled. When I was given a mission, I was expected to take the action necessary to complete it. The planning would not always be perfect. But I was a captain in the Air Force, highly trained in my job; and I had the authority to make the changes necessary to get the job done.

The major part of my new job was to supply Army troops on the battlefield. I learned to drop paratroopers and to get them to the combat zone without being shot down. I learned how to airdrop all types of equipment, using half a dozen different methods, to re-supply the paratroopers. And I learned how to land the C-130 on a short, primitive dirt runway to offload the supplies. Landing to offload supplies, instead of air-dropping them by parachute, made the C-130 Hercules a far more efficient machine.

Getting the paratroopers and supplies to the drop zone without being shot down by the enemy was the first challenge. The tactic used to avoid detection by radar was to fly low and fast, while attempting to keep high terrain between the aircraft and the enemy radar site. If the aircraft could be tracked with ground radar, it was vulnerable to being shot down with a radar-controlled missile. Route planning, done by the pilot and navigator together, was the first step to successfully getting to the drop zone.

A low-altitude, high-speed mission, sometimes as a single ship and sometimes in formation, required my total concentration. I needed the assistance of the copilot, navigator, and flight engineer pointing out obstructions, which I would fly over or around. Navigating was difficult at low altitude, and it was the job of the navigator, looking out the pilot's windows, to keep us on course. The copilot would back up the navigator, by map reading, to ensure we did not get lost. I used my flight engineer as my extra pair of eyes to make sure that I didn't fly into radio towers or electrical wires that I did not see and that were not on the charts. I flew these missions at only a few hundred feet above the terrain.

This was not a smooth, pleasant, plane ride for the paratroopers in the rear of the aircraft. This was one of the most unpleasant rides imaginable and frequently caused the paratroopers to get airsick. At this low altitude there was usually a lot of turbulence, together with constant sharp turns to avoid obstructions, and up-and-down motion to follow the terrain. We would always turn the air conditioning to full cold to keep paratroopers from getting airsick, but I have heard from a number of them that jumping out of the plane was easy after the miserable ride to the drop zone.

The C-130 was capable of carrying ninety-four passengers; but because of the size of the parachutes and the other required equipment, we could only carry sixty-four paratroopers. The troopers would ride to the drop zone in four rows of canvas seats; two rows for each door. When we were near the drop zone, the paratrooper doors, one on each side of the aircraft, were opened; and a red jump light was turned on, indicating that it was not safe to jump. They would stand up and hook their parachute-opening lanyards to a cable in the aircraft; and when the red jump light turned green, their indication that we were over the drop zone and it was time to leave the plane, they began jumping about one per second from each door. Their parachutes, which were on their backs, were automatically opened by the lanyards when they were about twenty feet below the aircraft.

Approaching the drop zone, we got busy in the cockpit. I had to fly exactly on track approaching the drop area, especially when I was the lead aircraft and there was a large formation following me. If the formation was not stabilized behind me, there was a greater chance of dropping troopers outside the established drop area—into trees or other obstructions. Being dropped into hostile territory was hazardous enough for the airborne troops; they didn't need the extra problems of being dropped into the trees.

The paratroopers couldn't be dropped safely at the low altitude and high speed we were flying. I had to perform a popup maneuver to get to about eight hundred feet above the ground; that was high enough that their parachutes could fully open; and it was low enough to limit their time descending, exposed to enemy gunfire. I also slowed my plane down to close to its minimum speed so as not to injure anyone when they exited. The popup to drop altitude also placed me in a vulnerable position if there were enemy forces in the area. I was only at eight hundred feet above the ground and at the slowest speed possible; our aircraft would probably draw gunfire from anyone near the drop zone. For my survivability, I would only subject myself to the undesirable conditions for the minimum amount of time.

After the popup, I had my first look at the drop zone and made final corrections, left or right, to adjust for the wind direction. If there was a wind from the left, I would fly down the left side of the drop zone, causing the troopers to drift to the right and land in the center of the area. The navigator made a rapid calculation using the latest winds and told me the number of yards I had to fly left or right of the centerline, to have my jumpers land on the centerline.

My navigator gave a five-second countdown, followed by the term "green light," the code words for beginning the drop.

Members of the 327th Tactical Airlift Squadron planning the route to the drop zone. Left to right: The author, squadron commander; Russ Dennis, pilot; Lou Amadio, pilot; Charlie Stanton, chief nagigator; Bruce Cairns, pilot

The copilot turned on the green light, and the jumpmaster started moving his troopers out the doors. I could feel a jolt as each of the troops left the aircraft. Dropping a full load of paratroopers would take about thirty seconds using both doors. An "all clear" from my loadmaster meant that all of the paratroopers had left the aircraft safely. I would then make a turn to my escape heading and raise the flaps, descend back to low altitude, then accelerate to high speed and the safety that comes with it, flying my exit route out of hostile territory.

I dropped troops hundreds of times and had the good fortune to drop the Golden Knights, the US Army parachute team. I once dropped a special Air Force team into the ocean, at night, a few miles off the coast of Norway, north of the Arctic Circle. I was on a training exercise in northern Norway, as were the jumpers. I didn't drop them from the normal low altitude but from high altitude to provide stealth. Because of the altitude, we all were wearing oxygen masks for the jump. Each trooper was dressed in a black rubber water survival suit over his normal cold weather gear. They each had a one-man life raft with them, in order to paddle to the coast. Their mission was to establish a paratroop drop zone about one hundred miles inland, which required enough supplies for them to move that distance without being detected. Their packs were too heavy to lift, so they slid the gear to the end of the aircraft ramp before jumping. The enormous load was attached to each trooper with a lanyard, so it would hang below him; it would splash into the ocean just before the trooper did. This team was the toughest and best trained, with the most difficult mission, that I have ever dropped.

Once the airborne troops were in the drop zone, we had to airdrop the vehicles, large guns and ammunition, and of course food and water. We had a number of different ways to accomplish this second phase of the operation; the most common was by using multiple large parachutes to get the load on the drop zone without damage.

The largest formation I have ever flown in was an exercise in southern Germany that was meant to demonstrate the capability of the Air Force to airdrop heavy equipment to ground troops in a forward area. Bleachers were set up for the numerous dignitaries and the newspaper and television crews, a safe distance from the drop zone. They were all invited to witness a show of force by the United States military. Thirty-six C-130s were to fly a low-level, high-speed formation to the drop zone and then drop the heavy equipment in view of the spectators in the bleachers. I was carrying an open trailer, six feet wide by eight feet long, that was loaded with equipment and covered with a cargo net; this would be the first pallet out of the plane. The second pallet held a small truck to tow the trailer, and the last pallet had a military jeep.

I was scheduled to be third in the huge formation. The first aircraft had a general in the cockpit, to direct the thirty-six C-130s; that crew also had two highly experienced navigators to ensure that they maintained course and did not miss the drop zone. If the lead C-130 had to abort the mission because of mechanical problems, the second aircraft would then lead the formation; that crew, too, had two navigators. As the number three aircraft, I had my basic crew, with only one navigator; I didn't have much to do other than fly the in-trail formation to the drop zone and drop my load. Easy enough. But then the number two aircraft had trouble starting an engine and required maintenance; so the lead aircraft began taxiing out with me right behind, in the number two position. The lead pilot then informed me that he was leaving the formation to get maintenance assistance. Now I was leading the massive formation. I taxied to the runway, with everyone following, and took my position. I was waiting for the planned takeoff time, so we would arrive at the drop zone precisely on schedule.

I was distressed that I only had one navigator on my aircraft, because an error in navigation would place me in a difficult position. I was preparing myself mentally for the task of leading the formation when I was notified that both the original lead and number two aircraft were repaired and they would replace me on the runway. I breathed a great sigh of relief when I got the good news.

Three dozen aircraft required an enormous amount of room to maneuver on the ground; they filled up almost the entire taxi space on the air field. Because of the limited taxi space available and the great number of planes, I was trapped on the runway. The only possible way to get off the runway and rejoin the formation was for me to taxi to the opposite end of the runway, a mile and a half away. Then I turned off of the runway onto the parallel taxiway and rejoined the formation as the last ship. That's how I became number thirty-six in the thirty-six ship formation; I was the end of the line.

We all took off with five seconds between planes. When it was my turn, the runway was engulfed in a haze of brown-gray smoke from the thirty-five aircraft that had just taken off in front of me. A stiff breeze would have blown much of the smoke off the runway, but the wind was light and variable. This created a problem: when the wings of any aircraft create the lift required to fly, they also create wingtip vortices—

miniature horizontal tornadoes—turbulence that can interfere with the next plane's takeoff.

The vortices dissipate in a few minutes or get blown off the runway along with the smoke—if there is a wind; but with almost no wind, I was expecting turbulence right at liftoff. Since I was the last aircraft, and I did not have to worry about anyone behind me, I advanced power rapidly during the initial portion of the takeoff roll, to take off before the normal liftoff point. Immediately upon liftoff, I made a turn to the side of the runway where the turbulence would be less. The tricks worked, and for a few seconds during liftoff it was a little rough, but not too bad. Once airborne I had to concentrate on getting into position two thousand feet behind the airplane in front of me; then all I had to do was follow him.

With everyone established at the proper interval, the formation extended for twelve miles. I decided to fly a little above the rest of the formation, which kept me out of all the turbulence and engine smoke. When the front of the formation turned, at a planned turning point, I could see all of the aircraft; it was a beautiful sight. I maintained my position in the formation visually, but I could also "paint" a few of the aircraft immediately in front of me on the radar. The biggest problem in holding my position in the formation was maintaining the required two thousand feet of separation. I relied mainly on my experience to visually gauge the distance between us, but I also checked the radar screen for a precise distance reading.

At the speed we flew, I was exactly five seconds behind the aircraft in front of me. When he started a turn, I would begin counting to myself and begin my turn when I got to five. If I was exactly two thousand feet behind him, my turn should begin at the exact location that he began his turn. If we both used the same angle of bank, thirty degrees, I would complete the turn without losing my position in the formation and would not have to maneuver to regain my correct position. After one hour of this low level, high-speed flight in formation, we were near the drop zone. We all completed the popup to get the thirty-six aircraft in position for the drop.

I could see that the drop zone was covered with about a hundred pieces of equipment and there were still parachutes in the air from the aircraft immediately in front of me. Some loads had only one large chute, but there were also loads with numerous chutes attached, swinging and floating to the ground. I watched three pallets extract from the plane immediately in front of me, and knew that my navigator would call "green light" in a few seconds. When he did, my copilot threw the switch that turned on the light and also deployed the extraction chute out the aft ramp and door. When the extraction chute fell, it pulled the ripcord, which opened the chute directly behind my plane, pulling out the trailer. The trailer was attached to the truck, and that was also pulled out. The truck was attached to the jeep, which moved but didn't leave the airplane. I had a problem.

The connecting strap between the truck and the jeep had broken, and the jeep was still in the aircraft. The loadmaster immediately called, "Malfunction." The loadmaster was in a dangerous position. The pallet with the jeep attached was loose on the rollers and would roll either forward or aft, depending on the attitude of the aircraft. If the nose of the aircraft was up, the jeep would roll aft; but if the nose was down, the jeep would roll forward to where the loadmaster was standing, possibly injuring him. Once I understood the nature of the malfunction, I pulled the nose of the aircraft up and the jeep slowly rolled out the back of the plane, approximately ten seconds late, and definitely off the drop zone. Then I got more bad news from the loadmaster; the parachutes on the jeep had not opened.

I don't know how many newspapers and TV crews reported the incident; but in the United States, the most popular TV evening news show was the Huntley-Brinkley Report, and they reported the snafu the next evening. The jeep was the last piece of equipment dropped from the enormous formation and the only one that came down with no parachutes; and it was all captured by the TV cameramen. I didn't see the Huntley-Brinkley Report the next day, but I spoke to people who did. The jeep fell one thousand feet without parachutes, and the touchdown was spectacular—in full view of all of the dignitaries watching from the bleachers, then replayed the next evening for the millions of Americans who watched the evening news on TV.

9

YA GOTTA HAVE LUCK

THE HOSTILE ENVIRONMENTS modern aircraft fly in, coupled with enormous speed, generate forces far greater than the human body can endure; and in some situations it is impossible to survive an accident. Over the years, many friends and acquaintances were unlucky: they had a malfunction beyond their control, leading to a fatal crash. This chapter is not about my skill as a pilot; it is about my being a lucky pilot.

I went to the Vietnam War Memorial and looked up the names of the people I could remember who were killed in the war. There are fifty-eight thousand names on the wall, and some of them were close friends. The three that I looked for first were Tom Case, Monty Shingledecker, and Harold Zook. There were eighteen people killed in Vietnam the day they crashed; the names are arranged by date of death and are alphabetical within the date. Major Tom Case was the aircraft commander of the C-130 that exploded that day, killing all on board. His name was the third one listed. Zook was the copilot on the crew; his was the last name of the eighteen killed that day. Harold Zook's name is on panel 07E, line 130; he replaced me on that mission, because I made a lucky decision.

It was late spring in 1966, and it was just starting to get hot—not only the temperature outside but also the war in Vietnam. I had been in the 61st Tactical Airlift Squadron for just a few months, as a pilot on the C-130, when word was put out by the Squadron Scheduling Section that they were looking for a volunteer to fly as a copilot for Tom Case on a drop mission in southern Arizona. As usual, the initial information was limited; and that was the story with this mission. At the time, I was flying as a left seat aircraft commander, but because I was still new in the airplane, sometimes I flew in the right seat as the copilot for the more experienced C-130 pilots. The initial information I received was that it was to be an experimental test flight developing the low altitude parachute extraction system (LAPES). It was in Arizona, a state I had never visited; and it was testing a new system, which sounded exciting. I volunteered for the mission.

LAPES was different from all of the rest of the airdrops I was familiar with. In every other drop system, the load was pulled out of the back of the C-130 and lowered to the ground with parachutes. LAPES was an airdrop from five feet above the drop zone. The load was pulled out of the rear of the plane by extraction chutes and then fell the few feet to the ground and slid to a stop. Since LAPES required that the C-130 would be only five feet in the air, there was the possibility of the aircraft hitting the ground, inadvertently, during the extraction. To prevent damage to the aircraft the drop was made in the landing configuration, with the landing gear and flaps extended. Then, if there were an inadvertent touchdown, it would be on the landing gear only, preventing damage to the belly of the plane. LAPES was a very accurate drop system and was capable of dropping the heaviest loads.

We were in Arizona for about a week, making a few drops a day. We were perfecting our technique as a crew, while getting some experience dropping heavier loads than we had ever dropped before. The feel in the aircraft when we dropped a heavy LAPES load was unusual, because we were flying at only a few feet above the ground and were conscious of our height. When the load was pulled out, the aircraft instantly became thousands of pounds lighter and the plane popped up to a few

An Air Force C-130 dropping a 30,000-pound Sheridan light tank, using the low altitude parachute extraction system (LAPES). The parachutes are used only to pull the tank out of the aircraft. Once extracted, the tank falls to the ground and slides to a stop. (USAF photo)

hundred feet. It was a strange feeling, and took a few missions to become comfortable with the unusual sensation.

We were scheduled to return to our home base near Nashville after the first week, but before departing for the few days at home, we were all called in for a briefing by the mission commander, a lieutenant colonel. We were told that we were practicing for a dangerous mission in Vietnam; before being given further details, we would have to sign paperwork to volunteer for the mission. To sweeten the pot, this one mission, which would take a few months to complete, would earn us credit for a one-year tour of duty in Southeast Asia.

This was a period of increasing buildup of our forces in Vietnam, and all C-130 crewmembers were expected to serve for a one-year tour in theater. Very few C-130s were based in Vietnam; most flew into the country from bases in friendly countries in Southeast Asia. The tours were unaccompanied, though: no dependents were allowed. I was under a lot of pressure. I knew that everyone was rotating through the tours and that my turn to leave my family for a year was right around the corner. The short duration of the mission was the bait for getting me, and the rest of the crew, to accept this unknown assignment.

I remembered my dad saying, "Never volunteer for anything"; and this time I heeded his warning. I was the only member of the crew that did not accept the mission. The other crewmembers and the mission director tried to convince me that this was a good deal and that I was silly not to sign on the dotted line. They were asking themselves, How dangerous could one mission be? Had I not made that lucky and difficult decision, I, too, would have been within the fireball when their cargo of forty thousand pounds of high explosives took all of their lives.

Harold Zook, another pilot in the squadron, volunteered for the mission and replaced me; I remained in Tennessee and proceeded with business as usual. After months had passed, and not having seen anyone from that crew, the seemingly minor decision I had made almost faded from my memory. One morning, though, word was passed that Tom Case and his entire crew had been killed in North Vietnam. I, along with the rest of the squadron, learned for the first time of the details of the mission for which I had refused to volunteer.

The crew was attempting to destroy the Paul Doumer Bridge spanning the Red River in North Vietnam. The bridge was part of the major roadway between Hanoi, the capital, and the port city of Haiphong. After numerous strikes against the target using conventional bombing techniques, the bridge was still usable. A large explosive device would be required to destroy the main structure supporting the road deck of the bridge, but the weapons systems available in 1966 were incapable of delivering the required amount of explosive force at one precise location. Also, it had become obvious that a fighter bomber, a relatively small aircraft, was not capable of carrying one bomb heavy enough to accomplish the task; so the C-130 was selected to do the job.

The C-130 model E that I was flying at the time could carry a maximum load of forty-four thousand pounds. That was the structural limit of the floor of the cargo compartment and was the weight agreed upon for the explosive device that Tom Case and crew were going to use to destroy the bridge. The week that I was involved in the mission was a test to determine if it might be feasible to drop such heavy a load using LAPES.

The initial drops that I made were nowhere near forty-four thousand pounds, and I assume that changes had to be made to the system, over a period of a few months, until they were capable of getting that enormous amount of weight extracted from the aircraft.

The plan was to have the C-130 fly a low-level mission to a point upstream of the bridge without being detected. A large strike force at high altitude was to divert the attention of the defensive emplacements on the ground, thus allowing the low-flying C-130 to slip under the radar, undetected, and follow the river. At the planned location upstream of the bridge, the explosives would be extracted by LAPES; the pallet would then float downstream until it was under the bridge. We were told in the briefing that the explosive pallet was designed to attach itself to the iron pilings of the bridge using magnets. I do not think it was feasible, and I suspect the briefer was misinformed. I think the plan was probably to use a magnetic fuse, which would have been activated when it floated under the bridge. Forty thousand pounds of high explosives would have been sufficient to destroy a substantial portion of the structure.

Planning for the mission took many months; but the mission did not proceed as planned. The first attempt to execute the mission was aborted because of the amount of hostile gunfire. The next evening is when the C-130 exploded, probably killing all on board instantly. I can envision a number of reasons for the aircraft to explode, the most probable being hostile gunfire hitting the high explosives. There are other possibilities, though: the aircraft might have crashed into the water, causing the explosion. Flying five feet above the river, at night, in hostile conditions, they may have just flown into the water and crashed as they tried to follow the river to their drop location. There is another possibility: the device might have detonated prematurely due to the high forces of the extraction or the shock of hitting the water. I doubt that anyone knows exactly what happened, but the pilots flying in the diversion overhead reported an enormous explosion.

Gene Stevens was a flight engineer in my Air Force Reserve C-130 squadron when I was stationed at Willow Grove, just north of Philadelphia. It was in the late 1970s, and I was flying for TWA as my primary job, but I was also a lieutenant colonel in the Reserves, flying the C-130. By this time I had been in the Hercules for over ten years and was a flight evaluator for the other pilots in the squadron, which means that I gave the check rides to evaluate their proficiency. I was on a routine trash hauling mission, going into Norton Air Force Base in southern California. I had flown into Norton dozens of times when the weather was good and was familiar with the field and the surrounding terrain. This, however, was a foggy, drizzly day and we were in the clouds, even though we were at low altitude, about ten miles from landing.

In the United States, there is radar coverage almost everywhere, and because Norton was a major Air Force base, I knew I could expect a ground-controlled approach (GCA) all the way to touchdown. This system, phased out for civilian aircraft in 1970 but still in use by the military at the time, had to be the easiest approach to fly; all that the pilot had to do was to follow the instructions of the radar controller, who told him to fly up, down, left, or right, until he was in a position to land. There was one drawback to that system, though: I was placing my life in the hands of someone else. The radar controller gave me headings and altitudes, which I followed blindly.

I was on the typical radar controlled approach to the runway, under the guidance of the Los Angeles Air Traffic Control Center. When I was close to Norton, I was instructed to change my radio frequency and contact the military controller, who would then give the instructions for getting me onto the ground. During the changeover from civilian control to the military, my aircraft went off the center's radar, and the military picked up my blip. The military controller was then responsible for identifying my aircraft on his radar screen with a positive ID; if he failed to accomplish this step, he might follow the wrong blip on his screen, thinking, in error, that it was my aircraft. That was precisely what occurred that day. The military controller was watching a blip on his radar screen about ten miles from me, which was flying parallel to my aircraft, thinking that the other blip was my plane. He was giving me instructions based on the position of the other aircraft.

TWA had a requirement to back up a GCA, a ground-controlled approach, with an instrument landing system (ILS) approach, if it was available. This TWA procedure seemed like a good idea, and I always used it as a backup when flying for the military, even though it was not required. Because I had the ILS tuned in, I knew that the controller had flown us through the final approach course, which was very unusual. His instructions did not correlate with where I thought I was, and I began to get confused and concerned. I had flown into this airfield many times when the weather was nice and had observed the hills, which I thought were now right in front of us.

I was beginning to feel uncomfortable. I asked the copilot to question the controller as to the reason why we flew through the final approach course and to ask him when we would be turned onto our final heading. He responded that we would be turned onto the final approach in five miles. This was a very confusing response and meant that one of us was misinterpreting the position of the aircraft. Then I asked the navigator to determine the height of hills directly in front of us. It could have been that we were higher than the hills, and everything was okay.

The navigator informed me that there were some hills in the vicinity that were above our altitude. Now I was on full alert. On two occasions, the copilot had expressed my concern about our location to the radar controller, with no success from him about verifying our position. I decided to speak directly to the controller, instead of relaying messages through the copilot.

Because of my concern with our situation, Gene Stevens, the flight engineer, unfastened his seat belt and shoulder harness and stood alongside his seat; from this position, he could look almost straight down through the side windows. By looking straight down, you can sometimes get a look at the ground through a break in the clouds, a view you cannot get from your seat. Gene took one glance down and shouted, "Trees!" He didn't have time to say more than the one word. In an instant, it all came together: I was correct in my concern, and we were now only seconds away from flying into the hill.

The C-130 was designed by Lockheed with turboprop engines because the turbine engine, coupled with a propeller, allows the pilot to increase power, from idle to maximum, in about one second. The change in power is almost instantaneous. A turbojet engine, in contrast, can take in excess of ten seconds to do the same thing. The Lockheed engineers designed the aircraft exactly for the situation I was in: I required instant power to fly away from the hill.

When Gene shouted, "Trees!" I went into my survival mode. I advanced all four throttles to maximum power, pulled the nose of the plane up steeply, to trade about fifty knots of airspeed for altitude, and began a sharp turn to the right, to get away from the hill. I knew that I might be interfering with other aircraft above me, so I instructed the copilot to squawk, "Emergency!" This transmitted a radar signal to the controller that I was taking emergency action, which might be in violation of his instructions.

The remainder of the approach and landing was routine, but I was angry. I wanted to ensure that the controller understood that he made a mistake, that there were no shortcuts when the loss of my life and the lives of my crew might have been the result of his complacency. After landing, I visited the base commander and explained to him what had happened. He was also a pilot, and he fully understood why I was so angry. The commander had the controller immediately placed in student status, pending an investigation. I filed a formal letter of complaint; and when the investigation was completed, I received a letter of apology from the base commander.

I was lucky that day. If Gene Stevens had not decided to stand up at that moment, the outcome of that routine mission might have been vastly different.

Not all of my good luck was a matter of life and death. Early in my career, flying the tanker as a copilot, I was on SAC alert at Morón Air Base south of Seville, Spain. I think it was in 1963.

Morón was a bomber base and had numerous turbojet, six-engine, medium-range B-47s on alert. My crew was the only tanker crew. We were there on SAC alert for a unique, highly classified, special mission. We were flying the only propeller-driven, reciprocating engine aircraft on the base; all of the other aircraft were jets. The mission had just been initiated, and the bomber crews knew nothing about our airplane or why we were on alert with them for the first time. I got many inquiries about our mission, including why there was only one tanker on alert; but I was not permitted to divulge any information. We were the mystery crew, flying a mystery plane.

On the third day we were living with the B-47 crews in their mole hole, we had our first alert. The Klaxon horn sounded and we proceeded immediately to the alert vehicle for the drive to the aircraft to start engines. I had endured hundreds of alerts, and never got conditioned to the shock the Klaxon caused to my nervous system. When I heard the first blast of the horn, I immediately put on my flying clothes and ran.

When I got to the station wagon, there were only four of us. We had only a few minutes to get to the KC-97 tanker and get the engines started, but we needed a full crew to do it. John was missing. John was the boss, the aircraft commander, and no one on the crew knew where he was. We had all been flying together for a few years and had responded to many alerts together. The few other times someone got lost, he always showed up at the plane, usually by riding with another crew; it always seemed to work out. Without John, I was in charge; I waited an appropriate amount of time and then decided to race to the airplane with the hope that he was already there. He wasn't.

We did everything required for the practice alert except to start the engines. I decided not to start the engines without John, and I expected that there would be consequences for my omission. In my five years in SAC, this was the only time that I'd ever heard of a crewmember not responding to an alert; so I had no guidance on what action to take, other than my best judgment. It was obvious that we did not have our engines started: the huge propellers were not turning. As soon as the alert was over, the Alert Force Commander was sitting in his vehicle near the aircraft entrance door, waiting for an explanation.

The KC-97 was a large aircraft with an upper and lower deck. I had to climb down a ladder to get from the cockpit to the lower deck, and then a set of steps, to get from the lower deck to the ramp and the waiting major. On the way out of the plane, I was thinking about an excuse but decided to simply tell the truth; it was not my fault that John had not responded to the alert. There was also the possibility that John was incapacitated for some reason and required assistance, so I decided not to make up some phony story. As soon as I was out of the airplane, the major shouted, "Why didn't you start engines?"

The aggressiveness of his voice caught me off guard, and I said the first thing that came to my mind, which was the punch line to a joke that was going around my squadron at the time. I said, "I did start the engines. I just didn't engage the props." Obviously, he hadn't heard the joke. Having no experience in flying propeller-driven aircraft and not wanting to show his ignorance, he took my smart-ass response at face value, said "okay," and drove away.

John had been in the shower when the Klaxon went off; he didn't hear it and didn't know that there was an alert until he left the shower room and realized that the alert facility was empty. He went to his room and closed the door, waiting to see what fate awaited him. When the alert was over, we were all concerned for his wellbeing and were relieved to find him in his room. We traded our stories and gloated over how lucky we had been.

10

LOST AND FOUND

WAS FLYING OVER the Pacific, on my way to Vietnam. It was 1967. My regular navigator, Harvey Manikovsky, was ill and had been replaced by a navigator recently out of school, who had little experience flying over water. The route we were taking in a C-130 was from southern California to Hawaii, then to Wake Island, and finally, to Saigon. This was the first time I had ever flown with this nice young navigator, and soon I realized that the kid was lost in the Air Force. Most crewmembers fit into a mold; if you don't conform to the mold, you are an outsider and might never be accepted into the fraternity. That's how it was with Gerald (not his real name): all of his life he'd wanted to be a minister; because of circumstances, though, he'd found himself a navigator.

On most flights I could have done without a navigator. I had plenty of radio navigation equipment at the pilot's station to be able to determine our position by myself, but the leg from Honolulu to Wake Island was an all-day flight with only open ocean in between. Wake Island is only a few square miles of land in the Pacific Ocean. If you cannot find Wake, there is no other place to land, so having a navigator on that leg was essential. Wake did have a long-range, low-frequency, radio beacon that I could pick up about an hour out from landing; but I would not bet my life that the beacon would be on the air and that the receiver in my aircraft was working. I needed Gerald to do his job.

On over-water flights we calculated an equal time point (ETP); this was the point somewhere around the middle of the over-water portion of a flight where it took the same time to turn around and fly back, during an emergency, as it did to continue straight ahead and land. On over-water legs, I always wanted to know exactly where it was so that I could make an instant decision on which way to proceed if I had an engine failure: would I turn around and go back or continue straight ahead? I asked Gerald on the intercom how close we were to the ETP but got no response. I called him on the intercom a second time. Nothing.

I looked over my right shoulder to see if he had his headset on, but he was not in his seat at the navigation station. This was not unusual; maybe he was getting a cup of coffee or using the urinal. Then I saw him on his knees with his back to me; his elbows were on the lower bunk, which was just aft of his seat. I had to look around the flight engineer, who was directly in my line of vision, to get a better view of why he was in this unusual position. As I was trying to figure out what was going on, the engineer, to solve my puzzle, placed his hands together, indicating that he was praying. I knew that Gerald was a very religious young man, but this didn't seem like the right time or place to be praying. In the past, I had flown with a Catholic pilot who crossed himself before every takeoff, but I'd never seen anyone in the cockpit on his knees, praying.

At first I was angry, but I realized that I had better analyze the situation a little more before taking any action. I got out of my seat, put my hand on his shoulder, and asked him what was wrong. He had tears in his eyes, and it was obvious that he was upset. His first words to me were, "We're lost, and I can't get a fix." This was just what I didn't want to hear in the middle of the Pacific, so I asked him to explain further what was going on. He was babbling and not making much sense; I couldn't really understand what he was trying to say. I knew enough about his job to give him a hand with his navigation problems, not only to help him, but to know if we were really lost. I looked at his navigation chart and saw that all of his fixes were right on our track, except for the last one, which was about a hundred miles north of our planned route. After plotting this bad fix, he was unable to confirm our position because of radio problems, so he decided that he needed divine intervention. I knew that we had not made a heading change for at least an hour and that the winds were light, so we couldn't possibly be that far off track. I convinced him to just ignore the bad fix, plot our assumed position using the basic time and distance calculation, and try to get a good fix based on our assumed position. I told him to do exactly what he'd been taught to do in navigation training and what every experienced navigator does every time he found himself in Gerald's situation.

We weren't lost; we were right on track the entire time. Gerald was lost. Eventually, he pulled himself together; and when at last I was able to receive the Wake Island low-frequency beacon, it was right on our nose. That night, while eating dinner at the club on Wake, Gerald got me to one side and told me how comforting it was to have had God helping him when he needed assistance. I was astonished at his comment and realized he had no business in the cockpit of a combat aircraft. I flew with Gerald just one more time after that flight.

Gerald's last flight with me was during the Six-Day War, later in 1967. He was with me for a flight from Athens to Wheelus Air Force Base near Tripoli and then to Italy. The C-130s were all painted in the camouflage colors of brown, green, and tan for blending in with the jungles of Vietnam. On this assignment, though, I was not working for the US Air Force but for the International Red Cross, so my airplane had the United States emblems painted out and replaced with an enormous red cross. Under the auspices of the Red Cross, my mission was to evacuate civilians of several nationalities who had been brought to Wheelus from all over the war zone. We were to fly them to their temporary quarters in Pisa, Italy.

I had only ninety-four passenger seats, but there were a little over one hundred scared and tired civilians who just wanted to get to a safe location. I thought it was ridiculous to leave behind a dozen people, so I just loaded everyone into the aircraft. Those without seats sat on the floor, and the loadmaster used cargo straps as makeshift seat belts for them. When we were airborne and everyone was settled in, the loadmaster called me on the intercom to ask if one of the passengers could come to the cockpit for a little quiet and privacy, in order to breastfeed her newborn infant. The only spare seats we had in the cockpit were upper and lower bunks, which were right next to Gerald's seat.

I told the loadmaster to assist her in climbing the few steps up into the cockpit. Immediately, Gerald began objecting. He came up with about half a dozen reasons why I couldn't have her breastfeed in the cockpit right next to his seat, but

I ignored most of them. She was Dutch and she spoke English very well. I had the engineer give her a headset so she could speak with us. The C-130 had so much engine noise that everyone had to wear earplugs and all communications were over the intercom, wearing a headset. She told us that her husband was a Dutch diplomat and that he'd stayed behind, but all of the diplomatic wives and children, as well as nonessential male personnel, were on the airplane. Her baby was only a week old, and she was just learning how to care for it. She was grateful for the ride out of the war zone and the opportunity to get out of the crowded cargo compartment.

While I was speaking to the young mother, Gerald was digging out numerous navigation charts and taping them to the ceiling of the cockpit in order to isolate himself from the lower bunk, where he knew the breastfeeding would be taking place. I knew that he was upset with what was about to occur and that he was building a screen between the navigation station and the bunk. The Dutch woman, realizing the extent of Gerald's distress, was discreet; she covered herself completely with a blanket while she fed her infant. At one point, when the tape began to come loose and one side of the charts hung down, Gerald decided that he could no longer stand to be in the cockpit; he went to the cargo compartment, holding his hand near his face to block his view. I don't think that he ever realized that the mother and baby were totally covered with a blanket and that she was as uncomfortable with the situation as he was.

After the flight, Gerald told me that he could no longer stand to be a crewmember and wanted to turn in his navigator's wings and quit the Air Force. He didn't care what the repercussions were. Everyone he flew with knew that he was out of his element in the cockpit and was extremely unhappy. These were my only experiences with him, and I can only wonder what else occurred on other flights with other crews.

Soon after the Six-Day War was over—which was soon after it began, of course—Gerald at last received the divine intervention he'd been searching for: instead of getting out of the Air Force, he was permitted to stop flying as a navigator. He earned an Air Force Chaplain's Cross. Gerald was no longer lost. He was found at last.

The only time I was really lost in an aircraft was on a flight from Frobisher Bay on Baffin Island, Canada, flying south to Selfridge AFB near Detroit, during my first year out of pilot training. If I knew then what I know now, this incident never would have happened.

I was in the left seat of the KC-97, and Tim Casey was in the right seat. We were both new copilots from the same pilot training class. The navigator was also a youngster, and none of us had the experience to realize that we had a malfunction in the compass system of the aircraft. The only person with any experience was the aircraft commander, who was sound asleep for the entire incident except for the time when he woke up and asked me how things were going. I told him that we didn't know where the hell we were. He looked at the heading indicator, which indicated that we were flying south, and his comment was, "Keep flying in this direction and we'll get to the United States"; then he went back to sleep. The heading indicator he checked was part of the system that had failed, and the failure was now unnoticed by everyone. This probably was the reason that he still had only the rank of captain, even though he was getting close to retirement: he didn't take seriously a serious responsibility.

Frobisher Bay was a forward base used by SAC Operation Reflex crews because of its location just a few miles from the Arctic Circle in eastern Canada. To get from there to any sort of civilization, we had to fly about six hours south over thousands of lakes, which all looked alike when navigating by radar, as we were. Also, we were flying in persistent clouds, so we could not use our sextant for celestial navigation. This left us with radio navigation, and we were so far from civilization that we didn't have much luck with the radio beacons. The real problem was that we had a malfunctioning compass directing the autopilot. The main aircraft compass system was precessing at about twenty degrees per hour, which means that every hour we were turning left about twenty degrees. After a few hours, we were flying east, but we thought we were still heading south.

Pilots learn to check their gyroscopic compasses against the old standby magnetic compass to prevent this problem, but we were so close to the magnetic north pole that the standby compass was almost useless. This far north, Air Force navigators were instructed to reset the main compass for grid navigation, which made a cross check with the standby compass impossible. Under these conditions, the navigator was supposed to check the aircraft heading with a sextant, but the clouds ruled out that technique. Last and most critical was that my heading indicator, which I was using as a directional gyro, was the final method of identifying a failed compass system. It was giving me the indication that we had a compass problem. But I was convinced that I had a bad instrument, and I kept resetting it to agree with the faulty compass. I reset my

heading indicator about half a dozen times and commented to
the other crewmembers every time that the instrument was
still screwing up. It wasn't; I was.

We were three young and inexperienced boys trying to
do a man's job and messing it up pretty badly. The average
person who knows very little about aviation thinks that the
best pilot is the one who can consistently make a great landing. After spending my entire adult life learning, teaching,
and piloting, I can tell you that a good pilot is the one who
knows everything about his aircraft systems, understands the
reason for the thousands of regulations and procedures, and
doesn't violate them. The pilot who brings this knowledge
into the cockpit and uses it to understand the conditions affecting the aircraft is someone I would call one of the best
pilots. Neither Casey nor I was a good pilot at that time. We
didn't understand what was occurring, and we found ourselves hundreds of miles from where we thought we were,
heading in the wrong direction, and getting farther off track
every minute.

What saved us was an emergency radio call from the radar
controller at Goose Bay, Labrador, asking the aircraft on the
easterly heading to identify itself. The unidentified aircraft
was entering his restricted airspace. The UHF (ultra high
frequency) radio the military used had a portion that was always tuned to UHF guard channel, the emergency frequency,
and we received the transmission on that radio. I asked the
navigator if it was possible that Goose Bay was calling us. He
said it was impossible; they were much too far away, and we
were heading south. I knew that we were lost pretty badly,
so, disregarding the navigator, I answered their call. The
radar controller then went through his identifying procedure

and confirmed that we were the aircraft he was painting. I explained to him that we were lost, and he then directed us to the field, using compass-inoperative procedures.

We spent the night at Goose Bay and had our compass fixed. I learned an invaluable lesson: I had to think when there was a problem, no matter how minor it appeared at first, or I would not live to be an old man. Goose Bay had the only radar for hundreds of miles around. If they had not picked us up on their radar or had not been able to make radio contact with us, we probably would have continued on the easterly heading, running out of fuel over the North Atlantic, never knowing that we were almost a thousand miles from where we thought we were. In aviation they say that an accident is a number of events all linked together like a chain; if nothing breaks the chain, an accident occurs. Thank you, Goose Bay Radar, for breaking the chain of events.

I played a small part in another incident, also caused by a compass failure, when I was on a three-month rotation to Lajes Field in the Azores. The mission to station tankers in the Azores was passed among the KC-97 tanker squadrons on a rotating basis. I had two rotations to those remote islands, located in the Atlantic off the coast of Portugal. Our mission was not part of the SAC war plan, just routine refueling of SAC B-47s crossing the Atlantic while proceeding to and from the States and their forward bases surrounding the Mediterranean. The refuelings were always scheduled missions; however, this time, my crew was asked to preflight a tanker and stand by to refuel a B-47 that was lost in the Atlantic and running out of fuel.

I received my initial notification of the incident while I was eating lunch at the Officers' Club on the hill overlooking the runway. Immediately, I located the rest of the crew and we preflighted an aircraft while we waited for our instructions. Our refueling mission was cancelled about two hours later when it was determined that the aircraft in trouble was not a bomber but a B-47 that had been transformed into a weather and reconnaissance aircraft and did not have in-flight refueling capability. While I was having dinner that evening, once again at the Officers' Club with the view of the runway and ramp, the B-47 crashed about a quarter mile from the runway and bounced onto the parking ramp, hitting three other aircraft. The crew had been lost for hours and finally ran out of fuel, crashing into the approach lights leading to the runway. If the pilot could have stretched the mission another two thousand feet, he would have reached the runway and it would have been just another incident, instead of an accident. There was no fire because there was no fuel; the three-man crew all survived.

The aircraft was flying from the States to Europe, and because of a compass failure over the Atlantic, the navigator was terribly lost and confused. They resorted to asking for and receiving a high-frequency, directional finding (HF/DF) steer. The high-frequency radios on aircraft are the long-range radios, with a range of thousands of miles. The land-based stations can provide a line of position to a lost aircraft by determining the bearing from which the aircraft was transmitting. As an example, the HF station at Lajes could tell a transmitting aircraft that it was on a north–south line, (or any other) that passed through Lajes. Then, if the aircraft was in the North Atlantic, it would turn south to get to the Azores. The problem with this very basic steer is that the navigator would have to know whether they were north or south of the Azores to turn in the correct direction. The crew of the B-47 in question was so badly confused as to their position that they turned in the wrong direction when they received their initial steer from Lajes. That crew had basically the same problem I'd had in Canada: a bad compass and no idea of where they were.

They made some other bad decisions, such as circling the field to land into the wind, when a downwind landing would have shortened the flight by a few minutes, permitting them to land safely. The crew flew for a few thousand miles, making bad decisions at every turn, and crashed, out of fuel, a few seconds from the runway. Just one good decision, saving one minute's worth of fuel, would have broken the chain of events that led to the accident.

I was not in the air but on a walk in Greenland, south of Sondrestrom Air Base. When I had a day off from alert, there were only two places to go if I wanted to walk off of the base—to the glacier, east of the base, or to Lake Ferguson, a few miles south. The glacier was an outcropping of ice and snow from the main ice cap and was flowing down the fjord, toward the ocean. The path to the glacier was well traveled and easy to follow. You couldn't miss the glacier; the face was three thousand feet high. At one time, the path went to a viewing area about a mile from the base of the ice; just a few weeks before my visit, though, a huge piece of ice broke off and killed some people in the viewing area. After this incident, the area three miles from the glacier was off limits. If this chunk of ice had fallen into the ocean it would have become an iceberg; Greenland calves all of the icebergs in the North Atlantic.

I have always loved to fly over the coast of Greenland, especially the east coast, where the main body of ice reaches almost to the ocean. The view of the numerous glaciers and the enormous icebergs is spectacular. When you see the glaciers from the air, you can see that the ice is actually in motion. The annual movement is just a few feet, but you can see the massive cracks and stress fractures caused by the glacier's squeezing out of the main body of ice before flowing down a fjord, toward the water. Flying for TWA in later years, I would always make a lengthy announcement to the passengers so that they could see and understand this phenomenon.

It was summer, the only time we could take a walk off base. The winter was far too cold, and the daytime hours were either too short or almost totally dark. During the summer months, there was daylight for twenty-four hours, and at the summer solstice the sun made just a circle overhead. Three of us decided to walk the few miles to Lake Ferguson, which was known as the best place to catch Arctic char, a freshwater fish related to salmon. I was not going to fish, though; I was looking for a caribou rack.

The walk to the lake took us just a little over an hour, so we decided to walk another few miles along the north shore to the end of the lake. The area had numerous caribou that lived in the green fringe between the ice cap and the ocean. They shed their huge racks every year, and I was looking for one to bring back to my home in Massachusetts. I was also carrying a hack saw with me. Many of the weaker caribou do not survive the harsh winters; so if we found a skeleton, I would use the saw to cut the rack from the skull. I knew I could not find what I was looking for on the trail, because it was long since picked clean; I would have to walk off the trail to get a good specimen.

When we reached the end of the lake, we were getting tired and not looking forward to the long walk back. Instead of walking the length of the lake and making a ninety-degree turn to follow the trail back to the base, we decided to take what we thought was the shortcut: straight back. This meant walking over a fairly high, long hill, but it was grassland, with no trees. And I had the added benefit that I might still find my caribou rack, walking where probably no one had been before.

It took about an hour to reach the top of the hill, where we expected to see the Air Force base; but all we saw was another hill exactly like the one we were on. We were positive that the base was on the opposite side of the second hill, so we never considered turning around and walking back to the lake. The hills were long and extended to the end of my field of vision on both sides. The distances were deceptive, and climbing the first hill was far harder than I thought it would be. The tops of the two hills were a few miles apart, and we figured that they must have been formed by the ice cap as it moved forward or receded over thousands of years. We started down the back side of the first hill and into the flat valley between the two hills, and then we realized that we were in trouble. The valley was a peat bog, nearly impossible to walk through. We sank into the spongy vegetation up to our knees. It was about half a mile across the base of the valley, and we decided to continue to walk through the peat and climb the hill on the other side. I was positive that the Air Force base was just over the next hill; and the walk back, the way we came, would be about a ten-mile walk.

Walking through the peat, and sinking in with every step, was tiring, but we continued to the top of the second hill, fully expecting to be in the mess hall on the base in a short while. We were getting hungry by that time and had finished all of our water. When we reached the top of the second hill, there was still no base—only another hill exactly like the one we were standing on. Because of the similarity, we were sure that the next valley would be torture to walk through, once again. We noticed, though, that the third hill had an antenna on it, the only manmade object we had seen for hours. The antenna was about forty-five degrees from the way we were walking, but we decided to head for it. We assumed that there must be a path or some sort of road from the military base to the antenna, which would make our walk much easier. Also, we hoped that there might be a phone near the antenna, and we could contact the base. We had been walking for about ten hours, and what had started out as a little fun was rapidly turning into a disaster, not yet a survival situation, but heading in that direction.

It took another few hours to reach the antenna, through a similar peat bog in the valley, and then to the top of the third hill. At last, we got lucky. There was not just one antenna as we thought; this was the base antenna farm. There was even a small building with two people on duty. They said that it was the first time they'd ever had visitors to their duty station, which happened to be seven miles from the base. I asked them which way the base was, and they pointed in a direction that I thought was impossible. We never would have found the base, going the way we were headed. They realized how tired we were; so after a long drink of water, they drove us the seven miles back to the base in their pickup truck.

I sat in the back of the truck, totally exhausted, along with the racks of about a dozen caribou the antenna crew had collected. They knew where to look for them; obviously, I didn't. I bought my caribou rack from the driver for a few bucks, but I lied a little about how I got it, after I hung it in my basement in Massachusetts. The driver dropped us at the mess hall, where they had just started serving midnight "supper"—an early breakfast that begins at midnight. It was June twenty-first, the summer solstice, and continuous daylight in that part of Greenland.

11

EVERYTHING GOES WRONG

THE RESULTS OF an overnight ice storm can be spectacular, especially if the next morning there is bright sunshine lighting up the hundreds of small limbs of a tree coated with ice, making them sparkle. There is, however, a downside to the beauty of the ice, as it can add thousands of pounds of additional weight when it coats every limb and twig of the tree. Occasionally, a large branch will break under the weight, causing it to fall on power lines, cars, or people. Ice is a problem not only on the ground but also in flight.

When an airplane encounters icing conditions, the problems from ice buildup are different from the problems ice causes for tree limbs and power lines. Ice on the wings of an airplane disturbs the airflow over the wing, causing a reduction in lift. At the same time, it increases drag and increases the weight of the aircraft. An aircraft in heavy icing conditions can accumulate thousands of pounds of ice rapidly; combined with reduced lift and increased drag, this can be deadly for an unwary pilot.

In 1968, shortly before I was released from active duty, my unit was responsible for maintaining a few crews trained to carry nuclear weapons, as a backup to the squadrons who had primary responsibility for this specialized task. I was an aircraft commander of one of the backup crews. Once a year, we had training on the dozens of requirements for loading and transporting these weapons from one location to another. I'd never heard of anyone in my squadron having to carry the weapons, so I never expected to have to, either. But then I got the orders.

The mission required flying to a location where I would pick up eight nuclear weapons, load them onto the aircraft, and move them to a location eight hours' flying time away. The flight would have been much shorter if I could have flown a direct route to the destination, but because of the sensitivity of the cargo, I could not fly over certain locations or over-fly countries that did not permit their passage.

The first problem I encountered was loading the weapons into the aircraft and getting them tied down in compliance with the exacting specifications in the hundred or so pages of instructions we had to follow. Each of the weapons was individually mated to a wheeled dolly and had to be handled with the same care we would have used with a Rembrandt painting. It took two hours to winch the first dolly into place and tie it down with precisely the correct type and pattern of tie-down chains. The rest of the weapons went more quickly, but loading them still took another eight hours. When we finished, it was getting late. I decided to fly about one hour to another US Air Force installation along my route of flight, where I knew we could get some sleep. More important, the base would provide the necessary security for the airplane and cargo.

We got an early start the next day, ate breakfast in the mess hall, and took enough extra food with us to have lunch in flight. Then I went to base operations to plan the mission and file our flight plan. Also, I sent an encoded message providing the information required for the Air Force to track my flight. The weather en route was bad, with icing in the clouds, but I thought I would be able to climb above the ice into the clear air that was forecast to be above the clouds. Another problem was that strong headwinds were predicted for the entire flight. Because of the headwinds, what had been planned as a seven-hour flight was stretched to eight hours. The weapons were very heavy, which limited the amount of fuel I could carry; however, I was able to load an extra few thousand pounds of fuel, which took me to my maximum takeoff weight. If everything went as planned, I would land with a comfortable amount of fuel.

I entered the clouds shortly after takeoff and immediately began to pick up clear ice. This was not an unusual occurrence, and it had been forecast in the weather briefing. What I did not expect was the intensity or the persistence of the icing. It usually occurs in a narrow temperature range; as the aircraft climbs, the temperature changes and the icing ceases. The icing didn't stop, though; it just changed in character from clear ice to rime ice. I continued in the icing conditions throughout my entire climb to altitude, with all of the anti-icing equipment on the aircraft operating. I checked continuously to see the amount of ice I was picking up by looking out the window at the parts of the airplane that were not anti-iced, and I realized that I had more ice than I had ever experienced before. I kept hoping that either we would get to a temperature where the accumulation of ice would end or we would break out of the clouds.

When you turn on all of the anti-icing equipment on the C-130, you pay a penalty in loss of available engine power. The wing anti-ice uses hot air from the engines to heat the leading edges of the wings and prevent the ice from building up, but by robbing the engine of air, the engine power available is reduced by as much as twenty-five percent. This meant that I was flying a four-engine aircraft, but I was using the power of one engine to remove ice. I had taken off at maximum weight; and with the weight of the ice buildup, I probably weighed more than my maximum weight. The ice was increasing the drag and decreasing the lift, and I was using the power produced by one engine just to run the anti-icing equipment. Finally, I reached a point where the aircraft was incapable of climbing to a higher altitude. I was at only fifteen thousand feet and still in the icing conditions.

This was unfamiliar territory for me. I had been a pilot for eight years and had about four thousand hours of flight time, but I had never experienced a situation where I was asking for more than the aircraft could give. I'd been briefed by the weatherman that the cloud tops were at sixteen thousand feet, and occasionally I could see blue sky above me. I knew that if I could climb another thousand feet I would be above the clouds. Above the clouds I would stop picking up additional ice; but more important, I could turn off the anti-icing equipment and get back all of my engine power.

At fifteen thousand feet, still in the clouds and the icing, I was fighting a losing battle. There was a slow decrease in precious airspeed, as the weight of the ice increased. I was considering my options, and concluded that my only recourse was to return to the base I had taken off from, and continue the flight when the weather conditions were better. If I continued to fly in the icing conditions, unable to climb, and with a steady decrease of airspeed, I would reach a point where I had to descend to a lower altitude or stall the aircraft. Was there some way to get that extra thousand feet to get above the clouds?

While searching for a solution to my dilemma, I remembered Major Tom Parry telling war stories late one night while I was on SAC alert. Major Parry was one of the few remaining World War II veterans still in the military at the time, and I enjoyed listening to his war stories. He'd said something years before that I remembered, and I wondered if I could use it to climb the thousand feet. He'd told a tale about having an engine failure at liftoff and making a one-hundred-eighty degree turn, back to the runway, to land. The runway was near the coast, built on a bluff a few hundred feet above the water. His aircraft was very heavy, and during the turn over the ocean, it descended below the level of the runway. It appeared, to the then Second Lieutenant Parry that they were going to crash into the cliff directly in front of the aircraft. The plane was incapable of climbing the hundred feet to get over the cliff, with the failed engine; and they didn't have the space available to turn away from the cliff. Then he told all of us young pilots to remember how to get out of a similar situation, something they never teach you in school. The pilot in the left seat ordered him to extend the wing flaps, and they popped up, over the cliff, and made a successful landing.

I was wondering if extending a small amount of wing flaps would work in my predicament and permit me to climb the thousand feet that I needed to get above the icing. I really didn't have much to lose; I was getting ready to abort the mission anyway and decided to give the wing flaps a try.

The wing flaps are on the trailing edge of the wing and extend aft and down, away from the wing, to change the shape and size of the wing. The flaps are used primarily during takeoff and landing, to allow the aircraft to fly at a slower speed during those two critical phases of flight. Technically, the wing flaps increase the amount of lift produced by the wing, which was just what I needed to climb above the clouds; but it comes with a penalty. The wing flaps would also add to the drag and would cause me to lose an additional few knots of airspeed.

I instructed the copilot to extend the flaps five percent. This was an almost imperceptible amount; the two settings we used for landings were fifty or one hundred percent. I figured that I would give five percent a try first, since I was in unfamiliar territory. This little change in the shape of the wing performed just the miracle I needed, and my guess about dropping only five percent was right on the money. After climbing about five hundred feet, I realized that we were almost out of the clouds and the ice. I then told the engineer to turn off only the wing anti-ice but keep the remainder of the anti-icing equipment on. It was the wing anti-ice that was the largest draw on our power supply and the one that I needed the least, if we were going to get out of the icing conditions shortly.

The combination of the added power and the increased lift from the flaps worked. We climbed above the clouds and out of the icing, but we still hadn't delivered our cargo of nuclear weapons to our destination. Now it was time to consider the fuel situation. Turbine engines are most fuel efficient at higher altitudes, and I had been stuck at a relatively low altitude with maximum power on the engines.

On long flights, when fuel quantity might be an issue, the navigator and flight engineer would construct a fuel chart. The chart was an instant depiction of the amount of fuel we had remaining versus the amount of fuel required to complete the flight. If I was above the line on the chart, I had sufficient fuel reserves; below the line meant that I would not be able to continue on to our destination but would have to land and get additional fuel. I was right on the fuel line. If I continued to my destination without stopping to refuel, I would have no cushion if some unforeseeable event occurred. Also, I had to keep in mind the nature of my cargo and the consequences of an incident or an accident if I ran out of fuel. I began planning to stop and get an additional ten thousand pounds of fuel.

Because of the political sensitivity of nuclear weapons, I was not permitted to refuel in the countries that prohibited over-flight. This greatly limited the options I had for refueling. At last, I selected an isolated military airfield in a country that I was confident I was authorized to enter. It appeared to be the ideal location to refuel; it had a suitable runway and was along my route of flight. Also, it was a military airfield and they carried the type of fuel I needed. Then I went through the long process of encoding a classified message and sending it to my controlling authority, to inform them of my fuel diversion.

My intention was to not inform anyone on the ground of my cargo, but just to get ten thousand pounds of fuel and continue on to my destination. I did, however, request remote parking for refueling, which was standard procedure when carrying hazardous cargo. The control tower operator was having difficulty understanding my request; we were both speaking

English, the international aviation language, but it was not his native tongue. After landing, once again I informed the control tower that I was requesting remote parking, as well as the type and quantity of fuel I needed. He understood my request, and I was met by a little vehicle that I followed to the remote refueling area.

The vehicle that guided me to the parking area was not a military vehicle, as I was accustomed to seeing, but an ancient civilian car that the driver probably drove to work. The only aircraft I saw on the parking ramp were a few old World War II reciprocating engine fighter planes. This was not the first-class Air Force base in a foreign country that I expected but rather a third-rate leftover from bygone years.

I taxied behind the little car for about two miles to a location that was about as far as I could go and still remain on the airfield. From my location, I could not see any portion of the small aircraft hangars or control tower, because of the intervening trees. The downside to my remote parking location was that it was right next to a small town, and I'd parked the aircraft about two blocks from the town center. All that separated the buildings of the town from the old tarmac I was parked on was a three-strand barbed wire fence. The four turbine engines of the C-130 are extremely noisy, and everyone who works around the aircraft wears ear plugs because of the high decibel level. The noise alerted the town that something unusual was occurring on the base, and the large camouflaged aircraft with United States markings, parked on the outskirts of their village, succeeded in bringing the entire town to the fence to look at the C-130.

The driver of the follow-me vehicle spoke a little English. He assured me that the fuel truck would be along shortly and that I would be getting the JP-4 fuel I had requested. Maybe things were looking up! I had the loadmaster hang a curtain over the forward entrance door so that no one could look into the cargo compartment and view the nuclear weapons. I stationed him at the door and gave him instructions that he was not to allow anyone, other than our crew, to enter the aircraft. Also, I ensured that all of the other doors were secured from the inside.

In a short time our fuel truck arrived, and it was something to behold. I had started to panic when I realized how close we were to the town, but I went into the full panic mode when I saw the fuel truck. It looked like the broken-down heap the Joads drove, in The Grapes of Wrath. The age of the truck and its condition were not what caused my panic level to increase; it was the size of the fuel tank on the rear of the truck. The house I was raised in had a five-hundred-gallon heating oil tank next to my play area, and I was familiar with a tank of that size. I was sure that the fuel truck had a five-hundred gallon tank strapped onto the back. I calculated that it would take three truckloads of fuel get the ten thousand pounds I had requested, and the truck would have to refill two more times. I would be on the ground for hours.

Then came more bad news. The engineer informed me that there was no place to ground the aircraft electrically during the refueling. Refueling an aircraft is a hazardous operation; fuel transfer can build up static electricity, which might cause a spark and explosion. The fuel truck and aircraft must both be connected to the ground to dissipate the static electricity and neutralize the charge, to prevent a spark. All normal refueling areas have metal rods driven deep into the ground beneath the tarmac; the grounding wires are attached to these rods. The refueling truck driver was familiar with our location, and found an old metal stake in the ground that he had used before, but I had reservations about using it. He then pointed out a water pipe under the fence that he thought we could use. I had no idea if the water pipe or the metal stake were adequate, so we attached our grounding wires to both of them.

I was visualizing an incident where the aircraft would have a fire and the weapons would be consumed. I was confident that a fire would not cause a nuclear explosion because of the safety devices built into the weapons, but they contained high explosives that might detonate in a fire. I requested that we have emergency equipment stand by for the refueling and was informed that it would be available shortly. When the old fire truck arrived, I realized that it was right in character with the rest of the base: vintage World War II.

With nuclear weapons, all of the rules change, and violation of the rules has serious consequences. One of the rules was the no lone zone: no one could be alone in the area surrounding the weapons; there had to be two people, each in full view of the other. The no lone zone extended throughout the entire cargo compartment where the weapons were loaded and included the latrine facilities we had in the rear of the aircraft. Anyone using the latrine required two additional crewmembers to escort him because, when the curtain was drawn surrounding the facilities, the escort would be by himself only a short distance from where the weapons were tied down in the aft compartment. Therefore, two escorts were required. My navigator, Shuminsky, must have eaten something that did not agree with him, and he had diarrhea.

As soon as we began refueling, Shuminsky informed me that he had to use the latrine, immediately! We had six crewmembers. A normal crew was five, but we had two loadmasters. The engineer was busy refueling, and one of the loadmasters was guarding the forward door. I instructed the second loadmaster and the copilot to escort Shuminsky to the latrine in the rear of the cargo compartment. That left only me with no apparent duties, other than to supervise the entire operation.

It's at this relatively quiet time that the driver of the follow-me vehicle, who had been chatting with the dozens of onlookers on the town side of the three-wire fence, decided to show everyone how important he was by inviting them to cross the fence for a closer look at the airplane. By the time I saw what was happening, I was surrounded by about fifty non-English-speaking civilians dispersed all around the plane. I was trying to refuel the aircraft without allowing anyone on the ground to have knowledge of my cargo, and now, about a dozen of them were at the front door of the aircraft, trying to look inside. They almost succeeded in squeezing past the loadmaster to get a better look. The two crewmembers escorting Shuminsky, upon hearing the commotion, came to the front door and succeeded in holding the curtain in place while backing the crowd away from the door. What helped was that it was very bright outside, and the cargo compartment was dark inside, so it took a few seconds to get your eyes accustomed to the darkness before you could focus on the exposed weapons. Although some of the civilians were able to get a peek into the rear of the aircraft, I don't think they realized what we were carrying.

I was having a far more difficult time than the crewmembers at the front door were having. At first, I tried to shout and make hand motions meant to convey the message that civilians were not permitted near the aircraft, but that was totally useless. I was surrounded by a crowd of curious well-wishers who were just trying to be friendly, apparently spoke no English, and had been invited into the area by the driver. There was so much commotion near the aircraft that one old man did not see the static wire that was grounding the fuel truck and tripped over it, disconnecting it.

While I was reattaching the ground wire, I was envisioning a spark and the consequent explosion; hoping that if it occurred, I would not survive the conflagration. The story would have been on the front page of every newspaper in the entire world! Death was preferable to humiliation. In my anger, I shouted at the old man who had tripped over the wire. My displeasure caused him to become distressed, so he took out a cigarette and was preparing to strike a match to light it. When I saw him about to light a match, I went ballistic! I was worried that a small spark from the grounding wire might ignite the fuel vapors, and he was going to strike a match to light his cigarette, ten feet from the fuel truck!

I ran over to the engineer, who was on a ladder refueling over the wing, and told him that the situation was totally out of control and to stop refueling. He informed me that the fuel truck was almost empty, anyway. Next, I went to the front door of the airplane, shouted to Shuminsky that how I didn't care how dirty his underwear got, but I wanted him out of the aircraft immediately. When Shuminsky was out, I had the loadmaster close the front door, because the crowd still wanted to see the inside of the C-130. Aided by the now embarrassed driver who had caused my problem, and using my entire crew, we herded the civilians away from the plane. Eventually, they retreated to their side of the fence.

I had taken on about thirty-five hundred pounds of JP-4 fuel, which was exactly the amount of fuel it takes to make a stop and then climb back to altitude. I decided that waiting for the fuel truck to refill and return with another five hundred gallons of fuel was a mistake, so we politely informed the control tower that we had sufficient fuel and took off. The remainder of the flight was uneventful, and I landed with the minimum amount of fuel required by the regulations.

Unloading the weapons was considerably easier than the loading was, and I had plenty of time to relax and let my blood pressure return to normal before flying out the next morning. Shuminsky still had a bad stomach, but at least he didn't require an escort every time he went to the latrine.

The mission was my last before returning to my home base and flying as an instructor pilot for the next few months. I was teaching new C-130 pilots the tactics and maneuvers that all combat-ready pilots had to master. A few months after unloading the nuclear weapons, I was released from active duty, with ten years and three months under my belt, and I was content to become a flight engineer for TWA. To get released from active duty, I had to refuse a promotion to the rank of major. If I had accepted the promotion, I would have incurred an additional two-year commitment to the Air Force.

I had worked for TWA for about a year when I was selected to work in the training center, giving other flight engineers their annual proficiency checks in a Boeing 727 flight simulator. Someone asked if I was sorry about giving up a great military career and not remaining in the Air Force as a thirty-year-old major. The first thing that came to mind was the mission carrying the nuclear weapons and the recurrent nightmares I had for a long time after the flight. I would dream about stalling the aircraft due to the icing and an explosion when the old man lit his cigarette igniting the fuel vapor. Next, I considered that I was now making fifty percent more money than I had been making in the Air Force and working half as hard. I answered, "Getting out of the Air Force was the best decision I ever made."

In December of 1968, when I was released from the Air Force, TWA hired only experienced pilots and trained them to fly as flight engineers, the third pilot in the cockpit. I was awarded my first flight engineer's certificate on the Boeing 727. My station was immediately behind the two pilots, sitting sideways, facing to the right.

The job title of Flight Engineer has almost totally faded into oblivion. In the United States these days, new cockpit designs have increased the automation of those systems that I operated manually; and the position is almost obsolete, just as navigators and radio operators were replaced by automation many years before. Modern commercial aircraft now have only two pilots in the cockpit.

Everything at TWA was based on seniority, including the type of airplane we flew, our flight schedules, vacations, and even our space-available flight passes. I was a new flight engineer at the bottom of a seniority list of over four thousand pilots. With a seniority number of 4,392 I flew the airplane that paid the least, and I flew the flights that no one else wanted.

Every month, each pilot bid for the flights he wanted to fly the following month. The bidding process established my days off, the length of the trip, and my destination or layover city. The number one man on the seniority list chose his schedule first, and then number two made his selection, et cetera, until it came to me: as a very junior pilot, I took what was left. I flew out of LaGuardia to places like Pittsburgh, Dayton, Cincinnati, Indianapolis, Chicago, and Kansas City: the least desirable flights. Occasionally, though, I would get to the West Coast cities or maybe to the Southwest. The senior pilots were flying to London, Paris, and Rome, or other, even more exotic, destinations.

Part of the engineer's job was to perform a preflight inspection of the exterior and interior of the aircraft before every leg. It took only about ten minutes and was basically just a visual look at about a hundred items to ensure that there was no obvious damage or abnormal condition. One of the first early morning flights of the day from Kansas City, where I'd had a layover, was to California, and I was performing the interior inspection on the 727. Normally, because it was so early in the morning, I would be the only person on the airplane. The first thing I'd do was turn on all the systems that had been shut down the previous evening; then I would preflight the passenger compartment. I began my preflight at the cockpit door and was working my way to the rear of the passenger compartment, starting a pot of coffee as I worked my way past the forward galley. I usually started the coffee on my way to the rear, and the brewing would be completed by the time I returned a few minutes later. The rest of the crew was always happy to see that the coffee was ready when they boarded.

I continued walking aft while inspecting the windows, seats, and emergency equipment, when I realized there was someone bent over between two rows of seats. I thought the person was hiding from me, so I approached cautiously. One moment, I was looking at the buttocks and back of a torso bent over between the seats, and the next moment I was face-to-face with an attractive, blonde, middle-aged woman. It was obvious I had startled her as much as she had startled me. After the embarrassing moment passed, I checked her authorization to be on the aircraft without an escort. She was a federal inspector who worked for the Department of Agriculture, and she also needed a cup of coffee. We went back to the first class galley, where we had a laugh about scaring each other and talked about what she was doing on a TWA 727 so early in the morning. She said there was an outbreak of some flying insect in the Midwest that was a menace to certain crops. The Department of Agriculture was trying to keep the insect infestation from spreading to the agricultural areas of California, where there were susceptible crops and no natural defenses. As the assigned inspector, she inspected this particular flight every day, looking for the insects by shining a flashlight in all of the dark areas, under seats, and in seatback pockets. If the beam of light illuminated an insect, its iridescent outer shell would glow, so it could easily be seen and identified. If an insect were found, the aircraft would have to be sprayed with an insecticide before departing for California. She had been doing this every morning for a few weeks, and all of the TWA station personnel who worked the early shift knew her, so there was no need for an escort.

As we continued our conversation, she asked me if I knew her ex-beau, also a TWA pilot. He was stationed in Kansas City, and I had always been based in New York. I explained that with a seniority list of four thousand pilots, the chances of us knowing each other were slim; when she gave me his name, I confirmed I had never heard of him. Near the end of the conversation, I asked her for the name of the insect she was looking for. She gave me a scientific name that an entomologist would use when talking to a colleague, so I asked her for the common name that might be more familiar to me. She answered: "I just call it the pilot bug because of the similarity with my last boyfriend." She could tell by the look on my face that I was confused, so she continued: "All it does is eat, screw, and fly away."

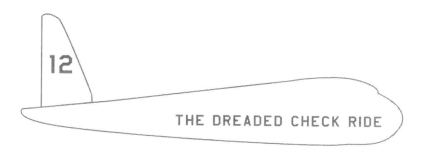

12

THE DREADED CHECK RIDE

NINETY PERCENT OF the job of being a pilot was moving an airplane from one place to another; the remaining ten percent of the job was going to school to learn how to do it and getting checked to see if I was doing it correctly. It seemed there was always someone looking over my shoulder when I was in a TWA cockpit, either giving me a check ride or just observing my actions. Airline flying may be the most highly trained and closely monitored of all possible ways to earn a living. Maybe that's because when the door closes on a commercial jet, the safety of the passengers is in the hands of the pilot and the rest of the crew. There are few times in your life when you have absolutely no control over your wellbeing; the two that come to mind are when you are at thirty-five thousand feet, flying at close to the speed of sound, and when you are on an operating table, under anesthesia. The few times my life depended on a surgeon and an anesthesiologist, I have thought about how much more comfortable I'd feel if they, too, were governed by federal regulations. Were they required, as I was, to have gotten a suitable rest period the night before? Had they ever been subjected to an unannounced drug and alcohol test, as pilots are?

For the latter part of my career with TWA, I was subjected to mandatory drug testing. This was a federal government program, administered by the airlines, to ensure that the crewmembers were not under the influence of drugs while performing their jobs. The testing was sensitive enough to detect a foreign substance in your body weeks after it was taken and was instrumental in weeding out the small percentage of crewmembers who smoked marijuana or used any of the other readily available street drugs.

The drug testing always came at the completion of a flight; at TWA, we were met by a supervisor after we landed and handed the computer-generated paperwork. A computer randomly selected an individual or sometimes the entire crew for the mandatory screening. We had to report to a laboratory within an hour or two, where they would take a urine sample under controlled chain of custody, to ensure that the sample was not switched or tampered with (there were all kinds of rumors about some drug abusers switching their urine with a clean sample). After seeing the extent of the precautions to prevent a switch, I don't believe that switching occurred. After the bugs were worked out of the initial system, it was effective in stopping drug use among the crewmembers.

Alcohol testing was instituted soon after the mandatory drug screening and was also effective. Drug abusers and alcohol abusers were treated differently, though. The drug abusers usually lost their jobs; but because alcohol was legal, it was treated as a medical problem. When I first started flying in the Air Force, alcohol was a problem; over the years, though, we all came to realize that the throttle and the bottle do not mix, and the culture changed: the image of the hard-drinking pilot was finally gone. Many modes of transportation now have the drug and alcohol testing that began with the aviation industry. Wouldn't it be nice if the legislatures that initiated those rules were required to have the same high standards as pilots? And don't forget about the medical profession.

As a pilot, I had to have a physical examination twice a year, done by an FAA-certified doctor. The physical included an annual EKG to see if I was developing any heart problems. The medical screening ensured that I was physically fit and reduced the chance that I would have a heart attack in the cockpit. With every physical, I was placing my license, and therefore my job, on the line. The doctor had a rigid set of standards to follow, established by the FAA medical department; and there was always the chance that he would find some medical problem that would ground me immediately. The EKG was linked to the FAA computer in Oklahoma City through a telephone line and was instantly evaluated by the computer. An abnormality in my EKG would ground me until a human cardiologist could read the printout.

All medications had to be approved by the FAA, and there were prescribed medications that I could not take because they would cause drowsiness or have other detrimental side affects. I don't know of any other profession where the routine problems that everyone has when they age could cause them to lose their job. The stress of getting a physical twice a year always raised my blood pressure the first time it was taken, and it usually had to be taken a second or third time before it returned to normal. This was not unusual with pilots, and the doctors were aware of the problem.

✪

Professional golfer Payne Stewart died in an accident in 1999 while flying as a passenger in a Learjet. The aircraft was at forty-five thousand feet when it lost pressurization; everyone on board died from hypoxia (oxygen deprivation). The autopilot was engaged, and there was nothing wrong with the engines; so, even though the flight crew was dead, the aircraft kept flying until it ran out of fuel a few hours after the loss of pressurization. I did not read the final accident report, but I assume the pilots were incapacitated before they had a chance to put on their oxygen masks.

Airliners are designed to cruise at approximately thirty-five thousand feet, roughly seven miles above the surface of the earth. This is a hostile environment, extremely cold and with limited oxygen; but the passenger compartment is heated and pressurized to provide a shirt-sleeve environment. Otherwise, the temperature in the cabin would be forty degrees below zero, and the passengers would lose consciousness from lack of oxygen in less than thirty seconds. The limited oxygen at that altitude is not sufficient to allow your brain to function, so you would progress from irrational thinking to death from hypoxia as the time or the altitude increases.

Air Force pilot training was more extensive than at a civilian flying school. One pilot training device, used by the Air Force but not required by the FAA and therefore not a part of my TWA training, was the altitude chamber. Air Force pilots had to have altitude chamber training every three years, as I recall; so I probably had eight or nine chamber rides.

The altitude chamber gave me a chance to experience hypoxia under controlled conditions, with the hope that if I found myself in the situation that the Learjet pilots found themselves in, I would be trained to recognize the condition and take corrective action before becoming unconscious. I do not know if either of the Learjet pilots had ever received training in an altitude chamber.

The altitude chambers used by the Air Force were in the shape of a shoebox and large enough to hold twelve pilots, sitting six on each side. There was space for two safety instructors, who were qualified to give emergency assistance if one of the pilots required immediate medical aid. The instructors received hazardous duty pay in addition to their regular salary. Outside, a few people operated the chamber and observed the proceedings inside through porthole-style windows, made of a plastic material that was capable of withstanding the great pressure. The altitude chamber was constructed of heavy, reinforced steel to withstand the pressure differential between normal atmospheric pressure outside and a partial vacuum inside. The heavy steel door on one end had a rubber gasket, making the entire chamber airtight once the door was closed. We began each session, before the chamber was pressurized, breathing one hundred percent oxygen, to reduce the amount of nitrogen in our systems, thereby reducing the chance of getting an altitude-related illness. When the door was closed, a vacuum pump started to remove the air from the chamber to simulate climbing to altitude in an unpressurized aircraft.

The chamber included a balloon holding a small amount of air. As the pressure dropped in the chamber, simulating an increase in altitude, the trapped air inside the balloon expanded; the same as the trapped air in a person's body. At eighteen thousand feet, the balloon was twice as large as at sea level. I loosened my belt at that pressure, because any bubble of trapped gas in my stomach or anywhere else in my body—a joint or a dental filling, for example—also doubled in size. More serious problems could occur because of the nitrogen dissolved in the blood. Such expanding gases caused different degrees of discomfort, from minor problems to extreme pain, as the altitude increased. When I first began flying, I was told to inform my dentist, before having a tooth filled, that I was a pilot and could not have any air trapped under the filling.

If one of the students experienced pain during a chamber ride, either the altitude of the chamber was reduced until the pain stopped or, occasionally, the student having the problem was removed from the chamber, to complete his training another day.

The altitude of the chamber increased until it simulated flying in a non-pressurized aircraft at forty-one thousand feet. At this altitude, breathing one hundred percent oxygen was not sufficient to prevent hypoxia; the oxygen had to be pressurized, and forced into the lungs. When the oxygen system automatically began supplying pressure, we had to begin what is called pressure breathing or reverse breathing. Normally, we use muscles to bring air into our lungs, and then relax the muscles to exhale. In pressure breathing, the oxygen is forced into the lungs, and the muscles are used in reverse, to force the air out. At that altitude, we had the opportunity to speak, using the intercom system built into our oxygen masks. It required a little practice to produce understandable words. When I attempted to relax my muscles and speak, the pressurized oxygen system forced the gas the wrong way over my vocal chords; and initially I produced no sound. I had to force the air out of my lungs to speak. It was an unusual sensation, but in a short while I trained myself to produce understandable phrases. At this very high altitude the balloon, hanging in the center of the chamber, which began at sea level with very little air, was fully inflated.

The altitude of the chamber then dropped to twenty-five thousand feet for the hypoxia demonstration, the portion of the simulated flight I enjoyed the most. At this lower altitude, we removed our oxygen masks, and as our brains were deprived of oxygen, we became hypoxic. I could then identify my personal symptoms of hypoxia so that if I ever encountered those symptoms in an aircraft, I would recognize them as the onset of hypoxia and put on my oxygen mask.

At twenty-five thousand feet, the time of useful consciousness (TUC) was close to two minutes, depending on variables such as smoking, age, and aerobic conditioning. TUC was the period that a pilot could function and make rational decisions, in the cockpit, when deprived of oxygen. We were given a series of tasks to accomplish while we became hypoxic. The tasks involved using a pencil and paper, so that we would each have a record of our actions; we added numbers or solved simple puzzles. I have saved these papers over the years, and recently I reviewed the results of my problem solving ability without sufficient oxygen. At the beginning of the demonstration, I was solving the problems correctly; at about one minute after removing my mask, I would begin to make errors. This progressed to the point where I was incapable of controlling my writing and started what looks like doodling or scribbling on the paper, with no problem solving ability at all. Without sufficient oxygen, my brain was incapable of performing the simplest reasoning.

We were supposed to put our own oxygen masks back on when we recognized our personal hypoxia symptoms, but the instructors were observing closely to assist if needed.

In my last experience in an altitude chamber, near the end of my Air Force flying career, I was determined to be the last person to put on my mask, so I'd get a good chance to really experience hypoxia. The literature talks about a "sense of wellbeing," and now I can vouch for that symptom. With my mask off, I began working on a series of simple tasks with pencil and paper, while constantly looking around the chamber to see which of the other pilots had put their masks back on. When I had done about ten of the puzzles, there were still a few pilots who continued to have their masks off; I, of course, was one of them. I recall thinking I'm doing great and can continue solving the puzzles because they are so easy; also, because of this sense of wellbeing, I was confident I would be the last one to put my mask back on. My next recollection is of the student next to me holding me in my seat while one of the instructors held the mask to my face! I'd progressed far beyond the point of being able to put my oxygen mask back on, and would have fallen out of my chair if I'd not been held in. I was unconscious. The sheet of paper with the puzzles showed my progression from solving the problem to doodling on the sheet to ripping through the paper with the pencil because of a lack of coordination. I was completely unaware of my true state! My brain was telling me that everything was fine, but I was actually in deep hypoxia and was totally incapable of doing anything, including remaining in my seat, that required muscle coordination.

Airline pilots have quick-donning oxygen masks that can be taken down and put on with one hand in about one second. Anytime the airplane is above forty-one thousand feet, one of the pilots has to wear an oxygen mask continuously. If there is an incident at altitude in which a passenger plane begins to lose pressurization, the pilot is notified with a warning horn and has to make an immediate emergency descent to a lower altitude. I never had this happen while I worked for TWA, but it did happen in an Air Force plane I was flying. I was between Midway Island, in the Pacific Ocean, and California when I had a pressurization failure in a C-130. I landed at Hickam

The author carrying all of his gear, after returning by helicopter from a four-day escape and evasion exercise. Mosquito netting, which was used to cover his face and neck during the exercise, is seen stacked on his head.

AFB, near Honolulu, for repairs. The part that was needed to fix the airplane was unavailable for a few days, so I stayed in a beachfront cottage at Fort DeRussy, a military R&R location on Waikiki Beach. You win some and you lose some.

Another military training device that civilian-trained pilots don't experience is the vertigo trainer. Vertigo is the sensation of spinning or disorientation that can occur in flight when the sensors in your body that maintain your equilibrium are confused. The primary sensors that tell us about the position of our bodies are the eyes and the semicircular canals in the inner ear. A pilot who cannot see the horizon or the ground—flying at night or in the clouds, for example—is deprived of the best tool for overcoming vertigo: vision. The balance mechanism in our inner ears helps us establish which way is up and whether we are turning or accelerating. In the vertigo trainer, neither system is available.

The vertigo trainer is a simple, enclosed cockpit simulator, positioned on the end of a long boom that rotates around the motor and mount in the center of a large room. The trainer has no windows; with the door closed, there are no outside visual references. The cockpit is elementary, with instructions and a checklist to prepare the simulated aircraft for takeoff. As a pilot works on the checklist, the trainer begins to rotate slowly.

After completing the checklist, the pilot lines up on the runway heading and requests takeoff clearance, on tower frequency. After takeoff, the pilot is told to turn right and climb to five thousand feet.

Having followed this procedure, I was on my way; the airplane was so simple that it almost flew itself. I rotated and lifted off, raised the landing gear, and began my climbing right turn, as I'd been instructed. When I was in my right turn, I received instructions to squawk a different code on my IFF and contact departure control, a typical after-takeoff instruction. I had to look down and to my left, to the location of the IFF. This triggered the most violent case of vertigo I could imagine, exactly what it was designed to accomplish.

The semicircular canals work just fine for the conditions under which they evolved: walking on the surface of the earth. These sensors can get really messed up in an airplane, though, and the specific maneuver I had to do was designed to maximize the mess.

When I looked down to the left, I had a violent sensation that I was tumbling rapidly and was totally incapable of functioning. I slammed my head back against the headrest to make this enormously uncomfortable sensation stop, and the tumbling ceased. I tried it a second and third time with exactly the same result: it came on and stopped instantly. It would have made it impossible for me to function if this had been a real aircraft and a real case of vertigo.

I learned from the training that a simple head movement can induce vertigo; if I ever got that spinning or tumbling sensation in the aircraft, I should immediately place my head back where it had been before the onset of the vertigo.

The design of modern cockpits takes motion-induced vertigo into consideration, and the operation of equipment and switches requires very little head movement. No doubt, many early pilots were killed before it was recognized that they were crashing because of vertigo and that something as simple as cockpit design could have prevented it.

The Air Force had a unique way to test the capability of their combat units, the operational readiness inspection (ORI). The individual flight checks given by the airlines were similar to those that were given to Air Force pilots; however, there was no civilian equivalent to the Air Force's ORI. This was an inspection of a flying squadron or wing to prove they were capable of performing their wartime mission. This was the only reason for the combat units' existence, and the ORI was their final report card.

I took part in more than a dozen ORIs as a pilot, but there is one that stands out in my mind. I was flying for TWA but was also flying for the Air Force Reserves. I was one of the most senior pilots in the 327th Tactical Airlift Squadron, and I probably had more flying time in the C-130 than any other pilot in the squadron. I was also a flight examiner, which was the top of the pilots' food chain: I was the alpha male of my pack.

We weren't doing very well, about halfway through the weeklong inspection; as a matter of fact, we were doing quite poorly. Each of the six of us had to fly an assault landing: a short, low-level route; and a landing on a three-thousand-foot runway, simulating supplying ground forces in a combat zone. We had to touch down within the first few hundred feet of the runway and stop on the remaining portion of the runway. The touchdown zone was marked with painted horizontal lines, and there was an inspector at each line to ensure that every airplane landed within the mandatory touchdown area. It was like landing on an aircraft carrier, except that we were flying large, four-engine planes, and we didn't have a cable to stop us. We stopped our aircraft with reverse thrust and maximum braking.

There was nothing gentle about an assault landing. Upon touchdown, the pilot yanked all four thrust levers into the full reverse position, with the hope that all engines would reverse equally. But with the inspectors watching, Ron Manion's number four engine did not reverse, and his plane pulled off to the left side of the runway, into the grass. He regained control of the aircraft quickly and got it back onto the runway without causing any damage, but the sortie was considered ineffective. It was a freak malfunction, just one of those crazy things that happen in aviation; and it could have happened to any of the six of us. We completed that phase of the ORI with five effective and one ineffective sortie—a failure. One more ineffective sortie during the remainder of the ORI, and we would receive an overall failing grade, with the humiliation that accompanies it.

The major flying portion of the ORI was a six-aircraft, low-level formation flight to the Coyle Drop Zone, including a heavy equipment drop. We had to drop all six loads within the boundaries of the large clearing; if any aircraft aborted because of maintenance or missed the drop zone with the load, it would be an ineffective sortie. The criteria for passing the ORI permitted only one bad sortie, and we'd already had it; the heavy drop mission had to be perfect. I was selected to fly the lead ship, and was designated the mission commander. The inspection team's lead C-130 evaluator, Major Dick Nagy, was going to fly in my aircraft, observing my every action and verifying that I complied with all of the regulations and procedures.

I hadn't seen Dick since he was a first lieutenant, ten years earlier. At that time, I was a new C-130 aircraft commander and Dick was assigned to my crew as my copilot. This was the safest way of making up crews; inexperienced aircraft commanders got the best copilots. Dick was now the inspector looking over my shoulder, and he was going to perform his duty to the best of his ability. I knew that if I did not lead the six C-130s to the drop zone and place the formation in the optimum position over the target, someone might not drop his load within tolerance, and we would not pass the ORI. I also knew that I could not expect a gift from my former copilot.

The Coyle Drop Zone was in the New Jersey Pine Barrens, north of Atlantic City, in simulated hostile territory. This is the southeast area of New Jersey and consists of glacial deposits in a coastal area that at one time was under the Atlantic Ocean; because of the poor soil conditions, there were only stunted pine trees that topped out at less than half of their normal height, which explains why this type of terrain feature is called a pine barrens. To get to the drop area without being detected by the simulated enemy radar, we planned a one-hour, high-speed, low-level route: south into Delaware, then a turn to the east, crossing lower Delaware Bay and the southern portion of New Jersey, to the safety of the Atlantic Ocean. Once over the ocean, I would turn the formation left and fly north until we were abeam of the drop zone. Another left turn would then place us on our westerly drop heading for our final lineup with the drop zone centerline.

All six planes were off exactly on time. We had just descended to the five-hundred-foot planned altitude for the low-level formation through the simulated hostile territory, when Jack Chambers, in the number two ship, called me and said he was getting what he thought was oil on his windshield, and it must be coming from my aircraft. Immediately, I scanned the four oil quantity gauges on the lower part of the center forward instrument panel, as did everyone else in the cockpit. It looked as if the number three engine was losing oil, because the gauge indicated slightly less than full. With a grease pencil, the engineer marked the position of all four engine oil quantity needles, and all we could do was wait and see if it was really number three that was decreasing. It could have been another engine, or possibly Jack was getting hydraulic fluid or something else on his windscreen. Time would tell if it really was engine oil from my number three engine.

In about five minutes, I confirmed that number three was losing oil, because the oil quantity needle was definitely below the grease pencil mark on the gauge. Without oil lubricating the bearings, the engine would fail, so I would have to shut the engine down before the engine quit by itself, causing damage. I was hoping to keep the engine operating for another fifty minutes, in order to accomplish my drop. Once the extraction chute pulled the load out of the rear of the aircraft it would be okay to shut the engine down and still have an effective sortie. My immediate concern was to keep checking the rate at which the engine was losing oil in order to determine if I had fifty minutes of oil left in the tank. I also had to determine if there was a risk of an engine fire caused by the oil leak.

I sent the flight engineer to the rear to scan the engine, and he said that the oil leak appeared to be coming from the oil filler cap. The engine oil is put into the engine through a line that is capped; it's similar to the gas tank on your car. The difference is that on an airplane, if the cap is not secured properly, the airflow may create a pressure drop that sucks the oil out of the tank; that's what was happening to my aircraft. A simple thing like securing a cap properly was now standing between my entire unit's passing or failing our inspection. There was absolutely nothing I could do in flight to fix the problem. If I had been on the ground, it would have been a ten-second fix.

I was relieved that there was no danger of an engine fire, and did not feel that shutting down the engine, if I had to, would present a problem. I was, however, highly concerned that the oil tank would empty before our reaching the drop zone, preventing me from making my drop. Just as everyone looked at the engine oil quantity gauges when we first received the radio call about the oil leak, now everyone was timing the rate at which we were losing the oil, to determine when the tank would be sucked dry. We all came to the same conclusion: the oil would last 'til just before we reached the drop zone. If I were lucky, we could make the drop zone with four engines; if this was my unlucky day I would have to shut down the engine before reaching the drop zone, cancel my drop, and have my sortie considered ineffective. I called Jack in the number two plane, described the situation to him, and had him prepare to become the formation leader. There was no question that I would be shutting down the engine; the question was when.

I realized that everyone in the cockpit was so involved with our oil problem that we'd forgotten that we were still at very low altitude with five airplanes behind us, relying on my navigator to stay on course and get them to the drop zone on time. That's when I instructed the copilot that he was to devote his full attention to assisting the navigator to stay on course and perform his other duties, such as watching for obstructions.

He was not to get involved with the engine problem, but was to devote his full attention to the safety of the flight. I would continue to fly the airplane, and would make the decision to shut down the engine, if necessary.

There have been accidents where the entire cockpit crew was so involved with correcting a maintenance problem that they forgot the most important thing—flying the airplane. I was not going to allow this to occur, and I used the procedures that I'd learned at TWA for cockpit management during an emergency.

In preparation for shutting down an engine under these conditions, I had to establish exactly when to call for the engine shutdown checklist. My flight engineer, just like the rest of my crew, was the best that the squadron had to offer, and I relied greatly on his judgment. We decided that we would not shut the engine down when the oil quantity reached zero, but rather when the oil pressure failed. This would allow us to keep the engine running for a slightly longer time. We then had a discussion about what constituted no oil pressure. Was it when the pressure fluctuated out of limits, or was it when it reached zero? We both felt that we were following the guidance in the flight manual, but we were doing it from memory. We didn't have the time to do the necessary research to find the section in the flight handbook that applied to our problem. Dick, the evaluator, was on the headset during this entire conversation, and because he had many thousands of hours in the C-130, he might have wanted to get involved in the conversation, but he didn't. He was also a highly experienced flight examiner, and he knew that the outcome of the entire ORI could rely on my decision, so it was not appropriate to get involved in my conversation with the engineer. Now I had all of the information that I needed and was prepared for making the engine shutdown decision when the time came. I let the engineer watch the engine and devoted my attention back to my duties as the mission commander. I still had to get the formation over the drop zone and get six heavy equipment loads on the target to pass the ORI.

As we all had calculated, the oil quantity gauge on number three engine indicated zero, meaning the tank was empty, just when I was getting ready to make my final left turn and begin my search for the drop zone. Normally, this was the busiest period of the entire flight, and now I had to deal with an engine failure. I had to locate the Coyle Drop Zone, visually, early enough to get the formation on the proper course and heading as soon as possible. This would allow the formation to be stabilized a few miles out, and would give everyone the best chance for getting their loads on the target. I had checklists to run before the drop, and I had to pop up to drop altitude and slow down the formation to drop airspeed. The navigator was feeding me time and heading information; the copilot was running the checklists and talking to the other five aircraft in the flight; and the loadmaster was getting the rear of the aircraft prepared so we could drop the loaded pallet out the rear of the plane. It was during these extremely busy few minutes that the engineer informed me that the oil pressure was fluctuating, just as we all had expected it would do.

When the navigator announced, "one minute warning," meaning that we had only one minute before his call of "green light," which would trigger the actions to drop the load, the formation was in perfect position. The engineer then informed me that the oil pressure was fluctuating ten PSI, which was the maximum allowable tolerance. It couldn't have occurred at a more critical time, but I had prepared myself mentally for this worst case scenario and had decided not to shut the engine down until the oil pressure went to zero. I was fairly confident that I would be in compliance with the flight handbook, even though the engineer hadn't located it in the manual during his quick search fifty minutes earlier. There was a lot at stake: I'd taken a big risk when I made the decision to keep the engine running, and it wasn't an easy decision for me to make.

I was close enough to see the combat control team and the ORI evaluators on the ground, near the center of the drop zone. I knew that in the next thirty seconds the engine bearings would get enough lubrication and not cause any engine damage, even though the oil pressure was fluctuating wildly. I had briefed Jack, in the number two ship, that if I could possibly keep the engine running and make my drop he would become the formation leader immediately after the drop.

The formation was in perfect position over the drop zone when the navigator called "green light" and the copilot activated the switch that dropped the load. There was never any doubt when a heavy load was pulled out of the rear of the aircraft because of the sound and feel of the plane. Watching a load extracted from the cargo compartment always reminded me of the speed and power of a freight train moving very fast: it was always exhilarating. The loadmaster called, "all clear"; I called for the engine shutdown checklist and made a left turn to clear the formation. I could see Jack making a right turn and descending back down to the escape altitude, with the formation following him. We had number three engine shut down in a few seconds.

The combat control team reported to me that all of the drops were successful, and I flew the half-hour route back to my base all by myself; the formation, flying at high speed once again, was far ahead of me. Dick, who was still standing behind my seat, observing and listening to everything that had occurred, never said a word during the entire flight. I knew that I had done everything within my power to get my load on the drop zone without jeopardizing safety or violating what I was pretty sure was the guideline for this problem. It would have been much easier for me if the engineer had been able to locate the appropriate paragraph in the manual, but he was just too busy.

After landing with number three engine shut down, I taxied to the parking area and shut down the remaining engines. After we completed the checklist and I signed the logbook, the flight was complete, at last. I was getting ready to leave my seat, when I realized that Dick was leaning over my left shoulder, trying to get my attention. I made eye contact with him and gave him a quick thumbs up–thumbs down signal, indicating that I wanted to know if we'd passed or failed. He knew that I was asking a question. Up to this time, I'd had no indication of how he would judge my decision to keep the engine running and drop my load with no oil quantity and the oil pressure fluctuating out of limits. He gave me a thumb down and left the cockpit; he still hadn't said a word.

When I left the airplane, Dick was in the right seat of the rental car we provided for the ORI team chief, a full colonel; it was obvious that Dick was briefing him. My commander, also a full colonel, was in his blue Air Force staff car, parked parallel to the team chief. I got into the front right seat, next to him, and told my boss that we got a thumbs down; his face paled. The information that he had received was that all six heavy drops were on the drop zone within the required tolerance; that was pretty much all that was required and he assumed that we had passed the inspection.

I explained to my commander that, if Dick was basing the failure on the fact that I did not shut down the engine when the oil pressure fluctuated out of limits, I thought that I could prove him wrong. I asked the commander to set up a meeting with Dick and the team chief, and we all would hash this problem out before the failure was chiseled in stone. I was keeping my fingers crossed that my memory was correct, and that there was something in the flight manual that would prove that I had done the right thing. I had one additional worry in the back of my mind, though: maybe Dick had given me a thumbs down for some other reason that I was still unaware of. I was tired, upset, stressed to the limit, under a ton of pressure, and I still had the biggest battle of the day ahead of me. First, I had to find something in the flight handbook that I thought existed, even though the engineer couldn't locate it during the flight; second, if it really did exist, then I had to convince the team chief to override Dick's evaluation.

I was right. It was right there in black and white in our bible, the flight manual for the aircraft. My heavy equipment drop was changed to an effective sortie, and we passed the ORI. In my mind, this mission was a preview of my remaining years in the military. When the position of squadron commander became available, some time later, I was selected as the new commander, ahead of more senior officers. I also held a parallel position to the one that Dick had; I became the Chief Operations Inspector at Air Force Reserve Headquarters. I continued to progress, and when promoted to full colonel, I was assigned the position of Director of Inspection; I was the inspection team chief for two years. Eventually, I held all of the positions of the major players who made the decision that I was correct, that day in the 1970s.

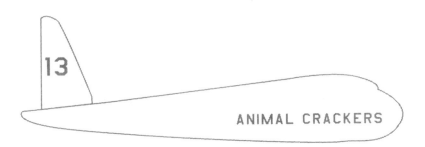

13

ANIMAL CRACKERS

WAS FLYING A C-130 returning from South Vietnam on what we called a trash hauling mission: an airplane full of war supplies on the westbound flight, and whatever had to be returned to the States on the eastbound flight. We had two routes that we usually flew. The northern route, a two-day trip with a stopover at Midway Island, was used when the winds were favorable. For this flight, though, I was planning to use the southern route, crossing the Pacific Ocean in three days, which meant having a night in Honolulu. On this trip, I picked up a stowaway that put the airplane out of commission for three weeks.

I was on final approach to Hickam Air Force Base, which uses the same runways as the civilian airport for Honolulu. I was only about a minute from landing, one of the few phases of flight that requires giving complete concentration to the task at hand. Experienced pilots learn that even in the best of conditions situations sometimes occur that can quickly degrade into a bad landing. When the weather is perfect, as it was that day, the pilot still has to look at the runway and make the necessary minor corrections, then look down to refocus on the flight instruments, interpret them, and make additional corrections. The average pilot probably makes a complete outside and inside scan once every five seconds, with his eyes constantly moving. The closer he gets to the runway, the more time he spends looking at the runway and the less at the instruments.

My feet were on the rudder pedals, which were on either side of a built-up area that supported the control column. On one of my downward scans toward the instruments, I saw something move near my feet. I had to divert my attention from my approach scan and look down to see what was between my lower legs—it was a rat! On the pedestal. Inches from my shins. Looking me right in the eye. It may as well have been a lion or a tiger: to me it looked enormous.

I was startled; I pulled away and let out a yelp. The rat was scared, too, and ran behind the instrument panel, which is a mass of electrical wires; that's probably where he'd come from. I told the co-pilot to continue the landing, and I just backed my seat all the way to the aft stops and pulled my legs away from the area where I thought the rat must be hiding. After landing, during the taxi to the parking ramp, I called the command post and informed them of the stowaway. I also told them that we had come from Vietnam, knowing that Honolulu wouldn't welcome this foreign visitor. It could have been carrying all sorts of strange things that we didn't want in the States.

My crew and I had just completed an all-day flight, and we were tired and hungry. But we were instructed not to open any doors until notified to do so. In an hour, the aircraft was surrounded by about two dozen federal and military personnel with sticks and brooms, one mop, and a few shotguns.

They definitely didn't want the rat in Honolulu. We got off the plane and they searched for the rat, but it couldn't be located. They placed poisoned bait and water in the plane and closed it up again, but when they searched the next day, there was still no rat. We stayed in Honolulu for a few days, waiting for the plane to be released; when it wasn't, we were sent to our home station as passengers on another plane. Three weeks later, my squadron was notified to send a crew to pick up the airplane. The rat was never found. It probably ate the poison and then died in one of the millions of places it could hide in such a huge aircraft.

I was a fully combat-ready C-130 pilot for the Air Force Reserve from 1970 until 1982. During my twelve years of reserve duty, the Air Force Reserve had the mission of supporting the diplomatic and military forces deployed in Central and South America. Approximately once every eighteen months, my squadron would deploy six aircraft and a suitable number of personnel to Howard Air Force Base in the Canal Zone. The task rotated through all of the Reserve C-130 squadrons; our job was to provide a mini-airline to deliver supplies and personnel to the major cities in the Americas, south of Mexico. I was the commander of the deployment, consisting of about 150 reservists, in the spring of 1982.

Upon returning from a mission that had made six stops throughout Central America, one of my pilots reported that they'd seen a snake in the rear of the aircraft. It had come out of the palletized cargo, and had slithered into the gap between the floor and the sidewall of the cargo compartment. I had the loadmaster who saw the snake write down a description of the reptile, so that the size and other identifying features would not change with time, as in a fish story. The cargo pallets were usually positioned on the edge of the tarmac before being loaded into the aircraft by forklift. It would have been easy for a snake to get into the cargo.

I had a serious problem. The flight crews were concerned about the snake being poisonous and were refusing to fly in the aircraft. This left me with a fleet of only five planes at a time when the normal six were not sufficient to fly all of the scheduled missions. The rumor that the snake was a "two-step" (its bite fatal before you take two steps) spread like wildfire among the crewmembers, and I needed additional information to combat the rumor. Of course, calling the snake a two-step was an exaggeration, but that didn't change the fact that the snake might really have been hazardous to the crews. I contacted an English-speaking reptile expert in Panama City to determine if there were poisonous snakes in Central America that met the description of this one and, if so, how to handle the situation. I learned a lot about snakes, and he learned a lot about airplanes.

He confirmed my worst fear that the snake might be poisonous. The large majority of the snakes were not dangerous, but one that fit the loadmaster's description was extremely deadly. The rumor was no longer a rumor; he had confirmed that it was possible that we might have a two-step living on the airplane. I asked the expert about flying at altitude while depressurizing the aircraft, with the crew on oxygen. I thought that if the snake didn't have enough oxygen, and the temperature was cold enough, the snake might die, as dozens of white mice had done on a TWA flight of mine, ten years before, when they were mistakenly placed in an unpressurized baggage hold. He assured me that the snake would just go into a state of hibernation and that the crew would die before the snake would. The only solution seemed to be to close the airplane up with poisoned bait and water and then wait. When I asked how long it would take, he informed me that if the snake had recently eaten, it could take a long time before it would feed again. That didn't solve the problem I had of flying all of the missions with an airplane grounded, so I decided to have the airplane flown back to our home base, north of Philadelphia, where we had extra planes. There, the crew would swap the contaminated plane for one that was snake-free. That way, I would have my fleet of six planes in Panama, where the workload was, and the airplane with the snake in it could sit on the ground back home.

We devised an elaborate plan for taking the necessary precautions for the safety of the crew, and then I asked for volunteers to fly the C-130 back to Philadelphia. The first part of the plan was to establish what the crew was to do if they saw the snake, and what weapon to use. We decided that the best weapon was a fifty-pound carbon dioxide fire extinguisher. The carbon dioxide is placed in the container under very high pressure; when it is discharged, the pressure is reduced to the outside air pressure, causing the gas to expand and cool. If the snake were hit with the discharge, it would be surrounded by a dense white fog that would prevent it from seeing, and the temperature of the gas would be below freezing, which would incapacitate the reptile. The second portion of the plan revolved around Doc Simmons.

In the Air Force, the doctors who specialize in caring for the flying crewmembers are called flight surgeons. I was fortunate to have Major Simmons, a Reserve Flight Surgeon who had deployed with us, as a member of my staff. He was concerned about the seriousness of the situation if a crewmember were to be bitten in flight, and he worked closely with me. A large portion of the flight would be over water, and it could be a few hours before a bitten crewmember could be taken to a hospital, so the major did a lot of research. He was a medical doctor, but he'd had no prior experience with snakebites. He decided the most efficient way to handle a bite in-flight would be to excise the puncture wound, including a few inches of flesh surrounding the bite, before the poison had a chance to spread from the area. This would be a large wound and would require considerable expertise; therefore, I assigned the doctor himself to the flight. To ensure he would have sufficient equipment for the flight, he obtained a complete surgical kit from the hospital and half a dozen cartons of additional medical supplies. We loaded more medical equipment onto the aircraft than was available in some third world countries.

The last part of the plan was accomplished after I had a volunteer crew to fly the airplane back home to Philadelphia. First, they each were trained in the operation of the fifty-pound fire extinguisher. This equipment was not standard on the aircraft, and I wanted to ensure that every crewmember was capable of using it. Everything was covered now, except for the scenario that Doc Simmons might be the one bitten by the snake. To cover this possibility, he gave all five crewmembers three hours of training on how to use the scalpel to scoop out the flesh surrounding a bite on his body, what medications to use, tourniquets, and so forth. He was very thorough; it was his butt.

A portable urinal was placed in the galley, so that no one would have to go to the rear of the cargo compartment to relieve himself on this long flight. The large fire extinguisher was also readily available to them. I wished them a bon voyage, and sent them on their way. They had an uneventful flight to Philadelphia and returned the next evening with a different C-130. The snake was never found.

A few years after the Bay of Pigs fiasco and the Cuban Missile Crisis, when our relationship with Cuba was at its worst, I went to the Norfolk Naval Air Station in Virginia to move a dozen guard dogs from there to Guantanamo Bay, Cuba. Guantanamo is a United States Navy installation on the southeastern end of Cuba and has been a thorn in Castro's side ever since he came to power in the late 1950s. I didn't like going there because the barracks we slept in were noisy; and if we arrived after nine at night, the mess hall was closed and we couldn't eat.

Landing to the east required that I fly a tight approach, staying inside the boundary of the base. If I strayed across the razor wire fence, I'd been briefed that I would be shot at by the Cuban border guards. Our side of the border was guarded by United States Marines, and it was considered to be a hostile border.

We were always quartered in the Marine barracks for our overnight stay, the same Marines that guarded the fence. The Marines had a late-night shift change, and when the troops got off duty after guarding the base boundary, they were all wound up and needed a few beers to calm down. There was a loud party at the same late hour every night, just when we needed our sleep.

The guard dogs I was carrying were to be used to secure the boundary in the no man's land near the razor wire fence.

When the dogs were loaded, my loadmaster informed me that one of the cages had a broken latch and that it was held closed with rope. I asked him if it looked secure and he said it looked okay. He also said the dogs had been fed and watered and we were not to disturb them; they would probably sleep for the three-or four-hour flight. I was surprised we didn't have a handler traveling with us, but I was assured that there would be no problem.

About two hours into the flight, the loadmaster came up to the cockpit and told me the dog in the cage with the broken latch was chewing on the rope and he was worried about it getting out. I decided to have the navigator assist him in turning the cage toward the sidewall of the aircraft; then, if the dog succeeded in chewing through the rope, the door would still be jammed shut. They both headed for the rear, but didn't get down the steps into the cargo compartment: the dog was loose. Now we were trapped in the cockpit, and I had no idea of how serious the threat was. I asked the load-master how big the dog was. He said, "Half German Shepard and half pony." That was enough to let me know that we had a big guard dog on the loose and it was probably trained to be extremely aggressive.

The cockpit floor of the C-130 is about four feet above the cargo compartment, with steps connecting them. The steps are next to a small galley with an oven, hot cup, coffee maker, sink, and small counter. A hinged platform covered the steps and acted as the floor of the galley. To protect ourselves from the dog, we lowered the galley floor, which provided us with some isolation from the cargo compartment. The mattresses from the two bunks in the rear wall of the cockpit gave us an additional barricade. The last step was to devise a plan of action if the dog succeeded in getting past the obstructions and into the cockpit. Our weapons consisted of the knives we all carried; two fire extinguishers, which were formidable weapons; and the crash ax. But I still wasn't sure we had the advantage. I directed the loadmaster to remain in the galley area, as our first line of defense, and to keep me informed. He was able to peek around the mattresses, and he said the dog was socializing with the other dogs, through the bars on the doors of their cages.

When I informed the Guantanamo control tower that I had a problem, they assured me they would have dog handlers waiting for us; we were to remain in the cockpit until the dog was under control. After landing, the forward entry door was opened from the outside after the handlers were in place near the door. I was watching the outside activity through the cockpit window, feeling relieved that help had arrived at last and I no longer had to worry about a 120-pound trained guard dog grabbing me by the neck. As soon as the door was opened, the dog leaped out and jumped on the first handler he came to. The dog was on his hind legs with his paws on the handler's shoulders and was licking the handler's face while the handler rubbed his flanks. Our menace turned out to be just an enormous, friendly animal that needed some water and attention.

Many millions of dollars have been devoted to solving the problem of how to deal with bird strikes. An aircraft hitting a large bird at hundreds of miles per hour is always fatal for the bird; sometimes it is fatal for the occupants of the aircraft. Many planes have crashed because of bird strikes, and probably thousands of aircraft have had damage to the engines, radome, wings, or windscreen; any forward-facing surface of the aircraft is at risk.

We always assume that birds fly near the ground; and within the aviation community, it is generally accepted that bird strikes occur only below ten thousand feet, far below the cruising altitude for most aircraft. But that assumption is incorrect. I had a bird strike near the Florida–Georgia border at twenty thousand feet. A small bird splattered on the windscreen when I was four miles above the ground. Perhaps during migration some species fly that high; or maybe the few ounces of muscle, bone, and feathers was carried to that altitude by a strong updraft. The bird strike did not cause any damage to my aircraft, but when one of the crewmembers looked at the mess of blood, guts, and feathers remaining on the windscreen, he offered the following riddle:

Question: What is the last thing that goes through a bird's mind when it hits the windscreen?

Answer: Its asshole!

Occasionally during my Air Force career I was hit by small arms fire. I never knew that the aircraft was hit until I'd landed and was informed by the maintenance crew that there was a bullet hole. While I was practicing a new maneuver to prevent getting hit by small arms I had an interesting bird strike at an interesting island in the Pacific.

The bullet hole was usually in the rear of the aircraft, because the shooter misjudged the speed of the plane. I think the hits occurred during takeoff or landing, when we would be at a low enough altitude, and slow enough, for someone to take a shot at us and actually hit the aircraft. During the

Vietnam War, the C-130s had sheets of acrylic armor plate surrounding the seats of all of the crew positions. When the hostilities ended, the heavy bulletproofing was removed and probably was stored for the next conflict. I never had a crew-member injured by being shot.

I always thought that the best method to keep from getting hit by the small arms fire was to stay away from the area that made me a target. The majority of the small arms were only effective up to 4,500 feet, and any bullets probably came from someone taking one shot at me from outside of the secure area surrounding the runway.

If I could avoid the low, slow flying which occurred during landing I could eliminate a large percentage of the hazard of the hostile small arms. There were three primary methods of flying the last few minutes of the flight, the final approach, and I would choose the method most appropriate for the conditions. First was the typical approach that airlines fly all the time: a gentle, continuous, descent to landing. This type of approach is wonderful for passenger comfort, but didn't work well in combat: it left me extremely vulnerable. Second, we flew the overhead approach, which was flown at high speed but we were still at low altitude. This approach left me much less vulnerable to the small arms fire but was still not the optimum, which is why the combat approach was developed.

For a combat approach, the technique was to fly over the runway at five thousand feet, which was above the effective range of the small arms. I'd begin the approach at minimum speed with my flaps and landing gear down for added drag, which I needed to accomplish a very steep descent. I would make one 360-degree turn, spiraling down to the runway, a drop of nearly a mile, while always remaining within the field boundary. The development of the combat approach did the trick; no more bullet holes from hits during the final approach. I don't think that other large aircraft were capable of the performance required to execute the approach, so the combat approach was a C-130 exclusive.

I was landing at Midway Island in the Pacific when the combat approach was first being developed. For practice, and to show off, I asked the tower if they would approve this new approach and landing. I was the only aircraft in their traffic pattern, and my request was granted. It was obvious to me that the tower had no idea what I was going to do; they questioned me repeatedly when they realized that I was beginning my approach from a mile above the runway. They had never witnessed the descent capability of the C-130 and they were amazed that I intended to land from that altitude. The spiraling approach and landing were perfect and really impressed the tower operators, but partway through my approach, I had a bird strike that penetrated the leading edge of the wing.

Midway Island is part of the Hawaiian island chain, even though it is over a thousand miles west of Honolulu. It was a United States Navy base, but it has since been deactivated and is now a National Wildlife Refuge. This small Pacific atoll was well publicized during World War II because of the naval battle that occurred near there between the Japanese and United States aircraft carriers. It was a huge victory for the Americans and was the beginning of the end for the Japanese fleet.

The bird I hit while flying the combat approach was a Laysan Albatross; there were dozens of them all circling in the rising air currents over the island. The aircraft had sufficient damage to the wing to require a temporary repair, which meant that I would have an extra day at Midway and a chance to explore the small island.

I was walking on the beach and began a conversation with the only other person in view: the wife of the Navy base commander. She had done a lot of research on the albatross and was very willing to share her vast knowledge with me. I spent about two hours with her, observing the birds, both on the ground and in flight, and absorbing her free-flowing knowledge.

The first thing that you notice about the albatross is how beautiful and graceful it is in flight. It stays aloft for hours, expending very little energy by soaring on the air currents. Then you see the birds on the ground and you can't imagine that they are the same birds that are flying overhead. On the ground they are extremely clumsy and have picked up the nickname Gooney bird. It appears that the bird cannot sense wind direction. If it lands into the wind, the landing is graceful; however, if the albatross lands with the wind, it may hit the ground too fast and tumble. The same applies for its takeoff. We watched one running down the beach, with the wind behind it. It was flapping its wings furiously in its attempt to lift off, with no success. After about fifty exhausting yards, it stopped, turned around into the wind, and was immediately airborne.

Midway and the neighboring Sand Island are the largest nesting locations for the Albatross. These two islands, only a few square miles in area, had in excess of four hundred thousand nesting pairs, taking up all of the non-paved areas of the islands. The birds mate for life, and are very noisy and demonstrative when performing their courting ritual, which I was fortunate enough to witness. The birds face each other and perform a dance, bobbing their heads up and down while rapidly clacking their beaks together. I had a ground floor room in the Navy barracks, and there was no sleeping once the sun came up and the birds began their mating dance. It had been their island for thousands of years; the Navy was only a temporary intruder for a short time.

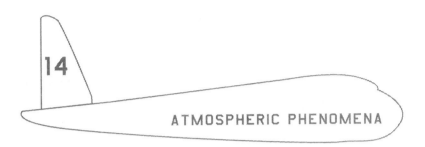

14

ATMOSPHERIC PHENOMENA

WE'VE ALL SEEN beautiful sunsets and marveled at the spectacular red color the sky becomes as the sun travels below the horizon. I've always thought of it as the end of a perfect day. When my wife was a child and saw the glowing orange and red cumulus clouds, she thought That is where God lives.

Physicists tell us the sky turns red because of the refraction of the sunlight by particles held in suspension in the atmosphere. After a large volcanic eruption, when there are an unusually large number of particles in the atmosphere, scientists predict the most spectacular sunsets. What they cannot predict, though, is the elusive green flash.

I have spoken to many pilots about the green flash, and occasionally one of them has told me of seeing it once. I'm lucky enough to have seen it twice. The green flash is an atmospheric event that occurs at the instant the top of the sun intersects with the horizon of the earth. If the conditions are perfect, at the first peek of the sun at sunrise or the last view at sunset, when the sun is just below the horizon, there might be a blaze of emerald green for a second or two—the green flash. The burst of green light occurs if the layering of the atmosphere is just right to allow the proper amount of refraction of the sunlight, similar to the common red sun at sunset.

When my children were teenagers in New Jersey, they learned about the green flash and decided they were going to see it. I told them that I had been looking for it for years and at the time had never seen it, so I knew that their chances of seeing it were remote. They decided to try, anyway. In order to see a green flash, you must find a location where you have an uninterrupted view of the horizon at the location where the sun rises or sets. In New Jersey, this would be on the Jersey shore, looking east over the Atlantic Ocean, at sunrise. That meant my kids had to get up early, collect their friends, drive the half hour to the beach, and get there before sunrise. The first time they tried, they were too late; the sun was already up. They were persistent, though, and tried a second time; however, this time clouds were on the horizon and by the time they were able to view the sun, it was well above the horizon. They tried a third time: this time, the conditions were perfect. The sky was perfectly clear and they were in position to view the sun as it first came up over the horizon, but there was no green flash. Wisely, that was their last attempt. They could have tried for years and might never have had the correct atmospheric conditions for the rare phenomenon, so how did I happen to see it twice?

For a number of years while flying for TWA, my seniority allowed me to fly international flights. I was based in New York and flew out of JFK. I began flying to Europe and the Middle East in the early 1970s on the Boeing 707, and over the years, as our equipment changed, I flew those same routes in the Lockheed 1011 and the Boeing 747. The takeoff time of those flights was evening, when the sun was setting in New York; by the time we were approaching Europe, over the Atlantic Ocean, the next morning's sun would be rising.

The initial hint of the coming new day was that I could begin to see a visible, backlit horizon. I was always amazed with how fast the sun rose when I was flying east. In this direction, the time it takes for the sun to rise is shortened by the speed of the aircraft, plus the usual tailwind. Taking everything into consideration, from my seat in the cockpit, I would watch the sun rise fifty percent faster than my children did while watching for the green flash from the New Jersey coast. I crossed the Atlantic hundreds of times, viewed hundreds of sunrises, and saw the green flash only two times. That's why it's called the elusive green flash.

The first time I witnessed this rare event, it was a typical Atlantic crossing. The takeoff from JFK was at sundown. With the time change, that meant that we'd be landing in Paris at breakfast time. We always tried to fly a route that would take the least amount of time so as to burn as little fuel as possible; fuel is the airlines' greatest expense. If every pilot could save a few minutes on every leg, TWA would save millions of additional dollars every year in fuel not burned. There was competition among the international pilots crossing the Atlantic, on any particular night, to get the most fuel-efficient route and altitude.

The North Atlantic Track System was devised to enable hundreds of aircraft to cross the Atlantic every evening in the most fuel-efficient and safe manner possible. The people who devised the track system have my highest compliments for their vision in devising this great aid to aviation. Every night, about half a dozen routes are established across the

Boeing 747 at the TWA International Terminal at JFK

North Atlantic, taking into consideration the best winds and avoiding any severe weather. Each parallel route has various altitudes available—usually from twenty-nine thousand to forty-one thousand feet, which are the most efficient altitudes for fuel conservation. The changing routes and altitudes are established twice a day and are made available to the airlines, which then determine which routes are the most efficient for their flights. Competing airlines also compete for the best routes, altitudes, and takeoff time slots. When you cross the Atlantic on a typical evening, you will probably have other aircraft above, below, to the right and left, as well as one in front and one behind your aircraft. It is imperative that every pilot fly exactly on course, altitude, and speed, in order to make the system work. To my knowledge, the system has never resulted in a midair collision over the ocean.

At night, when the wave of aircraft flies to Europe, the large majority of the tracks take advantage of the strong west-to-east winds that are prevalent over the Atlantic. During the daytime, when the flights return to the US, the tracks are devised to give the minimum head wind. Because of the strong westerly winds, if it took seven hours to fly from New York to Paris with a tailwind, it would take eight hours to return, flying into the headwind. When I first began flying in the Air Force, before the days of computers, it would take a

The author at the controls of a Boeing 747 over the Atlantic Ocean

few hours just for the flight planning, to determine the route, altitude, and fuel required for each trip across the Atlantic. After computers were introduced and the North Atlantic Track System was devised, planning the same flight for TWA took only fifteen minutes.

The dawn I saw the green flash for the first time, my aircraft was one of the many dozens of aircraft doing pretty much the same thing: first, flying to a North Atlantic Track entry point in the vicinity of the east coast of Newfoundland, Canada, then proceeding on our assigned track, altitude, and speed to the European track exit point, south of Ireland. When I was about three hours east of Newfoundland, over the Atlantic, the sun started coming up, and I prepared for the bright glare of the sun blasting through the windshield into the cockpit. I changed from clear eyeglasses to prescription sunglasses and placed the movable cockpit sunscreens in the correct position on the windscreen to keep the sun from shining directly into my eyes. My eyes were accustomed to the dimly lit nighttime cockpit: when the sun first breached the horizon, had I not been prepared, I'd have been quite uncomfortable. I always inspected the horizon for clouds to see if this was the morning when I'd finally witness the green flash, just as I had done hundreds of times before.

That morning, the distant sky did not look all that promising. There were some low stratus clouds, and on the horizon close to where I thought the sun would rise, there were a few large cumulus clouds—or maybe small thunderstorms. I put away the charts I used for departing the New York area, which I kept out in case of an emergency that might require a return to JFK. Then I began to shift my attention toward preparing for the end of the flight. The arrival information and approach plates for Charles de Gaulle Airport in Paris were removed from the binder to be reviewed and placed in the order in which I would need them. After reviewing the winds and weather in Paris, and relying on my previous experience, I made an educated guess about what the arrival instructions from the French air traffic controllers would be and placed the necessary charts on top of the pile. Sometimes I had difficulty understanding the French-accented English used by the Paris controllers, and I liked to be well prepared, in advance of what was usually a very busy approach and landing. After years of performing the same tasks, I had devised a system that worked for me and made one of the most difficult portions of the flight, the arrival and approach to the runway, somewhat easier.

I scanned the horizon, and saw that the sun was getting close to rising. It was time to stop my cockpit chores for a few minutes and devote all of my attention to the instant the top of the sun would rise over the distant horizon; with it, the new day would begin. I noticed that something strange was occurring just where the sun would rise. Two vertical cumulus clouds were forming a V, with blue sky between them. The bottom of the V was sitting on the horizon exactly where it appeared that the sun would rise, and the clouds seemed to be on fire. The back lighting, from the still invisible sun, turned the legs of the V a bright red, accented by the dark centers of the clouds and the clear sky viewed through the notch. The intensity of the red on the edge of the clouds increased until it was almost too painful to watch, even with my sunglasses on, and then I saw it: a blaze of bright emerald green exploded right at the base of the V. It lasted only about two seconds, then the clouds stopped glowing red and the bright sunlight replaced the green flash; a new day had begun. It was an exciting moment for me: at last, I had seen the elusive green flash, after searching for it for many years. Immediately, I asked the other two pilots, "Did you see it?" Each of them answered the same: "See what?"

The Boeing 747 was the most senior aircraft that TWA had, and the most senior flights were the longest ones. When I had the opportunity to fly the "seven-four" as a flight engineer, I was usually on reserve, since I was at the bottom of the seniority list on a very senior airplane. Being on reserve meant that I would not be assigned a scheduled flight, but was used as an extra to fill in for the more senior engineers who were unable to work their flight; possibly because they were sick or did not have the crew rest mandated by FAA regulations. I was on reserve when I was notified by crew scheduling that I was to deadhead (fly as a passenger), to Los Angeles and work from there to London's Heathrow Airport, then back to LAX. This was a very long, very senior flight; it was close to the maximum range for the early 747s.

A twelve-hour flight in a 747 would consume about three hundred thousand pounds of jet fuel, or about the amount of fuel that the average person burns in their car in a lifetime. Conserving fuel, without degrading the safety of the flight, was one of the primary concerns of the pilots, and we began our planning using a great circle route: the shortest route to fly from one point to another on the earth. The easiest way to describe a great circle route is to use a globe of the earth and a piece of string. For my flight from the Los Angeles airport to the London airport, using the globe, if I put one end of the string on LAX and the other on LHR and pulled the string tight, it would describe the great circle route.

There are a number of other factors that must be considered for fuel conservation other than the route; the most important is the winds. For the return flight from London to Los Angeles, because of the headwinds, we calculated that the most efficient route would be north of the great circle route: over northern Greenland, northern Canada, and then southwest to LAX.

The takeoff from London in the 747 was at mid-morning during the early winter, very close to the winter solstice, the shortest day of the year. It was daylight when we took off, but within a few hours, as we proceeded northwest on our flight to Los Angeles, I realized that we were flying into the daytime darkness of the polar winter. About six hours after takeoff, it was totally dark outside except for a visible horizon to the south. We were approaching the North Magnetic Pole; the location where the particles from a solar flare, which had occurred on the sun a few days prior, were now concentrated above the earth.

Solar flares cause disturbances of the high frequency radio we used for communication with the air traffic controllers, and we were briefed to expect the problem. I noticed that it was becoming harder to use the HF radio, and I was constantly changing frequencies in an attempt to have clear communications with the controlling agency. It was about the same time that I began having radio problems that I first noticed the Aurora Borealis, the Northern Lights.

The light show began with a few bursts of light of varying colors in the distance. Because there were no reference points in the dark sky, I could not determine how far away the light was emanating from. We had a discussion in the cockpit about the possible connection of our radio problems to the visual display we were seeing out of the cockpit windows.

As we continued flying into the glowing photons caused by the collision of the solar particles with the air, seven miles above the earth, the display increased in intensity until it was bright enough to turn out the cockpit lights and still be able to see and to perform our cockpit duties. The distance the northern lights were from the aircraft was now easy to establish: we were in them. When you fly through snow, few of the snowflakes actually hit the aircraft; rather, they are deflected around the aircraft, with the slipstream. This is what it looked like was happening with the lights. I had the feeling we were flying through pulsing waves of vertical rays of constantly changing colors that were parting to make way for the 747. Visualize flying through thousands of sheer curtains, hanging vertically and randomly spaced, rippling in a breeze and lit from within with all the colors of the rainbow. And yet that doesn't really capture the sensation. Austrian explorer Julius von Payer wrote of the Aurora Borealis, "No pencil can draw it, no colors can paint it, and no words can describe it, in all its magnificence."

It was eerie enough to be somewhat scary, but it was a visual treat that few people have ever witnessed. I didn't just see them; I was in the Northern Lights.

Flying in the clouds is an everyday occurrence for the professional pilot. Inexperienced pilots require years of practice, using only the instruments in the cockpit, to become capable of controlling an aircraft without looking out of the windows.

The pilot must be able to determine if the aircraft is climbing or diving, if the wings are parallel to the earth or in a bank, and whether the airspeed is increasing or decreasing. When you fly in the clouds, there is no way to answer these questions without relying on the instruments, but that is only part of the problem. The pilot also has to know where he is and how to get to where he is going. Additionally, the pilot has to get to the destination without flying through weather conditions that might be a hazard to the aircraft or to the passengers. All of this information must be discerned by the pilot without looking out of the cockpit windows, because a large portion of a pilot's life is spent within the clouds.

Meteorologists have technical names for all the different types of clouds, but pilots associate the clouds with the problems of flying through them. Stratus clouds, to a meteorologist, means layered horizontal clouds, usually at low altitudes; but to the pilot they indicate low ceilings and poor visibility for landing, with the possibility of fog. When you see what looks like a cotton ball floating in the blue sky, technically, it is called a cumulus cloud; however, take that same friendly cumulus cloud and add moisture and some method of lifting it to a higher altitude, and it might turn into a cumulonimbus cloud—a thunderstorm. Thunderstorms are a major hazard to aviation, and are avoided by pilots by using the weather radar in the cockpit.

I remember one particular flight on the Lockheed 1011 from JFK to Madrid when I was a first officer for TWA. From a few minutes after takeoff until we reached the coast of Portugal, we were over the Atlantic Ocean, and for the first four hours, we were mostly in the clouds. There was an intense weather system along our route of flight, with lines of thunderstorms embedded within the other clouds. Because we couldn't see the thunderstorms, the only way to avoid them was with our weather radar. In the first row of the first class cabin, we were carrying the former President of the United States, George Herbert Walker Bush. He slept through one of the nastiest weather nights I have ever had while crossing the Atlantic.

When you fly within the United States, the air traffic controllers know where the most severe weather is; to minimize delays, they route aircraft around the thunderstorms. Over the Atlantic, on a black and stormy night, the pilots are on their own, though, getting almost no assistance on the location of the worst weather, other than the hours-old information provided before takeoff. This is especially true on the lightly traveled routes from New York to Spain and Portugal; because there are fewer flights on those routes, there are few reports from other pilots on the location of the storms. On that night, we were totally on our own and were dodging storms for a few hours, relying only on our weather radar.

I'd been flying with Tex Luedtke for the entire month. As was usual, we alternated jobs on every other leg. That evening, it was my turn to operate the radar and navigate while he controlled the aircraft and maintained the heading I gave him, to keep us from penetrating the thunderstorms. I was busy scanning the radar a few hundred miles ahead of us to look for the best route through a line of severe thunderstorms. Then, as we approached the storms, I'd change the radar to scan closer to the aircraft and revise the heading Tex would fly, so we could pick our way around the individual storms. I also had to be careful that we would not penetrate a line of storms only to find ourselves trapped by additional storms directly behind the first line. It takes a lot of experience and knowledge to fly an aircraft through multiple lines of severe thunderstorms, keeping track of your position using the inertial guidance system for navigation, without awakening the 260 sleeping passengers, whether or not you're carrying a former President of the United States.

We were descending into the New York area in a Boeing 727. It was late in the afternoon, and we were completing a three-day "see the USA" trip; we had been all over the country, making a few stops every day. We'd been cleared by

Cockpit of a TWA Lockheed 1011 Tristar, Madrid, Spain. Left to right: Tex Luedtke, George H.W. Bush, the author

the New York Air Traffic Control Center to descend to and maintain eleven thousand feet. When we were a few thousand feet above the top of the clouds, one of the other pilots commented that the clouds looked like ocean waves. For some reason, the clouds below us had formed into a symmetrical series of waves that were exactly perpendicular to our flight path. It looked like the height of each wave, from the trough to the crest, was a few hundred feet. By using a little imagination, I could fool myself into believing that we were going to descend into the ocean. As we got closer to leveling off and I had a better sense of our altitude in relation to the clouds, I realized that we would penetrate the clouds at an altitude halfway between the base and the top of the waves. It looked like there were about ten of these cloud waves in a row, lined up exactly north and south.

We were flying east, so we were going to penetrate them at a ninety-degree angle. As we began our level-off and approached the first wave, I realized the sun was directly behind us and low on the horizon, just about to set, because I could see an ill-defined shadow of our airplane on the cloud directly in front of us.

The closer we got to the cloud, the more defined the shadow became. I had seen the shadow of my airplane on the clouds many times, but my airplane shadow had always occurred when the sun was above the airplane, so the shadow had been on the cloud tops below the airplane. This time, the shadow of the airplane was directly in front of us. When I first noticed the shadow, it was just a darkened blob on the cloud, but as we approached the cloud at over three hundred miles an hour, the shadow became more defined. I could begin to distinguish the wings and the circular fuselage as the shadow continued to increase in crispness. As we continued to get closer to the cloud, the shadow shrank to the exact size of the 727. I could clearly distinguish the T tail and the wings joining low on the fuselage.

Initially, I did not notice the halo. Similar to the halo surrounding a full moon, there was a halo surrounding the shadow. It formed a perfect circle slightly larger than the wingspan and completely surrounded the aircraft shadow. As the shadow shrank, so did the halo. What began as a white, circular band of light slowly transformed into a sharply defined circular rainbow. The water droplets in the cloud acted like prisms, causing the white light from the sun behind us to refract into the rainbow. Our plane was the tip of an arrow flying into a colored target, and the bull's-eye was the shadow.

I was mesmerized by what I was seeing; and a few seconds before flying into the cloud, I had the illusion that we were going to fly into the side of a vertical cliff! Adrenaline began to pump into my system with the sudden thought that I had misinterpreted our conditions and that I had only seconds to live. I had to calm myself by repeating silently, "It's only a cloud, it's only a cloud."

We entered the cloud, flying right through our perfect, full-sized shadow, and instantly we were in the gray of the interior of the cloud. The gray lasted about five seconds, and we popped out the back of the cloud to be greeted with the same image we'd just flown through. Ahead of us was a second, identical cloud, with the same indistinct shadow of the aircraft surrounded by a white halo. This time we knew what to expect, and we were able to fully enjoy the spectacle of flying through our own shadow. Again I had the illusion that I was going to fly into the side of a vertical mountain;

however, this time I did not feel the adrenaline shot that I'd had upon entering the first cloud. As the shadow shrank and gained definition and the halo glowed with color, we again flew through the bull's-eye, through our shadow, and into the cloud, with the instant change to gray.

We'd had the same experience about half a dozen times when we received instructions from New York Center to turn right twenty degrees. As soon as we began our turn, the conditions changed and the visual treat we'd been enjoying for the previous two minutes was gone; possibly never to be duplicated.

15

INTERESTING MISSIONS

FLYING CERTAINLY INVOLVED hours of boredom, but the interesting and exciting flights that occasionally fell into my lap more than compensated for the boredom. When I look back on the unusual things I've done and the interesting life I've had, I can say that I wouldn't trade my profession for any other I can think of, even though I do have to admit there were times when I was bored to death, or scared to death, or so tired I couldn't stand up, or so hungry I could have fallen down. Still . . . I wouldn't change a thing.

I was on a three-month tour in England when I was given a mission to take a C-130 to Belgium to show off the capability of the aircraft, then spend the remainder of the day placing the aircraft on static display for the public to view. The occasion was a country fair outside of the small town of Spa, a resort town famous for its hot springs, which made it a popular tourist destination. (The town's name has evolved into today's usage: we call a hot tub, or other hot water therapy, a spa.) Putting on a little air show would not have been anything special, except that at Spa there was no runway.

The fair was to be on a Sunday, so on Saturday we flew the short flight from Mildenhall, in the Midlands of England, to Liege, Belgium. Liege had a suitable airport for us and was less than an hour's drive to Spa by car. We took an Air Force station wagon with us in the airplane; after we landed and the car was unloaded, we locked the airplane and all six of us drove to Spa. We met our local contact who took us all to lunch, then we followed him in the blue Air Force station wagon to the fairgrounds. We had to inspect the place where we were going to land the next day, to ensure that it was suitable for landing the aircraft without causing any damage.

What was described as a fairgrounds, in the correspondence I'd received when I was assigned the mission, was nothing more than a large field where cows were grazing. I was told that the cows would be removed for the events of the next day. The field had been cultivated during prior years, so we could be fairly certain it did not contain any hidden obstructions that could damage the aircraft. We drove the station wagon across the field a few times to check the suitability for landing, and we didn't see any reason not to bring the C-130 in the next day. The area we selected for landing was almost a mile long, which was far more than was required, and though the entire field was sloping, I didn't think that would affect us. After memorizing the landmarks and determining that the field was long enough to land and then take off again, we drove the station wagon back to Liege.

The next morning when we filed our flight plan for the short hop to Spa, we immediately realized that we had a problem. All airports have a four-letter international designator used to indicate your destination on a flight plan; however, we weren't flying to an airport: there was no four-letter designator for the farmer's field in Spa. We explained our problem to the clerk when I filed our flight plan, and in-flight, every time we changed to a new controller, they wanted to know our destination. One of the controllers even asked us if we were sure we were going to land at Spa, because there was no airport for us.

We were all proficient at reading topographical maps and had no difficulty in locating the town from the air. Once we located Spa, we were able to immediately locate the fairgrounds, which now had some activity in the area nearest to the road. There was some smoke near the field, which I assumed came from a farmer burning some trash—just what I needed to check the winds. I scanned the entire field to ensure the cows had been moved to another pasture; they had. I wanted to let the people on the ground know where we were going to land and I didn't want anyone to drive a car near our landing strip, which looked like any other part of the pasture. I had decided to first make a low pass to a few feet above touchdown, then level off and fly the length of the field to see if everything looked okay to land. On the second approach I would land. The only difference was that I decided to use fifty percent flaps for the low pass and one hundred percent flaps for the real landing. I flew about a three-mile final approach, dropped flaps to fifty percent, put the landing gear down, and completed the landing checklist.

I encountered no surprises on the low pass, so now it was time to land. I used the same checkpoints I used for the first pass to find the correct lineup, then dropped full flaps. After a quick review of the checklist to ensure that everything was complete, we were ready to land. I established my rate of descent and adjusted the throttles to maintain the final approach speed, which would also be the touchdown speed. I kept aiming for the imaginary touchdown point while trying to stabilize the approach, so that nothing would change until we hit the ground. This approach is different from a normal approach and landing and is designed for landing on a short runway. This type of landing is not smooth because there is no round out or flare just before touchdown, which breaks the descent of the final approach during a normal landing. There is some cushioning, however, as air gets trapped between the airplane and the ground just before touchdown, making the landing a little smoother; it's called ground effect.

A few seconds from touchdown, I dropped the right wing a few degrees to be parallel with the sloping ground, making the touchdown equally on both main landing gears. If I hadn't done this, we would have touched down initially on only the left main gear, which might have overstressed that side. At the same time that I dropped the right wing for landing, I added a little left rudder to keep the plane from turning to the right. That's the same technique a pilot uses to make a crosswind landing. We touched down hard, just as planned, and bounced about five feet back into the air. Immediately upon first contact with the ground, I slammed all four throttles into maximum reverse thrust. I had to be ready to keep the aircraft moving straight ahead by using the rudder pedals if the propellers did not all reverse at the same speed, but everything worked exactly as designed. I kept the throttles in full reverse until I began blowing the freshly cut grass forward of the engines. At slow speed the propellers pick up anything loose on the ground, in this case grass, and because they were in reverse the grass was blown forward of the aircraft. I was constantly adjusting the amount of reverse thrust to keep the grass from getting sucked into the engine's air intakes. When I was slow enough to use wheel brakes, I took the props out of reverse. We had half of the field remaining in front of us when the plane had slowed enough to turn and taxi back to where the activities were taking place. The touchdown and stopping technique I used was called a maximum effort landing: we stopped in less than two thousand feet.

It turned out to be a pleasant day. The events of the day included airplane flyovers, aerobatics, and a very good multiplane group that performed loops and rolls in formation. But ours was the only plane that could land on the sod, so it was the only one on the ground. The C-130 was opened for inspection, and we must have answered a thousand questions, mostly about how we'd landed such a big airplane in the grass. The crowd loved it. In the afternoon, we cleared the area of spectators, started engines, and made a short field takeoff and

C-130 on static display at Spa, Belgium. The aircraft is on a sod field.

maximum effort climb to demonstrate our takeoff capability. After a couple of low passes, we headed for England. It was the end of a perfect day.

During the cold war with the Soviet Union, there were occasions when a Soviet bloc country would attempt to lure an American military plane into unfriendly airspace so they could shoot or force the aircraft down for "violating" their airspace. They could then claim that they'd done it "legally." The term the Air Force used for this deception was spoofing, and it happened to me while flying in international waters along the coast of Albania.

I was flying south over the Adriatic Sea between the heel of the boot of southern Italy and Albania. Italy was friendly territory; however, at the height of the cold war, Albania was the enemy. To stray into enemy territory probably would have caused an international incident; and it would've ruined my entire day, especially if the modern, Soviet-made fighter planes based there had shot down my defenseless C-130. I used the term "stray into enemy territory," which is not quite accurate: I was being lured into enemy territory by the Albanians.

My route of flight was to fly southeast over the Adriatic Sea to the Greek island of Kerkyra, which had two independent radio navigation facilities: a VOR, and a low-frequency radio beacon. These were the standard navigational facilities used throughout the world to establish the airways or air routes, similar to the interstate highway system, on the ground, in the United States. The stations at Kerkyra were operated by the Greek government, and were consistent with tens of thousands of others around the world. Each one transmits on a published frequency, and you ensure you have the correct station tuned in by listening for the three letter identifier, which is transmitted by the station in Morse code. At high altitude, you begin to pick up the stations about two hundred miles away. I had two VOR receivers and one ADF radio receiver on the C-130; they were all tuned to Kerkyra. As soon as I received a strong radio signal, I adjusted my heading for the high altitude winds, to fly a direct course for the Greek island.

At two hundred miles from the navigation station, the initial heading was not precise. As I flew closer to Kerkyra, the reception became stronger and I adjusted the heading a few degrees. When flying with radio aids available to me, I usually kept the airplane on course, while my navigator only monitored our position. About one hundred miles from Kerkyra, my navigator alerted me that I was on a course that would take me about thirty miles to the east of Kerkyra, which was just where we didn't want to be: over Albania. I immediately cross-checked all three radios for confirmation that I was correct and that the navigator was making an error. All of my radio indications were that I was correct; however, this was not the time to be proud and not take the navigator's advice. I made a right turn, disregarding my navigation instruments. My radios relied on information received from the ground, whereas the navigator was relying on information derived only internally, from our aircraft.

We were all aware of the spoofing that had occurred in the past, especially the case of another C-130 that was shot down in the Soviet Union a few miles north of the border with Turkey, in what is now Georgia. The information we'd received on that incident was that the Soviets had deceived the US Air Force pilot into believing he was flying to a VOR in Turkey when he was in fact flying to a VOR in the Soviet Union. The spoofing was accomplished by transmitting on the same frequency as the VOR in Turkey, using the same identifying call sign, but at a higher power output. Two radios were transmitting on the same frequency, but one was much stronger than the other. The instruments in the aircraft had picked up the stronger signal, and the pilot had no indication that he was flying to the wrong navigation radio.

All of my mental sensors were now alert. Was it possible that the Albanians were trying to draw me from international airspace into their airspace and make me the headlines in the newspapers the next day? Once again, I double-checked both VORs and the ADF and had the copilot perform the same verification, independent of mine. I listened to the navigator explain what he was using to determine the position of Kerkyra and decided that the safest course of action was to rely on the navigator and disregard the radio signals.

As we approached and then flew over the Greek island, I knew I'd nearly been spoofed. I was able to calculate the exact position of the bogus VOR and its low frequency beacon: about twenty-five miles from the real navigational facility, and inside Albania. After landing, I contacted the appropriate authorities and gave a detailed report of the incident, so no unwary pilot would fall into the trap.

For the three years before I began working for TWA in late 1968, I was stationed at Sewart Air Force Base near Nashville. The base had two tactical C-130 squadrons and a third squadron that taught new crewmembers to fly the aircraft.

The three squadrons made up an Air Force wing, which was commanded by the wing commander, a colonel.

The base had thousands of Air Force personnel who lived in the nearby towns and pumped millions of dollars into the local economy. It was a walled city within the civilian community. The wing commander was in a position analogous to that of the mayor of Nashville: he interacted with the local authorities on behalf of the base personnel; and he represented the Air Force in dealing with the state government. The commander was not only in charge of the largest military operation in Tennessee, but he was one of the most powerful players in that part of the state. When it was important to impress a local civilian dignitary, the colonel would conduct an unusual business lunch; occasionally, I was involved.

The nicest place to have lunch at Sewart was at the Officers' Club. The base was neat and clean, but the old wooden buildings had probably been constructed during World War II, if not before. The club provided acceptable food, but it had been built to be functional; not to impress anyone. In contrast, Fort Campbell, fifty miles north of us, had a beautiful new red brick Officers' Club, built on a knoll overlooking the surrounding terrain. That nice new building definitely was the place to take someone you wanted to impress. The wing commander decided that he would prefer to use the Fort Campbell Officers' Club for his important business lunches, even though it was fifty miles away. The most impressive part of the lunch, though, was getting there.

Fort Campbell was the home of the 101st Airborne Division, an Army unit that relied heavily on our C-130s; and we relied on them to provide drop zones and paratroopers, so that we could maintain our airdrop proficiency. Because of our close proximity, my Air Force C-130 wing and the Army's 101st Airborne Division had a symbiotic relationship. When a luncheon date was arranged, my squadron was notified to schedule a specially qualified crew and airplane to fly the commander and his guest to Kentucky. The Officers' Club at Fort Campbell would also be notified to prepare for the dignitaries.

I was an instructor pilot at the time, and I also worked as the Squadron Flight Scheduling Officer. I was responsible for deciding who would fly on which flight, and I did the initial planning for the mission before scheduling the pilot and crew. My Scheduling Section was the Squadron Command Center, and I was there every day when I was not flying. When a flight was scheduled to go to Fort Campbell with the commander, sometimes on short notice, I usually took the mission myself. That way, I didn't have to look for another pilot, plus it got me away from the office for a few hours and I got a break from my stressful office duties.

When the commander and his luncheon guest were leaving his office, he would call me on a handheld radio to notify me that he was on his way to the airplane. This was my clue to start engines and open the ramp and door in the rear of the airplane so that the cargo compartment would be ready to accept his staff car. The commander would drive his car onto the lowered aircraft ramp and into the cargo compartment, following my loadmaster's hand signals. As soon as he was parked safely in the calculated position, with the emergency brake set, I would taxi to the end of the runway. During the short taxi, the loadmaster would tie the car down, using four chains that he would attach to special fittings welded to the axle of the car. Once the car was tied down on the airplane,

I was ready for takeoff, about five minutes from the time the colonel had left his office.

I used the runway direction closest to the heading for Fort Campbell, regardless of the winds, so that I wouldn't have to waste a few minutes in turning, immediately after take off. I flew the fifty-mile flight at high speed, to save time. The flight always received priority treatment and I made a straight-in, high-speed, approach and landing at the Army airfield. I was in the air less than fifteen minutes, and the colonel and his lunch guest never got out of the car. Immediately after landing I would exit the runway, the chains were removed from the car, and the aft ramp and door were opened. I would taxi a short distance to an established offload area, the emergency brake on the car was released, and the commander would back out of the C-130. He would then drive to the Officers' Club, where he parked in his reserved spot at the front door. I would wait at the airplane while they had lunch, then we'd reverse the process for the trip back to Sewart. I had a chance to get out of the office for a while and also get some flying time; the commander would impress his guest by taking him to Kentucky for lunch, and the guest is probably still wondering how it all happened so fast.

Zero–zero weather conditions means the fog is so dense that you have no visibility. I have had zero–zero weather reported a few times in my career.

During one of my three-month tours in Mildenhall, England, the temperature was near freezing for about a week. In the early 1960s, most of the home heating in England was done with soft coal, which was mined in Great Britain and therefore inexpensive. There was a lot of moisture in the air; and smog resulting from the mixture of fog and coal smoke—what the English called pea soup—kept the visibility at a few feet for days.

I was a KC-97 tanker copilot during one of those pea soupers when we were told by the command post to prepare for a flight to refuel a B-47 flying from the States to Spain and desperately in need of in-flight refueling. For some reason, there was no available tanker in Spain. My crew was on standby and was the most available crew in England. The visibility at the time was about twenty feet, which made it possible to drive our crew vehicle, very slowly, to the aircraft. We prepared the tanker for the mission and then had a long discussion with the command post concerning the requirement to make an instrument takeoff. Because of the extremely poor visibility, we required special permission for that hazardous maneuver.

I was the copilot on John Garrison's crew, and was the only person to voice an objection to the mission, on the grounds that it was too hazardous. The KC-97 was designed shortly after World War II, and its instrumentation was primitive by today's standards. I didn't feel the instruments were accurate enough to permit this zero–zero takeoff; we did not have a written procedure for it; and neither John nor I had ever performed one. The normal takeoff at the time was ninety-five percent visual, with only a few glances at the airspeed indicator to see how fast we were going. This instrument takeoff would require total reliance on the instruments. In later years, flying more sophisticated aircraft, the takeoff technique changed, relying far more on the accurate instrumentation that had been developed by then. If we'd had modern instruments, it would have made what we were going to attempt much safer.

We were the last chance for the B-47 that was in trouble; if we didn't get airborne and transfer fuel to it, it would probably run out of fuel and ditch in the Atlantic. I finally said okay and stopped objecting. After we started our engines, John began to realize that his go-go attitude might have been a mistake. The visibility was now only about ten feet. From the cockpit, we could not see the yellow taxi line, which made it impossible to taxi to the runway. We talked about it, and John decided that if we had a vehicle drive in front of us, the driver could see the yellow taxi line, and we could follow the vehicle. I asked about not seeing the white centerline painted on the runway, used to locate the center of the runway during the takeoff. I knew what the answer was before I asked it, but I wanted to talk some more about what we were agreeing to do. John said he would fly a constant heading down the runway, so he wouldn't need to see the centerline. He planned to control the position of the aircraft during the liftoff by using the attitude indicator. It all sounded perfectly logical; however, our take-off roll required about one mile of runway. I told John that if he could not see the runway centerline to make corrections during the takeoff roll and we were off only one degree on our heading, we would be off the side of the runway before we were off the ground.

I could tell that Robbie, the engineer, and Dick, the navigator, were both beginning to understand my reasoning and were changing their minds about feeling comfortable with this hazardous maneuver. I made another radio call to the command post and informed them that we had engines started; but since we couldn't see the taxi line, we were requesting a follow-me vehicle to get us onto the runway and pointed in the takeoff direction. All I received from the command post was "Stand by." I think everyone, including the command post, was now having second thoughts about the degree of hazard involved; maybe they were wondering whether it was a mistake to risk losing our tanker in addition to the bomber.

I soon received one of my most memorable radio calls. The command post told us to shut down our engines; we were no longer needed for the refueling mission. A tanker was in the air from a base in Spain, where the weather was beautiful, and was on its way to a rendezvous with the bomber. I still feel that if we had attempted to take off without seeing the runway centerline, our chances of making it off the ground would have been very close to zero, and that does not factor in an emergency, such as an engine failure, during the takeoff roll.

Once we shut down the engines and secured the aircraft, the remainder of the crew got the true picture of my concern for our safety. We all got into the crew vehicle for our short drive off the flight line and to our quarters. John was driving. With a visibility of only a few feet, we had to find and follow the white line, painted on the center of the road, which would guide us back to the gate and out of the restricted area. We knew the line was close to the car, but with only a few feet of visibility, we still had to search for it. Once we found the white line, we still had a problem: John could not see the line from the driver's seat. We decided that I would walk on the line near the left front fender of the car, and Dick would walk along the right front fender, while John drove the car.

After I'd proceeded about a hundred yards walking along the side of the car, with my right hand on the front fender, I began shouting to the guard who was stationed at the entrance to the restricted area, in order to be able to judge which left turn line we had to follow. There were left turn lines going to the hangers on the edge of the flight line, but I wanted the line that would get us through the gate. Shouting for the gate guard was common practice when the fog was this bad; once in verbal contact with him, I was able to guess at his location and guide the car along the line that I expected would lead us to his position.

We all thought that we were doing fine and heading out the gate when Dick, who was walking along the right front fender, shouted, "Stop!" By the time John was able to react to the command, we'd run the bumper of the car into an enormous, gray hangar door. The visibility was so bad that I hadn't seen the hangar, which was only about three or four feet in front of me, until the bumper of the car hit it. I was so disoriented in the fog that I had selected the wrong left turn line. I'd followed a line that led to the last hangar instead of the line thirty yards away that would have taken us through the guarded gate. When we tapped the hanger door with the bumper of the car, moving at walking speed with a spotter at each fender, I'm confident that everyone had a vision similar to the one I had. I envisioned us traveling down the runway in excess of one hundred miles an hour, with no idea of where we were in relation to the edge of the pavement.

I breathed a great sigh of relief when I was finally back in my room. It was cold outside, about thirty-five degrees Fahrenheit, and my fingers and toes were cold from walking outside the car for about half a mile. When I blew my runny nose, the tissue turned black from the coal particles that had collected in my nose.

In later years, heating with soft coal was banned in England, and everyone switched to gas heat, greatly alleviating the smog problem.

When Germany was defeated after World War II, the country was separated into four sectors: the Soviet Union controlled the eastern sector, later called East Germany; and France, the United Kingdom, and the United States controlled the western sectors, together called West Germany. The line that separated them was part of what Winston Churchill called "an Iron Curtain." Berlin was in the Soviet Sector and was itself divided into East and West Berlin; separated by the Berlin Wall, which the Soviets built to keep East Berliners from escaping to the West. The wall was rebuilt numerous times, and after years of fortification, it had become almost one hundred percent effective in isolating East Berlin from the West. There were openings, called checkpoints, protected by heavily armed guards at each end; only a few vehicles passed through the checkpoints every week. I went to East Berlin, the Soviet Sector, through Checkpoint Charlie, at the height of the cold war.

The West was determined that West Berlin would not be isolated within the Soviet sector, so three air corridors into the city from West Germany were established. Before flying into Berlin, every Air Force pilot and navigator took specialized training to learn the procedures for flying the corridors. The corridors passed through what eventually became hostile airspace, so it was important that Air Force aircraft not appear aggressive. High-altitude flights and high airspeeds were not permitted. It was impressed upon me that my aircraft had to remain within the airspace carved out for the three corridors and that failure to respect East German airspace would probably result in a confrontation with a Soviet-built MIG fighter. It wasn't necessary to remind me to remain in the corridor; the very first time I flew to Berlin, I was escorted by two MIGs for almost the entire flight. They flew below me, and slightly aft, on the left side of my aircraft, flying at the same speed I was. It was thrilling and scary, but I knew that I would have no problem as long as I followed the rules.

In the 1960s, navigation all over the world, except for the Berlin corridors, was done with VORs. In contrast, the primary method of navigation within the corridors was by flying the radio beam of a high-powered localizer—the same radio aid used to guide an aircraft to the centerline of a landing runway. It was a far more accurate means of navigation than the VOR, because it prevented distortion of the radio wave, which might allow a plane to stray out of the corridor. The approach into Berlin was interesting because of the proximity of the aircraft to the buildings along the approach path. I think the surrounding buildings were closer to the airplane than at any other large city's airport I have flown into.

The highlight of my Berlin layovers was a tour through East Berlin. The United States insisted that East Berlin not be totally isolated, so they provided free bus tours and encouraged us to take the bus ride through the checkpoint and into the eastern side of the divided city. By operating a bus through East Berlin at regular intervals, the United States was diplomatically letting the East German leaders know that we were going to keep the border open, at least to the military, in accordance with the agreement that had divided the city.

Compared to West Berlin, the part of the city east of the wall was gray and dismal; it lacked the vibrancy of the West. After passing back through the checkpoint to West Berlin, my crew stopped for a beer. Seeing the vast difference between the two sides of the Wall and relaxing in a beer garden in West Berlin made up for the tension caused by being escorted through the corridor by MIGs.

We transported everything required in the Vietnam war zone—not only vehicles and heavy equipment but also all types of things that were necessary to keep the troops supplied. On one flight, my plane's cargo compartment was half-filled with whole blood, so we had to keep the temperature very cold. That was the only time in my career that a temperature controller was stuck in the full hot position. I had to make an emergency landing to get the controller repaired, or else hundreds of cartons of blood would have been destroyed by the heat.

I was always surprised at the heavy weight of ammunition. A full load of ammo in wooden boxes, distributed throughout the entire cargo compartment, was only a foot and a half high. At first glance, a C-130 at maximum weight, loaded with ammunition, looks empty.

This was the first war in which we had a large number of females in the military, other than nurses, and I once carried a pallet full of feminine items. If it was used in Vietnam, the C-130s carried it.

Frequently, I carried troops out of Vietnam to a location where they could get more suitable transportation back to the states, rather than riding in the very uncomfortable troop seats we had in the cargo compartment of the C-130. I had engines running, preparing to take off from Da Nang, when I was instructed to delay my flight for a few minutes to take a Marine, on emergency leave, with me to Okinawa.

A helicopter landed alongside my airplane, and something that vaguely resembled a human hopped out and entered my C-130. I was responsible for briefing him before the flight, so I climbed out of my seat and spoke to him for a few minutes in the rear of the aircraft. He was just a kid, and he was going to catch a flight home because his mother was dying. They had just picked him up with the helicopter from some forward location and he didn't have time to clean up—obviously. My initial observation was that he was caked with dry mud, from head to toe. He looked like he had been the loser in a mud-wrestling match. I couldn't get too close to him because of the stench; I guess it was a combination of body odor and the aroma of decomposed swamp mud. He looked corroded, and he had teenage stubble from not shaving for a week or two. His uniform had holes, but not from being torn; it looked like he was rotting away. He was wearing the standard-issue jungle boots that did not have leather uppers but rather had webbing to allow ventilation. One boot had khaki colored military tape wrapped around it; I guessed it was to hold the sole on. What bothered me the most were his eyes. He was trying very hard to focus on my face, attempting to understand what I was telling him, but every few seconds his eyes would dart away, and I guessed that he was still looking for the enemy. He must have been through hell; what he needed most was a long vacation from the war.

Occasionally, I transported human remains from the war zone to someplace where they could get the dignity and respect they deserved. I felt sorry for this American kid having to go through what was obviously a terrible existence, but at least he was alive.

After takeoff, the two loadmasters gave him some of the in-flight rations we always carried and some hot coffee, and he went into a restless sleep. They didn't want to get too close to him, because of the obnoxious odor. One of my loadmasters, also a youngster, said, "He was more like an animal than a human." Also, he said that he was extremely thankful he was in the Air Force and did not have to live in the swamps of Vietnam like that young Marine.

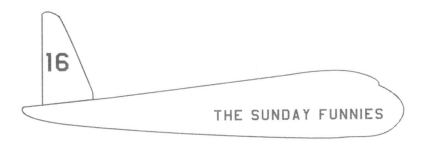

16

THE SUNDAY FUNNIES

I WAS AT HOWARD AFB in the Canal Zone with my C-130 reserve unit when I was assigned a five-day trip to Montevideo, Uruguay. It was unusual to have a flight to Montevideo and unheard of to have a five-day trip with just one destination. Usually, a long trip would entail visiting most of the capital cities of South America, with a lot of flying but very little—or no—chance for resting or exploring. This mission left on a Monday, had three days in Montevideo, and returned to Panama on Friday.

The United States had had a poor diplomatic relationship with Uruguay for a number of years; this was our first attempt to soften our relations with this small country on the south Atlantic Coast, between Argentina and Brazil. My mission was to transport a three-star Air Force lieutenant general and his wife on this official visit, the first in many years. The general, the commander of Southern Command, had been acting as the unofficial ambassador to Uruguay, performing his duties from his headquarters in Panama. The second highest dignitary on the flight was the soon-to-be-appointed United States ambassador, also accompanied by his wife. There were about half a dozen aides and assistants, making a total of ten passengers. This was everyone's first visit to Uruguay.

The general told me there would be an arrival ceremony upon landing and that he wanted to land as close to five in the afternoon as possible. The time request was right up my alley; we constantly trained to get to our destination at a specified time to drop supplies or paratroopers on a distant drop zone exactly on schedule. After the eight-hour flight, I touched down on the end of the runway just a few seconds from my planned time, and everyone was suitably impressed. The flight down to Uruguay had been fairly comfortable for the dignitaries because we used what we called a comfort pallet. It transformed the interior of the cargo compartment, which was normally pretty bleak, into a first-class, airline-type interior. In addition to airline seats, the pallet also had a galley and a latrine; and, in an addition to my crew, there was a steward who cooked steaks for all of us and tended to the passengers.

When we landed, I was met by a follow-me vehicle, to guide me to the ramp and the reception area. The general and the new ambassador, with their wives, came up to the cockpit after landing to look at the reception area and get a feel for what to expect when they deplaned. The cockpit of the C-130 is enormous; it easily accommodated the four crewmembers plus the four dignitaries, with room to spare. When we reached the ramp, it was obvious that this small South American nation was doing its best to welcome the diplomats from the United States. There were temporary bleachers set up, and dozens of people were waiting to view the festivities. The deplaning area was red carpeted, with a reception line of about a dozen people, both military and civilian. There was also a large military troop in formation, standing at attention, plus a band in elaborate, royal blue uniforms with bright red sashes that crossed diagonally, front and back. Their uniforms included red and blue plumed hats that were about a foot tall. All told, there were a few hundred people on the tarmac waiting to greet us.

I taxied behind the follow-me vehicle, assuming that the driver knew exactly what he was doing; I hadn't considered that he might have been given the position because of his low IQ.

The primary entry and exit door on the C-130, similar to every aircraft I have ever flown, was on the left side. I could tell as soon as I was guided onto the crowded ramp that the follow-me driver had not planned on making the general's and the ambassador's exit from the aircraft a simple matter of stepping out of the entry door and onto the red carpet. He was bringing the aircraft in backwards, as if our door were on the right side; we'd have to turn around, on the crowded tarmac, to have the door facing the red carpet. The general was standing on my left side. When I told him what I thought was going to occur, he said, "I told them I didn't want a large arrival ceremony, and they assured me it would just be a few people. Let them figure it out."

As we approached the waiting local dignitaries, I could see the people putting their hands over their ears to protect them from the engine noise. Noise was only the beginning of their problems, though. I was more concerned about having to make a 180-degree turn on the crowded ramp, which would place the tail of the aircraft toward the crowd. The C-130 is a large aircraft with four very powerful engines that produce oily jet exhaust fumes as well as high velocity wind from the propellers. It could be dangerous to be behind the aircraft, getting blasted by the engines.

I was becoming increasingly concerned that there was no one in charge on the ground who was aware of the approaching problem, so I stopped the aircraft and had the loadmaster open the forward entry door and signal to the follow-me driver that I wanted to speak to him. We were about fifty yards from the red carpet, which was on the right side of the plane. When we opened the forward entry door on the left side of the aircraft, everyone on the ground immediately realized that we would have to make a 180- degree turn. I was watching the receiving line: everyone had one hand on his ear for noise protection; the other hand was making circling motions, signaling that we had to turn around. The noise level from the engines was too loud for them to speak to one another, but there was no doubt that everyone realized they had a problem. The general made some comment into my left ear about them really screwing this thing up, and said, "Let's see how they recover." One of the dignitaries in a military uniform, possibly the Minister of Air, left the receiving line and got into the follow-me vehicle with the driver. With the windows closed, they were able to speak with one another, and I could see their hand motions as they devised a new plan for getting us turned around.

We were almost out of turning space, and their new plan would have worked, if the hundred-piece band were not to the right of the aircraft. The follow-me vehicle, with the driver and the dignitary, made a left turn and indicated that I should follow. I turned to the general and told him that if I complied with their instructions the engine blast was going to blow the band off the ramp. He told me that's their problem; so, using as little power as I possibly could, I turned the aircraft to the left, which directed the engine blast right at the band. I considered shutting down two of the engines in order to reduce the air blast behind the aircraft, but decided against that plan because I would then have to increase power on the two operating engines. I informed the crew on the interphone that we were going to sandblast the band and to let me know what was happening behind the aircraft, if anyone could see it.

I was concentrating on staying behind the follow-me vehicle and trying to second-guess what their new plan was, when I looked at the general and thought that he was getting airsick. He had his head pressed against the side windscreen, attempting to see what had happened to the band, and I noticed that he was red in the face. I asked him if he was okay, but he couldn't speak. That's when I realized that he was laughing hysterically while at the same time attempting to maintain his dignity in front of the crew by suppressing his laughter. The veins in his neck were standing out and he still looked like he was going to throw up. I took a quick look to my left, behind the left wing, and saw what remained of the band. What began as a neat formation of about ten across and ten deep turned into dozens of individuals, all running around picking up the foot-high plumed hats that had blown off of their heads when they turned their backs to the hurricane-force winds behind the engines. The only thing the general said to me was, "I told them not to plan an arrival ceremony."

The follow-me vehicle then surprised me with its next maneuver. I was expecting a 90-degree right turn, but it made a 180- degree turn to the right. I knew that there was now a high level government official giving the instructions to the driver, so I turned to the general and put both of my hands in front of me, palms up, indicating that I had no idea what they were doing. He said to just follow their instructions. I did.

The driver of the vehicle turned his automobile to the right, expecting me to follow in his tracks; what he didn't realize, though, was that a large four-engine aircraft might not have the turning capability of an automobile. The C-130 has tandem wheels on each side of the fuselage, limiting the turning radius of the aircraft. My 180-degree turn to the right required much more space than the driver expected, and now I was headed for the red carpet and the reception line. The dignitaries saw the aircraft taxiing straight towards them; and out of the corners of their eyes, they could see the havoc the band had experienced. They began to run to get away from the path of the aircraft. I was getting concerned about following a vehicle driven by someone with no effective plan and probably no experience in guiding a large aircraft. I was also concerned about the poor people on the ramp, probably some of the highest dignitaries in the country, who were now running from the aircraft thinking their life was in danger. The conditions were rapidly degrading; if I continued to taxi, I would be unable to turn away, because of the limited space. I stopped the aircraft, set the brakes, had the loadmaster open the forward entrance door and stand outside, and expected someone to come to the aircraft to give me their new plan. There was a huddle of some of the dignitaries, and then someone signaled with a hand across his throat, meaning I should cut my engines. One of the locals came to the aircraft and apologized for the fiasco, then asked the general if it was okay with him not to deplane until they were once again set up for the official arrival ceremony. The two wives complained about not getting off the aircraft after the long flight, but we all remained in the cockpit to watch the second half of the comedy show.

The band was recovering from its disarray; members were exchanging hats, finding ones that fit. They were also gathering into exactly the same formation and location they'd been in before the fiasco. The aircraft was now at ninety degrees to their original plan, so the red carpet was moved to where the forward entrance door now was, and the receiving line then formed near the red carpet. The band, still on the right side of the aircraft, was isolated from the red carpet on the left side of the plane. I was expecting to get the word at any moment that the general, the ambassador, and their wives could deplane.

My cockpit was now packed with about a dozen people who were beyond eager to get out into the fresh air, as well as to see what was happening on the ramp and the reason for the delay. The cargo compartment of the C-130 has only a few porthole-style small windows with a limited view. I stayed in the left pilot's seat, speaking to the general, who was still standing on my left. We were both chuckling about the lack of planning when the bandleader decided to move the band to a more suitable position, near the red carpet, and attempted to march the band to the front of the aircraft and back into the picture.

From the instant the first command was given to move the band, it was obvious that this was not a marching band and that the leader of the band had no experience in moving a large group in formation. It isn't easy to move a formation with a ten-man front, and the most difficult maneuver is a right or left turn. This marching band maneuver requires practice, because the people on the inside of the turn have to take very small steps, while the people on the outside of the turn have to take large steps, in order to rotate the group with some semblance of military discipline. The order to turn right was given by the bandleader, but it was heard by only half of the band; they turned right and marched away, leaving the left side of the band either in place or running to catch up. The pivot man on the right front corner turned right as directed, and proceeded to march away from the rest of the formation, while a few of the first rank attempted to stay with him. The center of the formation, not knowing what was occurring in the front, was marching straight ahead instead of turning, and the rear of the formation was not moving, probably because they hadn't heard the order to march. Mack Sennett couldn't have directed it better. Everyone in the cockpit broke out into hysterical laughter, watching the slapstick comedy.

The band members, when they realized what a mess they were in, did the sensible thing: they stopped attempting to march in military formation, and just wandered over to where the bandleader had moved, then assembled into their formation once again. I guess practice makes perfect: this was the third time they had done it that day. When everything was rearranged, the general and the ambassador, with their wives, wiped away their tears of laughter, put on their serious faces, walked onto the red carpet, and greeted the dignitaries in the reception line. In spite of our disastrous arrival, we now have much better relations with Uruguay.

All airlines have an occasional problem with a passenger who refuses to follow the regulations or the directions of the flight attendants, and TWA was no exception. A passenger might be under the influence of alcohol or drugs or possibly have mental or other medical problems, causing disorientation. The most common problem was the anxious passenger who was stressed-out by the frustration of getting to the airport on time, then being searched while going through security, which might lead to having words with the gate agent. By the time such a passenger was on the airplane, already feeling abused, the first order given by the flight attendant might cause the person to fly into a rage. The flight attendants were trained in handling angry or uncooperative passengers; however, at TWA, the policy was that when additional authority was required, one of the pilots would assist.

The typical scenario was to have the pilot put on his black uniform jacket with the gold stripes and his pilot's hat, to portray a symbol of authority, before leaving the cockpit and confronting the unruly passenger. In ninety-nine percent of the situations, explaining to the passenger that we will land the aircraft and have them removed from the flight or that we have the authority to place them in police custody upon arrival at our destination was enough to intimidate the passenger into compliance. In the other one percent of the situations, however, the passenger might be a Golden Gloves boxer who hits the pilot with a right cross to the jaw. It was because of the possibility of the unruly passenger injuring the pilot, and therefore jeopardizing the safety of the flight, that TWA changed its policy and decided that the pilots should not leave the cockpit in-flight to assist the flight attendants with passenger problems. This was especially true after the newer aircraft changed from three pilots in the cockpit to only two pilots.

Soon after the change in TWA policy that kept the pilots in the cockpit, I was working a flight from San Juan, Puerto Rico, to JFK, when a disturbance occurred that directly involved a dozen passengers and, indirectly, about another hundred; about half of the passengers were greatly amused. We had eight flight attendants on board, and each of them came to the cockpit to report on what was occurring in the passenger compartment.

TWA flew a number of daily flights from New York to San Juan, and for many months in a row, while I was a first officer on the Lockheed 1011, I flew the nine a.m. flight. At that time, I lived only a few miles from JFK, and a nine a.m. takeoff was gentleman's hours; far easier for me than flying the all-night flights to Europe. The flight time to San Juan was three and a half hours, so I arrived at my beach-front layover hotel early in the afternoon. We left the next day at dinnertime, which meant that I'd had over twenty-four hours in a tourist hotel in the Caribbean, compliments of my wonderful airline job. The flight was short, and the routine so familiar, that I considered it more like going on vacation than going to work. We carried so many people between the two cities that we used to joke that one-third of the Puerto Ricans were in Puerto Rico; one-third were in New York City, and one-third were always in the air, between the two locations.

The Puerto Ricans were mostly very polite, easy-going passengers, but they did have their own peculiarities. I was on the morning flight to San Juan on the first day that security screening was initiated because of hijackings, and pocket-knives were no longer permitted in the passenger compartment. We had 270 passengers, and security had confiscated 110 pocketknives, which were placed in a cardboard box in the cockpit to be returned to the owners when we arrived in San Juan. The knives came from youngsters like the gang members in West Side Story. These were exactly the kind of kids who participated in the uproar on my flight from San Juan to New York.

I was able to piece together what was occurring because of the steady stream of information we were receiving in the cockpit from the excited flight attendants. It appeared that a young lady (I use the term loosely) went into the aircraft lavatory and washed out her panties. Not having a suitable place to hang them up to dry, she placed them on the seat back in front of her, hoping to have them dry before our arrival in New York. She was in an aisle seat on the wide body L-1011, which had two aisles; so the panties were in plain view of everyone in the area, including two young men across the aisle from her. The guy closest to her leaned into the aisle and asked her whose panties are on the seat back and why are they hanging up? She answered that they are her panties, and they are hanging up to dry.

Now they have gotten the attention of all of the passengers in the immediate area. The second male, who was one seat from the aisle, got out of his seat and stood in the aisle to join the conversation. A little deductive reasoning on the part of the guys progressed, logically, to: "If these are your panties hanging up, what are you wearing under your skirt?"

She answered, "Nothing."

In the cockpit, we received the first report from a female flight attendant. She was relaying to us what she had observed only because it was so humorous, not to request assistance or advice. By the time we received the next report from a second flight attendant, there were half a dozen guys in the aisle, all surrounding the young woman's seat and all discussing whether she was wearing panties or merely teasing them. She continued to insist that she wasn't wearing anything under her skirt, and as the testosterone levels increased in these young males, the guys began to egg her on, looking for a free show. With their hormones raging, these young men convinced the young lady that the only way they could confirm that she was not lying to them was to have someone get a peek. She eventually volunteered a quick peek by pulling her skirt up and then immediately back down. All of the guys said that it was too quick, and they still couldn't tell if she was lying.

In the cockpit, when we heard there was a commotion in the aisle, we turned on the fasten seat belt sign, making our standard announcement that everyone had to return to their seats and fasten their seat belts. Naturally, that was as effective as telling a bunch of sharks in the middle of a feeding frenzy that it's not lunchtime. No one returned to their seats, and a few female passengers in the area, who didn't want to be involved, left their seats and went to the rear of the aircraft. This made more room for additional males to squeeze into the area surrounding the drying panties.

The flight attendants now wanted to know how to handle the situation; we told them it seemed to be innocent fun and not to interfere. That may have been a mistake, but we figured the show would finally come to an end and everyone would settle back into their seats. We asked the flight attendants if she may have been drunk or displaying unusual behavior before the beginning of the incident and no one had noticed anything out of the ordinary.

After she gave the second peek, then the third much longer look, she was surrounded by so many cheering males that she got out of her seat and danced into the crowded aisle, swinging her skirt up and down, giving everyone a good look.

The male gang began pushing and shoving one another, attempting to get closer to the action, and we had a situation that was totally out of control and was getting dangerous. The flight attendants were frantic by that time and were not able to stop the show. What had started as a group of routine passengers had degraded into a hormone-fed mob that was getting nasty. In the cockpit, we were getting the story from the excited and frantic flight attendants who were going to the fringe of the crowd to see what was happening and then running back to the cockpit to make their report and maybe get some advice.

Since the company policy had recently changed and we were not to leave the cockpit to get involved with the passengers, I was relieved that I didn't have to go to the passenger compartment to attempt to defuse the situation. The entire show came to screeching halt when a tall, elegant, well-dressed, Spanish-speaking woman in her fifties, who obviously was not intimidated by the twenty-five-year-old guys, marched her way down the aisle to where the free show was taking place. She slapped the young woman across the face and shook her shoulders, and gave her a tongue-lashing in Spanish. She then marched the now embarrassed younger woman to her seat, took the panties off the seat back to be placed out of view, and informed the men that the show was over. She was far more effective than the crew had been in quelling the near riot, and she got everyone to return to their seats.

After we landed at JFK, the entire crew was still buzzing about what had occurred, and the three of us from the cockpit wanted to see what the woman who had caused the commotion looked like. She was pointed out to us in the lobby of the architecturally famous TWA International Terminal by one of our flight attendants; and by that time, she was surrounded by a dozen of her family and friends who came to greet and welcome her to New York City. She was now wearing a jacket with her skirt and blouse, and appeared to be just another well-dressed and attractive woman on vacation. She didn't appear to be embarrassed, so I assumed that her relatives and friends had no knowledge of the show she'd put on. I guess what happens in flight stays in flight.

In 1972, tropical storm Agnes moved north, up the east coast of the US, dropping large amounts of rain and causing minor flooding in a dozen states. When it reached the northeastern corner of Pennsylvania, it stopped its forward movement and remained there for a few days, dropping enormous amounts of rain on the area. The Susquehanna River, which drains the basin, was incapable of handling that quantity of water and overflowed its banks, flooding the neighboring cities of Wilkes-Barre and Scranton.

At the time, I was in the Air Force Reserves, flying C-130s out of Willow Grove, Pennsylvania, less than a two-hour drive from the flood. My squadron, being so close, was given the job of aiding the relief effort by flying supplies into the Wilkes-Barre/Scranton Airport which was built on a bluff above the flooded area and was the headquarters for the distribution of the supplies. Many of the pilots in my reserve squadron were airline pilots, and because I was working for TWA and stationed at JFK, I was given the mission to fly to Kennedy and bring a load of fresh water back to the flood area.

JFK gets airplanes from all over the world; however, my brown, khaki, and tan camouflaged C-130 received a few comments on the ground control frequency. I taxied to the Pan American hanger, which was next to the TWA hanger, and was met there by a representative of the Rheingold Beer Company, who came from their brewery on Long Island, only a short ride from JFK. He informed me of the weight of the load of water; and after making a few calculations, I realized that someone had planned the load, because it was close to the maximum weight I could carry. I asked him why I was taking Long Island water to Pennsylvania; his answer was that his company had volunteered to package the drinking water in beer cans for easy distribution and storage. He also told me that the only cans and packing cartons available were their standard Rheingold Beer materials, with the preprinted labels. From the outside, it was impossible to tell that the cans contained water instead of beer; you had to open a can and drink the contents to know that it was water.

It was only a short flight back to Wilkes-Barre, where I was met by the unloading crew leader. The boss, after looking at the beer cases, decided that our plane could be unloaded by hand instead of tying up an urgently needed forklift. I taxied to the edge of the ramp, overlooking what normally would have been passenger parking. During the flood emergency, it was being used for parking the personal vehicles of the volunteer workers who were unloading the planes. Dozens of volunteers got the entire plane unloaded in only a slightly longer time than it would have taken a forklift.

We were starting engines to return to Willow Grove when I noticed some very strange behavior by the crew that had just unloaded our cargo. They were running to their private cars, which were parked adjacent to the ramp, and loading their trunks with cases of water. At first I thought that they must be desperate for drinking water at home, and then I realized what was going on. No one had told them that they had just unloaded a plane full of water, and that it was not a plane full of Rheingold Beer.

Coors Brewing Company, in Colorado, did not distribute east of the Mississippi River in the 1970s, so it was a real treat for someone on the East Coast to get a case of Coors.

I flew to Colorado to pick up an Air Force Reserve civil engineer squadron that had just completed their mandatory two-week summer encampment, and I was to return them to their home base on the East Coast. There were about fifty reservists with their two weeks' worth of baggage, plus seven thousand pounds of Coors beer they were taking home with them. When I gave the troops the standard briefing about the weather, the time for the flight, and most important, what to expect during an emergency, I also told them that there was to be no beer drinking during the flight.

A few hours into the flight, I had an engine failure on the number two engine, (the inboard engine on the left side) and decided to land at Pope Air Force Base, North Carolina, to get maintenance. Pope was the largest C-130 base at the time, so I knew they had a big supply of spare parts and highly experienced maintenance personnel. I had a good chance of having the engine repaired and getting on my way without having to remain over night. At the time, I was a highly experienced instructor pilot on the C-130, with many thousands of hours of flying time in the aircraft. The weather was beautiful at Pope, so this was certainly not a nail-biting experience. For all landings with an engine inoperative, I was required to have the ground emergency equipment standing by, so I complied with the regulations and was followed down the runway, after landing, by the fire trucks. If I had a choice, I would not have requested the emergency equipment; I didn't consider a routine engine failure on a four-engine aircraft an emergency.

After maintenance checked the problem, they decided to change the engine, about a three hour job. When I informed the troops in the rear that we had three hours to kill while waiting for the engine to be changed, they asked if they could break into the Coors. I agreed, provided they stayed in the plane. We opened all the doors on the aircraft to make it as comfortable as possible for the beer drinkers. I went with my crew to the snack bar for something to eat and then to Base Operations to file our flight plan for the remainder of the flight. When we returned to the aircraft, my crew and I sat in the shade under the left wing tip, while the passengers remained in the aircraft, playing cards and drinking Coors. I asked their commander if everything was okay.

He said, "It doesn't get much better than this."

Killing time in the shade of the left wing, and enjoying a brisk breeze, we began watching the beer drinkers exiting the rear of the aircraft to empty their now-full bladders. The left side of the aircraft had my five-man crew and the maintenance personnel changing the engine; for a little privacy, everyone who came out to pee chose the opposite side of the aircraft.

The Lockheed engineers who designed the C-130 chose to make the cargo compartment low to the ground to make it easy to drive vehicles into and out of the aircraft. From my position under the left wing, I could only see the person on the other side of the plane from his knees down. We began to watch some of the beer drinkers do a little dance as they unloaded the beer, which had now been filtered through their kidneys. With the warm summer wind blowing at about twenty knots, if they peed into the wind it would blow back and splash all over their boots. As we watched each of them exit the rear of the plane and look around to decide which side they were going to use to pee, we tried to decide from his actions whether he would pee into the wind and all over his shoes or if he was sober enough to turn around and pee downwind. It was about half and half. My biggest laugh came from the guy who had removed his combat boots in the aircraft to cool off his feet, walked out in his stocking feet, and still peed in the wrong direction. He never knew that five of us had watched him pee all over his socks.

The center of TWA's domestic operation was St. Louis, also the home of Anheuser-Busch, brewer of Budweiser beer. I was a 747 first officer deadheading back to New York after an all-night flight from Honolulu to St. Louis. While relaxing in my first class seat, I began a conversation with the passenger next to me, an executive with Anheuser-Busch who was responsible, in some minor way, for the type of beer that his company produced. I told him I had spent time in Germany and had developed a liking for the dark, heavy, flavorful German beers. We got into a pleasant conversation, and I asked him why Budweiser couldn't produce the same type of product that Germany makes instead of the pale and thin beer that they were manufacturing. He opened my eyes when he answered that they could brew any color or flavor of beer they wanted to brew. But they were making beer for the American market, and their beer was what American consumers demanded.

Before we both dozed off, I told him this beer story. In the summer of 1987, my TWA seniority permitted me to be stationed in Cairo and fly the L-1011 between there and Bombay. In Cairo, the airline provided me with a room in the beautiful Sheraton Hotel, which had seven very nice restaurants. The restaurant of choice for breakfast or for getting a sandwich for lunch was an upscale coffee shop. Their primary menu was in Arabic, of course, but there was a shortened version, in English. The hot summer temperatures in Cairo called for having a beer with lunch, and I began drinking what the menu called domestic beer, for about a dollar a bottle. The domestic brew was Stella, which was not bad, but my palate was craving something more interesting or heavier—perhaps one of the German or Dutch beers.

Next to the domestic beer on the menu was imported beer, but the price was almost three times as much. I used "pointy-talky" with the non-English-speaking waiter: I pointed to imported beer on the menu in an effort to determine what brands of imported beer they had; I was hoping for a Beck's dark or something similar. Not having any success with the waiter in determining the brand, I decided to gamble and see what I got. I pointed again to imported beer on the menu, and I received a thumbs up signal from the waiter, his indication for one beer. I nodded. While I was dreaming of something dark and heavy, he brought me a Budweiser, the King of Beers. Imported? Yes. Imported from St. Louis, Missouri, USA.

In Tel Aviv, the most popular beer was Maccabee. I'd had a few flights to Tel Aviv for the Air Force. But with TWA, I had several dozens of layovers; flying either the nonstop from New York with the 747 or the L-1011 flight from Paris. Our layover hotel was the Tel Aviv Hilton, which is right on the beach, on the eastern end of the Mediterranean. The beach in Tel Aviv is lined with a beautifully paved promenade, one of the nicest I have ever seen, that extends along the coast for at least a mile. There are shops, restaurants, and, of course, bars along its length.

If you order a beer in Tel Aviv, you automatically get a Maccabee, pronounced in English with the accent on the first syllable: MAC-uh-bee. In Hebrew, the beer is pronounced with the accent on the second syllable: Muh-CA-bee.

Almost everyone in Israel speaks some English, including the young waitresses working in the numerous tourist bars near the beach. The waitresses had a running joke: they all pronounced Maccabee with the accent on the opposite syllable from the way the tourist pronounced it.

American tourist number one: "I'll have a MAC-uh-bee."

Waitress: "One Muh-CA-bee."

Customer number two, after listening closely: "Bring me a Muh-CA-bee."

Waitress: "That makes two MAC-uh-bees."

If you then asked the waitress how to pronounce the name of the beer, with the accent on the first or the second syllable, she immediately forgot how to speak English.

17

QUESTIONS AND ANSWERS

PEOPLE ARE ALWAYS asking me questions about aviation, and I always answer them to the best of my ability. Even though a large portion of the population flies on a regular basis, most of them know little about what is occurring other than whether they had a good flight or an unpleasant experience.

I always get asked: "Is turbulence unsafe?" "Does being hit by lightning injure the passengers or cause the aircraft to crash?" "Have you ever had anyone injured on your aircraft?" "Have you ever had to parachute out of an airplane?" I'll get to those, but first . . .

At a party, when I was talking about my career to a group of about a dozen interested listeners, one person asked me, "Does a pilot need a key to start the motors?"

I never heard anyone in the aviation community refer to the power plant on the aircraft as a motor; we always call it an engine; there are technical differences between a motor and an engine. Does the pilot need a key to start the engines? No. Not on any of the airline or military aircraft that I flew. The only reason you use a key to start your car is to keep other people from driving it. It would be a simple matter to install a lock in the ignition of the large aircraft that I flew and give a key to the pilot, but it didn't seem necessary.

You need two things to start a jet engine: high-pressure air to make the engine start turning, and electrical power for ignition. Sometimes the air and electricity are transferred to the airplane from the specialized carts or trucks that you see in the vicinity of the parked commercial jets at the airports, but it is also produced right on the plane by an aircraft power unit (APU).

The APU is a small jet engine. Don't confuse it with the large engines hanging under the wings. The APU is hidden from view within the fuselage. The exhaust from the APU leaves the aircraft at a location where it should not cause a problem.

I was flying an Air Force Reserve C-130, taking a few dozen military schoolteachers from Colorado to their home base in Warner Robins, Georgia. Robins Air Force Base had its own grade school; and the teachers, who were not part of the city school system, were provided military transportation to their annual convention. On arrival at Robins, the teachers' bags were unloaded at the forward entrance door of the aircraft. When it was safe to exit, they climbed down the few steps to the ground, picked up their suitcases, and boarded the waiting bus. I boarded the same bus as the teachers.

The C-130 had two doors on the left side: the forward entrance door, forward of the wing, which had steps to the ground; and the paratroop door, aft of the wing, which was about two feet from the ground and didn't have any steps. Passengers always used the forward entrance door, because of the steps. All of the grade school teachers were on the bus except for one, and the rest of the teachers were making unflattering comments about her. I gathered from their comments that she typically was late and everyone had to wait for her, and now she was still on the aircraft while everyone else wanted to get to the restroom in base operations. Finally, she peeked out the aft paratroop door. She saw there were no steps and it was too high for her to step down, so she sat in the door frame and hopped to the ground. I realized what was keeping her so long: she was looking for her suitcase, which had been unloaded by the loadmasters and was still at the forward door. She was way back at the aft door, but I could detect her relief when she spotted her bag up front.

The ramp area outside the C-130 can be a hazardous place, and I had briefed the teachers to stay away from the propellers, even if they were not turning. I saw the straggler look at the propellers; to remain clear of them, and following my orders, she stayed close to the fuselage and began walking forward to get her bag near the forward door. I raced down the aisle of the bus in an attempt to stop her before she walked another twenty feet. She was headed straight for the exhaust of the APU.

The APU was located in the left wheel well. The jet exhaust exited from a hole in the fuselage a few feet above the ground. My guess is that the exhaust speed was a few hundred miles an hour and the temperature was probably a few hundred degrees. She was going to walk unawares right into it.

I charged out of the bus at top speed, waving my arms and shouting for her to stop, although I knew she couldn't hear me. The APU is an unbelievably loud piece of equipment, so loud that if I had shouted directly into her ear, she probably would not have heard me. All of the teachers had been given earplugs before the flight; maybe she still had hers in because of the loud noise. In any case, she was just focused on picking up her bag and probably was disoriented by all the noise as well as the totally unfamiliar, scary location she was in. I knew my only hope of saving her from injury was to get to her before she reached the APU exhaust. I was running as fast as I could to grab her; I thought I would be successful in getting to her just before she reached the exhaust. She then glanced over her left shoulder, saw me running at full speed, and for some reason started to run.

She ran right into the exhaust, which probably hit her in the right thigh. She was only about a foot from where the exhaust exited the plane, insufficient distance to cool the temperature or slow the velocity. If she had been walking, she might have sensed the hot air and stopped before getting into the center of the exhaust, but because she was running, she took the full brunt of the core. The blast moved her about eight or ten feet to her left before she began tumbling—scraping and bruising herself on the pavement. Eventually, she lay—in a daze—about twenty feet from where she started. I was with her immediately and dragged her, on her butt, out of the range of the hot gas. At that distance, the exhaust was greatly dissipated, but it was still an uncomfortable place to be. I was concerned not only that she had broken something but that she might also have been burned by the hot gas. In just a few seconds, people surrounded us—the other schoolteachers had seen the entire scenario, as well as crewmembers and ground personnel in the area.

Initially, the woman was confused and did not know what had happened, because it was so sudden. The teachers had been briefed to wear jeans or slacks for the flight, and she was wearing a long sleeved shirt; both of those things gave her a lot of protection. She had no burns, and she didn't even realize that she had been in contact with the hot exhaust.

She had scrapes and bruises, but nothing that would not heal in a week or two. We were both lucky there were not more serious injuries.

I'm often asked if I have ever had to parachute out of an aircraft. My grandson Jake, when he was thirteen, and my great-nephew Noah asked me that. The answer is no. I was trained in the use of the ejection seat for the aircraft I flew while I was in pilot training; thankfully, I never had to use it. If I ever had to put on a parachute and bail out of one of the multi-engine military aircraft that I flew, I would not have hesitated for a second. The decision to bail out meant that the conditions within the aircraft were hazardous to my life, and my best chance for my survival was to get out. Why hesitate?

I did have a terrific experience, which included descending in a parachute from five hundred feet, when I attended Sea Survival School near Homestead Air Force Base, south of Miami. The school lasted one week and taught me what would be necessary to survive in the ocean in case I ever had to bail out or ditch. Some of the training was in a classroom, but a large portion of it took place either in a large swimming pool or in the salt water of Biscayne Bay.

The training was extensive. I learned, and had to demonstrate, such things as how to get out from under a sinking parachute if it landed directly on top of me and was pulling me under and how to keep from getting pulled under the water if my parachute did not collapse when I hit the water but remained inflated in the wind, dragging me across the surface of the ocean. For this last lesson, I was pulled behind a boat and took a pretty big gulp of seawater before I was able to get my body into the hydroplane position and disconnect the parachute riser, collapsing the chute. The highlight of the entire week was the last day, which I spent by myself in a one-man life raft. I used the survival equipment to make fresh drinking water, practiced alerting a passing ship or plane with a signal mirror, and basically learned how to survive in the ocean by myself. I wasn't just dropped off a boat with a life raft and told to survive; I got into the water the most realistic way: from a parachute descent.

I was on a small ship with a flat, unobstructed top deck, like a mini–aircraft carrier. Over my flying clothes, I wore a life preserver and a parachute harness with everything attached, just as if I had bailed out over the ocean. The outfit included a survival kit and a one-man life raft. I was attached to a parasail, which was attached to a small towboat. When the towboat in front of me began moving, I began running across the deck. I was airborne after about ten steps and was hanging, in my parachute harness, supported aloft by the parasail. As the tow boat increased speed and let out line, I rose to a height of five hundred feet.

The instructors in the towboat let me enjoy the view for a short while and then waved a flag, which was the signal to release myself from the line attached at my chest. Once I disconnected, my forward motion ceased, and I began descending. During the descent, I had to prepare myself for the water landing and review the steps necessary to inflate my flotation equipment and separate myself from the parasail. There was a safety boat near my touchdown location, with rescue swimmers standing by. Throughout the entire week the instructors were watchful to prevent any injury; however, swallowing salt water was my problem, not theirs.

I inflated my life vest and my one-man life raft. The blue-green water in southern Florida in December was warm, and

I sat in the bottom of the life raft and relaxed for a minute, thinking about how the entire ride had been easy and fun. I signaled to the safety boat that I was okay, and they left the area. I was on my own.

There's always the possibility of sharks, and we were instructed to use the shark repellant, if we needed to. It was readily available, hanging from the bottom of my parachute harness. The repellant was an intense, dark purple sea dye that would dye the water and restrict the shark's vision, preventing an attack—I hoped. I was expecting the life raft to be full of water when I climbed into it; what I didn't expect was that my shark repellant would be open and the raft would be full of purple water. I immediately found the faulty container and threw it overboard, but not before getting undiluted dye on my hands. Next, I located my survival kit and found the collapsible bucket. I bailed out the purple water and used a sponge to dry the inside of the raft—luckily for me. I learned later that the graduation gift from the instructors to each of the students was a faulty sea dye container. Anyone who sat in the purple water instead of bailing out the raft as we'd been instructed was dyed purple from bellybutton to toes for the next few weeks. I only had purple hands; they had purple everything.

The next question (but you already know the answer) is whether I have ever had anyone injured on my plane. The answer is yes; the school teacher who ran into the APU exhaust was injured. But there are a few other injuries that I'll tell you about. One serious injury occurred to a flight attendant during taxi in a TWA Lockheed 1011 at JFK. I was the first officer and was not taxiing, but I would not fault the other pilot, who had to stop that very big plane a little faster than normal.

You might think the flight attendant fell when the brakes were applied and the aircraft came to a sudden stop. That's a common enough occurrence, but this accident was different. The flight attendants have a physically demanding job, standing for hours at a time while serving the passengers; but that's only a small part of it. The most physical part of their duties was to push the heavy carts, loaded with food and drinks, through the aisle. The carts were loaded by the commissary workers before the passengers boarded the aircraft. They stowed the carts in the galleys, to be taken out later by the flight attendants, when it was time to feed the passengers. I would guess that the carts weighed over a hundred pounds; they were on wheels, so they could roll in the passenger aisle.

The carts have a locking system to secure them in their storage location in the galley; there's also a latch on the door of the storage cabinet. When the aircraft brakes were applied aggressively during our taxi to the runway the cart flew forward, out of its storage position. The locking device holding the cart in place had not been properly secured, and the cabinet door was open. There was a double error. The cart slammed into the flight attendant, pinning her against the front of the galley, causing serious crushing injuries. We had to taxi back to the gate and have her transported to a hospital.

There was only one passenger in first class on our short hop from New York to Pittsburgh in a 727, the sports announcer Howard Cosell. If you are too young to remember him or did not follow sports, he had a peculiar and distinctive speaking voice, somewhere between a wood rasp and a foghorn. And. He. Would. Pause. After. Every. Word.

I have not flown into the Pittsburgh Airport for many years, and my memory may be failing, but I think we landed on runway 27. That means we landed to the west, on a heading of 270 degrees. The terminal building was at the landing end of the runway, so we had to reverse direction and taxi the entire length of the runway to get back to the terminal and our gate. There were no intersections, just a mile of straight taxiway, and it looked like a drag strip.

Jay was the captain; and he was really moving down the long taxiway, about as fast as I have ever taxied. I was the flight engineer, and after landing I had a number of things to accomplish in preparation for shutting down the engines. So I wasn't looking outside. The first officer also had things to do, so I guess he was not looking out of the windows, either. In the middle of my checklist, I sensed we were moving rapidly, and I glanced outside to see how fast we were taxiing. I saw a maintenance truck on the right side of the narrow taxiway, and the two maintenance personnel were frantically signaling us to slow down and move to the left. They thought that we were going to hit the truck with the right wing; I thought that we were going to hit the truck with the right wing; I have no idea what Jay was thinking. But he wasn't slowing down.

I shouted at him that we were going to hit the truck, and he clamped on the brakes. The anti-skid system that is now on most cars was initially developed for the aviation industry and was installed on the 727; we probably went into a full anti-skid stop. The 727 also had a nose wheel braking system that was deactivated by TWA in later years because it was never used, but we used that automatic nose brake system that day. It was the kind of stop I'd made in the C-130 when landing on the shortest runways, applying maximum braking and letting the automatic systems do what they were designed to do: stop the aircraft in the shortest distance. I have never been on a commercial aircraft that stopped as suddenly as we stopped that day. The two maintenance workers, who had parked the truck in wrong place, were so sure that we were going to hit the truck at high speed that they dove down the embankment on the far side of the truck, to get away from what they thought was an imminent collision. After we stopped, the truck was so close to our right wing that I couldn't see it from my flight engineer's position; I had to get out of my seat and press my head against the side cockpit window and look aft to see it. We stopped only a few feet from hitting the truck.

I assume that Howard Cosell, seated in the second row of first class on the right side, must have unfastened his seatbelt after landing, in preparation for getting off the aircraft when we reached the gate. The sudden stop propelled him forward, out of his seat and onto the floor. He was sitting with his butt on the floor, and his feet wedged under the seat in front of him; he couldn't get himself out. The flight attendants had to assist him in getting out of the unusual position and back into his seat. He didn't have to be told why we'd stopped so short; he could see the truck right outside of his window. When we reached the gate, he was the first passenger in line to get out. He stuck his head through the open cockpit door and said to me, "I. Didn't. Know. You. Could. Stop. So. Short." The moral to the story is that you may not understand the reason for all of the rules and regulations; but if you keep your seat belt fastened when the sign is on, you will be much safer.

Jay bought me a lobster dinner that evening in the best restaurant in town for saving his rear end. If I had hesitated an eighth of a second before shouting to him to stop, we would have hit the truck.

I'm often asked, "Have you ever been hit by lightning?" The answer is yes; I have been hit by lightning—well, my plane has been—about half a dozen times. One time I was hit twice, about ten seconds apart, while in a holding pattern, waiting to land at LaGuardia. It was always a terrifying few moments until I realized that the flash and bang were a lightning strike and that we were still flying and still in one piece.

I was in a Lockheed 1011, which I believe was the largest aircraft authorized to use LaGuardia at the time. The runways extend into the waters of Flushing Bay and the East River and are supported by pilings sunk into the bottom. The L-1011, which weighed slightly less than half a million pounds, was too heavy to be supported by the portion of the runway over the water; it had numerous restrictions concerning maximum weight and taxi procedures.

A thunderstorm was over the field. We decided to enter a holding pattern and wait until the weather improved before landing on the short runways. As soon as we arrived at the holding fix, we got our first lightning strike. Just as I was recovering from the fright of the first lightning strike, we had a second one. Immediately, I informed ATC that we wanted to hold in a different location; the holding fix was probably right under a small thunderstorm.

The bottom line is that, to the best of my knowledge, lightning has never injured anyone on an aircraft. Scary? Yes.

Very dangerous to the aircraft? No. I say not very dangerous, because it might cause minor damage to the structure of the aircraft. One time when I had a lightning strike, it caused the anti-collision light to fall off; another time, I had a small hole in the radome, in the very front of the plane; but I never got more than minor damage. Aircraft are designed with static dispensers that disperse the electrical charge, keeping the aircraft and passengers safe.

It was summertime at Willow Grove Air Reserve Facility, Pennsylvania, where I was a reservist for twelve years. I was preparing to fly a training flight, which I did once or twice a week, on my days off from the airline. My crew was at their stations in the plane, preparing to taxi after starting the engines, but the crew chief, who was not going to fly with us on the two-and-a-half-hour flight, was outside, talking to me through the intercom. His job was to remain outside and watch the engines during the engine start, remove any outside equipment in preparation for taxi, and do a dozen other outside chores.

The late afternoon was hot and humid, typical for a summer day. There were a few cumulus clouds in the area that could cause a rain shower at any time, but there was nothing around that looked like a thunderstorm. If there were no thunderstorms in the area, there was no reason to expect lightning.

We had already removed all of the ground wires that kept the airplane and the surrounding ramp at the same electrical charge and prevented static electric arcing between the airplane and the ground. The crew chief was hooked to the aircraft with a headset plugged into the front of the plane so that he could speak to me on the intercom. During those hazardous few moments, before he disconnected his headset, there was a lightning strike somewhere behind the aircraft. There was a flash of light and an instantaneous crash of the thunder. The crew chief, whom I could see out of the windshield, was lying unconscious on the asphalt.

I immediately called the control tower for emergency assistance, describing to them what had occurred. A few of my crewmembers ran out of plane and went to the crew chief's assistance. They had to ensure that he was breathing on his own, which he was. In a short time, professional assistance was on the scene. They transported him to the medical facility on the base, where he regained consciousness and it was determined that he had no permanent injury.

After reviewing the incident, we concluded that the lightning must have electrically charged the ground in the vicinity of the aircraft. When we disconnected the ground wires, the aircraft had no way to equalize the charge with the ground, because of the rubber tires. The path of least resistance to balance the charge was through the crew chief's feet to his head, through his headset that was over his ears, and then along the electrical cord to the aircraft. The electrical charge went through the crew chief's heart and brain and was powerful enough to cause him to lose consciousness, fortunately without killing him. He was also lucky not to have been burned near his feet or in the vicinity of the headset. His only problem was headaches, which persisted for a while; but they eventually stopped.

I have worn reading glasses since I was forty-five. Someone seeing me take out my glasses might comment they were under the impression pilots had to have perfect eyesight. Is this true? The basic answer is that when I was accepted to Air Force pilot training, and then when I was screened by TWA, they selected the individuals who had the best medical qualifications. One of the criteria was near-perfect eyesight, which was easily obtainable in the applicants in their twenties. If they'd been selecting applicants in their fifties, no one would have been selected, because almost everyone at that age wears glasses.

I once asked my FAA medical examiner, while he was checking my eyes during one of my mandatory physicals, why I'd been required to have perfect eyes years before, but the FAA was now satisfied if glasses corrected my now fifty-year-old eyes. He told me that poor eyes in a youngster were a possible indication of other conditions in the body that might cause problems in later years; therefore, why not select what the statistics told them would be the strongest pilot.

Since almost everyone begins to have vision problems around their mid-forties, and pilots are no exception, almost all older pilots wear eyeglasses. The need for eyeglasses caused unique problems for me, especially when flying the final approach and landing. If they were designed to improve my distant vision, focusing on the runway, for example, they would not work when I had to scan the dials on the instrument panel. Pilots had to devise workarounds for this problem. Some wore multiple pairs of glasses on strings around their neck, constantly changing the pair they needed to look through. Some pilots had tri-focal lenses specially made so that they could have near vision for the instrument panel in front of them and for the panel over their head, with lenses for distant vision in the center of the eyeglasses, for looking out of the windscreen. I solved my problem by having two pair of bifocals specially made for landing; one pair were sunglasses for the daytime, and the other were clear, for nighttime landings. The upper part of the lenses were ground for focusing at a distance so that I could see the runway; the lower portion was for the instruments and had a focal length of three feet. I had the dividing line between the upper and lower sections placed exactly where my vision crossed the top of the glare shield, so that I only had to move my eyes when making the outside–inside scan; I didn't have to move my head.

When I was a youngster in the cockpit, the conversation was about girls and finances, with a few dirty jokes. When I was an old man in the cockpit, the conversation was about eyeglasses, plus the same dirty jokes I'd heard years before.

The question I'm most frequently asked concerns turbulence and takes many different forms, all leading to the same thing. Everyone hates turbulence, and they judge the quality of the flight by the amount of turbulence received. It is really unfair for a passenger to judge an airline or the skill of the pilot, by how comfortable the flight was. To make a fair judgment, it would be necessary to compare your flight with others at the same altitude, at the same time, and with the same type of aircraft. Some people think that the pilot is God, but I was never able to control the normal turbulence that occurred in the atmosphere. All that I could do was to use my knowledge and experience in an attempt to avoid turbulence; sometimes I was successful and sometimes I failed.

I remember one cross-country flight from Los Angeles to JFK in particular. After landing, I commented to one of the other pilots that it was one of the least turbulent flights I'd ever had. My statement to him was, "We didn't have a ripple for the entire trip." Walking through the terminal, I recognized a middle-aged woman who had been one of our passengers. She was being welcomed home by a man, probably her husband. I just happened to walk past when he kissed her cheek and asked her how the flight was. I was amazed when she responded that she'd been bounced around for the past five hours and that she would never fly TWA again. They say that beauty is in the eyes of the beholder, and I thought it was a beautiful flight.

Turbulence at altitude might be caused by many different phenomena; I will give you a short lesson on two of them: the jet stream and thunderstorms. A jet stream is a band of high velocity wind flowing through the upper atmosphere; it is similar to a river meandering through the countryside. A jet stream close to the cruising altitude of my aircraft might have winds well above one hundred miles per hour, causing uncomfortable turbulence. When I experienced turbulence caused by a jet stream, I would attempt to change altitude to avoid the worst choppiness and provide the passengers with the best possible ride.

Another type of turbulence is caused by thunderstorms— massive storms that can be dangerous to any aircraft. A pilot avoids thunderstorms by using the weather radar in the cockpit. Pilots are not permitted to fly into a thunderstorm, but sometimes there is turbulence in the clear air surrounding the storm. To avoid thunderstorm turbulence, I would not change altitude, as I would have done for jet stream turbulence; instead, I would deviate horizontally around where I thought there might be some up or down motion of the atmosphere. The horizontal distance I would maintain from a thunderstorm was a judgment call, and I relied on my years of experience in the cockpit, using such factors as the severity of the storm and my altitude.

Turbulence is just as uncomfortable for the pilot as for you, and he is doing his utmost for your comfort and safety. A few times when I have been in a sudden severe updraft or downdraft, I thought it might have caused some damage; but after a maintenance inspection when I landed, there was never any damage found.

You've heard pilots tell the passengers to keep their seat belts fastened while they are sitting in their seats. I always keep mine loosely fastened, and I advise you to do the same. If you sense that there is turbulence, I recommend that you tighten your seat belt right away, to keep you firmly in your seat. If you do not have your seat belt fastened and the aircraft suddenly moves downward only about three feet, you are going to fly upward, out of your seat, and hit your head on the cabin ceiling. If you do not break your neck when you hit the ceiling, your next maneuver is that you are going to fall the few feet back down, and if you don't land squarely back into your seat, you'll probably break something else. For your safety, and the safety of those around you, keep your seat belt fastened whenever you are in your seat, even if the seat belt sign is not illuminated.

I was flying a military C-130 at a few thousand feet on an evening training flight, and, as was typical, there were a few extra crewmembers on board the aircraft. I was flying practice instrument approaches and had flown the same pattern about half a dozen times. While waiting for me to finish my practice session, the extra pilot was not in a seat with his seat belt fastened; he was resting, lying on the floor on my left side, between my seat and left wall of the cockpit.

I had been around the traffic pattern a number of times, with no turbulence and no indication that there might be any, when I flew into a sudden downdraft. The aircraft probably moved downward less than ten feet, but it was enough to lift the resting pilot off the floor and slam him into the curve where the side of the cockpit transitions to the top. I watched him move up and bounce off the ceiling directly over my left shoulder. I knew what was going to happen next: he was going to land on top of me. I reacted without thinking, because it happened so rapidly; I leaned to my right, to prevent his injuring me. It was exactly the correct move to make. When he came down, he landed on my left shoulder and arm, slid off my left armrest, and back to the floor, where he'd started. If I had not leaned to my right, he probably would have landed on my head and shoulder; he could have broken my neck.

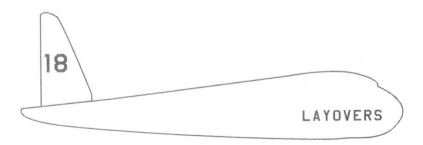

18

LAYOVERS

THE BEST PART of my job was the interesting places I flew to, especially when the layover was long enough to do what the tourists did. I had the opportunity to stay in some wonderful hotels, eat in some of the most interesting restaurants, and play tourist for days at a time. Without the layovers, the job would have become routine. Boring.

For a while in the late 1960s, I was getting to Wake Island on a regular basis while crossing the Pacific. The island was initially developed by Pan Am as a layover location for their flying boats, which island-hopped across the Pacific Ocean, much as I did during the Vietnam War. Early in World War II, the Japanese captured the island after a fierce defense by the US Marines, assisted by the Pan Am employees based there. I began reading about the island; and during my layovers, I would walk to the locations described in the books. There were still remains of the fortifications from the war, and it was a thrill to be able to stand on the same beach where the

Marines had been twenty-five years before, while I envisioned the enemy invasion force on the horizon.

I walked the beach alone, searching for relics, and soon realized that there were unusual collectibles to be found. Besides seashells, I used to pick up the purple spines of the sea urchins common to the area and began collecting little colored glass balls that would occasionally wash up on the beach. When I asked about the one-and-a-quarter-inch colored glass balls, I was told Japanese fishermen used them as floats for their fishing nets. I considered them a treasure because they were so unusual, and I still have some of them, mementos of a few terrifying moments I had trying to get one floating in the surf. It was bobbing in the waves, never making it to shore but moving parallel to the beach about ten or fifteen feet out from where I was walking. I was afraid that the surf would carry it away from the beach, so I decided to step into the water to get it.

I was wearing shorts and beach shoes. I took my wallet out of my pocket and placed it on the dry sand, thinking I was being more careful than I needed to be. I never really expected the water to wet my shorts if I timed the small waves properly. I stepped into the water from the safety of the deserted beach and immediately realized the sandy bottom was unstable. I was in the water just above my ankles, so I was not concerned for my safety. I thought about the "No Swimming" signs posted along the beach, but I was not going swimming. So I was not violating any rules. I had no idea why the signs were posted; I assumed it was because the beaches were desolate and there was no one available in case of an emergency.

I was still about five feet from the float but just couldn't get to it, so I decided I would have to get my shorts slightly wet.

I took another few steps into the deeper water and grabbed the ball, but just then my footing disappeared. I was no longer standing on the sand that made up the bottom of the Pacific Ocean; I was in the sand. I lost my balance because there was no firm support under my feet; in few seconds, I was gulping salt water and didn't know what was happening to me. I tried to walk out of the surf but couldn't find anything to walk on, even though the water was only a few feet deep. I could feel the sand around my calves and thighs, but it was like being in a vat of Jell-O with no bottom. I was being pulled rapidly down and out by the undertow. Between that and the shock of an unexpected mouthful of salt water, I panicked, which didn't do me any good.

A strong rip current just a few feet from the shore had liquefied the sand under my feet, making it impossible for me to stand up and walk back to the dry beach, which was now about thirty feet away. I was terrified of being dragged away from the beach in the rip current. When I realized that it was impossible to walk out of my predicament, I wiggled my feet out of the shifting sand and began swimming as hard as I could in the sand and water mix. I did not stop swimming, for fear of being pulled back out, until I was hitting hard sand with my hands, then I crawled on all fours to the safety of the dry beach; exhausted and scared. I never did get the glass ball I coveted.

When my seniority permitted, I enjoyed flying a Boeing 747 on the nonstop flight from St. Louis to Honolulu. We had twenty-four hours on the ground; and I would get up early in the morning to walk to the top of Diamond Head, the volcanic cone on the east end of Waikiki Beach. The walk up the side and down into the caldera, through tunnels and rocky paths, took a few hours. After eating a substantial brunch, I would return to the layover hotel and be tired enough to get a few hours of sleep, so I'd be rested for the all-night flight back to St. Louis.

When I was flying to San Juan, I took my snorkeling equipment to the beachfront hotel and left it with the bell captain, so I didn't have to drag it back and forth every trip. I did the same thing with my ski equipment for my winter flights from JFK to Seattle and Portland, where we had thirty-three-hour layovers. The long layovers always provided opportunities for great entertainment and were the best part of the job.

On long layovers, I have often rented a car or hired a car and driver to get away from the city and visit a remote tourist destination. This was common on layovers in Israel, where I would land at Lod International Airport and lay over at the beachfront Hilton hotel in Tel Aviv. I sometimes visited one of the famous destinations on the other side of the small country, only a few hours away: Jerusalem, Bethlehem, Jericho, the Dead Sea, or Masada.

I was traveling with Dennis Cox and his wife Kappy. We had five days off and had taken great pains to plan our driving trip to a Club Med resort near Hurghada, Egypt, on the Red Sea. The tiny stick-shift rental car, a ten-year-old Fiat, was the best of the dozen or so vehicles available to us when we began our trip from the Sheraton Hotel on the outskirts of Cairo. The car was one of the tiny, older models with space for four cramped people; we were pretty crowded, even though there were only three of us. For a trip of seven hundred miles through remote desert, we needed supplies for a few days.

We packed the rear left seat with food, a few small tools, the flashlights we carried in our flight kits, and most important of all, several cases of bottled water.

We had no idea what we were getting into, and we were concerned about two things. First, we didn't want to get sick from the food or water; Kappy and I had both recently recovered from stomach problems (we had eaten something not suitable for our delicate American stomachs); and we didn't want to be that miserable ever again. Second, we were concerned about running out of gas. Our road map indicated the locations of the petrol stations, and they were about a hundred miles apart. The gas pump symbol on the map became a standard joke with us, because there were no stations of the type we were accustomed to back home. After not finding the first gas pump, we were concerned about the possibility of missing the second one; so we stopped at the only building we'd seen in the last twenty miles, looking for someone to indicate where we could get some gas. In our search for a person to talk to, we found a single gas pump behind the building, hidden from the road; there was no sign indicating gas, no indication of anyone in the area, and certainly no electricity. We pumped the gas by cranking the handle! From then on, when the map indicated gas, we searched for the only building for miles around; the gas pump was always in the rear. Once we learned how the system worked, we were okay for the remainder of the trip.

We started in Cairo and drove east about a hundred miles to the narrow waterway that makes up the southern portion of the Suez Canal. Then we drove south, on the only paved road in that part of the country, along the Gulf of Suez and the Red Sea. We reached Club Med after dark, so all we did was eat and make arrangements for a mechanic to come the next day to make the car repairs we needed to continue our journey. We were at the only location we'd seen all day with a large enough population to warrant having an auto mechanic; luckily for us, the old Fiat had held together until we reached it.

Club Med was great, because of its location right on the Red Sea; the entertainment revolved around water activities. Never have I been to a location with a greater abundance of fish, which were readily visible in the remarkably clear water. We were the only English-speaking guests for the few nights we were there; nearly everyone spoke French and Arabic, so we relied mostly on what I call pointy-talky. The staff was pleasant, and we had a wonderful few days.

We departed before sunup after the third night; we'd made the choice to drive south about fifty miles, in the wrong direction to get home, to get to the only east–west road since we left Suez. We didn't want to drive home the same way we came; instead, we planned to make a big circle by heading west to the Nile, then driving north in the Nile valley, back to Cairo. It was a four hundred mile trip, which we planned to do in one day; Dennis and I had to fly the following morning. We had misjudged how difficult the drive would be, because up to this point, we'd seen another vehicle only every half hour, and that was usually a long-haul, eighteen-wheel truck. When we reached the Nile, the road passed through the main street of every town along the river. They were spaced only a few miles apart and we were slowed down to the speed of the bicycle, donkey cart, or camel that was invariably in front of us. Most of the population of Egypt is concentrated in the northern part of the Nile valley, and we traveled right through it.

We were unable to read any of the road signs, since they were all in Arabic. Our map indicated one prominent two-lane road along the west side of the river, but occasionally, we had a routing decision to make. Soon we learned the trick for choosing which road to take. There was an enormous amount of truck traffic along the north–south road, and all we had to do was follow the trucks; if they were headed north, they were all going to Cairo, and they knew the route. The few times we realized there was no longer any truck traffic, we backtracked to the main road, but this usually only caused a few minutes of delay.

By the middle of the afternoon, we were exhausted. We must have gotten off the main road, because it was about twenty minutes since we'd seen trucks. The cultivated area along the Nile extended a few miles from the river, and the road we were traveling went through fields of grain. There was no other traffic on the road nor were there any buildings or people—only our old Fiat and the unending grain fields on both sides. We were pretty sure we were on a spur parallel to the main route and we would probably come to a crossroad that would connect with the highway. We were way behind our planned schedule and decided to continue straight ahead instead of doubling back.

After driving another ten miles, we discovered why there was no other traffic using the road. We came to a small tributary of the Nile where the bridge was washed out, making it impossible for us to continue. We had probably passed a sign in Arabic informing us of the closed road; but we'd ignored it, just as we'd ignored hundreds of other signs we couldn't read. This was a depressing situation! Doubling back meant the loss of about an hour, and we still had a few hundred miles to drive.

Before reversing our course, we decided to pull out the map to determine if there might be an alternative solution.

The only vehicle we'd seen in the last half hour then pulled alongside our car, and the driver actually spoke a little English. He appeared surprised that the bridge was out and told us that he knew a shortcut. If we followed him, he would lead us to the main road to Cairo. We both turned our cars around and backtracked a few hundred feet; he made a left turn off the paved road and drove into the grain field, on a tractor path.

Dennis was driving, and I asked him to stop and not follow the car in front of us. We were isolated from the rest of the outside world, and the entire episode of someone coming to our rescue at exactly the right moment seemed to me to be too much of a coincidence. There was also the fact that the man didn't know that the bridge was washed out, but he did know exactly where there was a path to follow through the enormous field. I was concerned for our safety, concealed from view as we were by the seven-foot-high grain. I was envisioning a land pirate with a gang of cutthroats waiting to board our vehicle, with cutlasses drawn, once we were out of view of the paved road.

Our new best friend was waving his arm out of his car window, indicating that we should follow him into the field.

Dennis and Kappy were intrepid travelers and voted me down. We followed him into the field, scraping the high grain with both sides of the small car, unable to see anything other than grain and the dust from the car fifty feet in front of us. When we had driven for about a mile, I was expecting to come upon the main road back to Cairo, which the three of us assumed was at the far end of the enormous field. One time our guide stopped and walked back to our car to reassure us that we were doing the correct thing by following him. But he was really lost, himself. By speaking to us, he was trying to gain the confidence to continue. It was shortly after this brief conversation that we came to a clearing along the path where there were about two dozen people lying around. They were as surprised to see us as we were to see them. They didn't have cutlasses, as I had envisioned; they had hoes and shovels. They were taking a break from their work of maintaining the irrigation ditch that brought Nile water into the field. Without irrigation from the Nile, we would have been driving in a barren desert, like the majority of the country.

Our guide spoke with the workers for quite a while, their hands pointing in different directions, obviously providing our lost guide with various options. Finally, we were driving again, on a similar path, at a forty-five degree angle to the one we had been on, when we came to a single railroad track. Both cars stopped. The workers had informed our guide that the main road was about five kilometers away. Maybe I was naïve when I asked him which way. He pointed down the tracks.

I looked at the shiny rails and knew that this was not an abandoned stretch of track. The three of us had a little powwow, and I pointed out that we were about to drive on an active train track for five kilometers. Dennis said that if a train came along, we would simply drive off the track into the grain. This time we all decided to follow our guide, driving on the cross ties instead of turning back through the huge field by ourselves. At first, because of the jarring ride, we tried driving with one wheel on the railroad ties and one off to reduce the bouncing, but after much trial and error, we finally settled on an acceptable speed with both wheels bouncing on the cross ties.

When we came to a small railroad bridge, crossing what was probably the same Nile tributary that was once spanned by the washed out automobile bridge, we stopped the car and listened for any sounds of a train before bumping the length of the bridge, a few hundred feet.

We also drove for a quarter of a mile through an area where the train track was cut about eight feet lower than the surrounding field. Because of the steep embankment on each side of the track, had we encountered a train it would have been impossible to clear the track; we planned to exit the car and climb the bank to save our butts; to hell with the Fiat.

We did end up on the main road to Cairo at an intersection with an American-style gas station that had its own convenience store selling packaged food and drinks. Either the bumping along or the fear activated all of our kidneys. It was great to finally find a real bathroom, even though it was only a truck stop. We didn't get back to Cairo until after midnight and had to fly early the next morning. After rolling out of bed, when I had my first cup of coffee, I still had a smile on my face. Bouncing on the railroad cross-ties was a once in a lifetime opportunity for me.

I was sitting in a pew in Saint Patrick's Cathedral in New York City, relaxing for a few minutes away from the hustle and bustle of Fifth Avenue, when I noticed a woman sitting near me in the rear of the cathedral who appeared to be resting, just as I was. She was wearing an Egyptian cartouche around her neck, and I asked her if she had been to Egypt. She was an American who had married an Egyptian and lived in Giza, right next to the pyramids. Her husband's family owned one of the two stables where tourists can rent horses for riding in the desert surrounding the pyramids. I told her I knew the stable and knew exactly where she lived. When she heard that I would be in Cairo in a few weeks, she invited me to her home for a guided tour of the pyramids.

She'd met her husband while she was a student in Egypt, studying the ancient history of the country; she described herself as an Egyptologist. When I visited, I met and had tea with her extended family; then I had a tour of the family's multistory home and the horse stable. When she went to change her clothes for my private tour of the pyramids, I waited in her American-style kitchen in front of a large picture window with an unobstructed view of the Great Pyramid, about a hundred yards away. Her home was the sixth floor of the family compound. The parents and their children each inhabited one level of the family home, and there were provisions being made for a seventh floor to be constructed when the youngest child was married. My new friend had married into a prominent and wealthy family; and they treated me, their American guest, royally.

When she came back into the kitchen, she was wearing a flowing, long-sleeved white gown made of many layers of light, airy, gauzy material. When I told her that my last visit to the Great Pyramid was a difficult and dirty walk, she said we were going to a smaller pyramid, her favorite.

My host was not just an Egyptologist but a spiritual Egyptologist. She had been doing a lot of spiritual work in the small pyramid. She felt that she was getting close to the spirit of the pharaoh, who had been dead for twenty-five hundred years; and she wanted to show me how she was doing it. We walked to the pyramid in five minutes. She was a local guide and was let in for free; I had to pay less than an Egyptian pound. There were no other tourists around, just as she'd expected; they were all at the Great Pyramid of Khufu. We had the entire burial chamber to ourselves, which was what she needed to make contact with pharaoh's spirit.

We were in the very center of the pyramid, in a chamber the size of a large living room, where the king had once laid in his sarcophagus. Everything relating to the king had been removed long ago by grave robbers, and the only object was the bottom of an empty stone coffin near the far end of the dimly lit room. Perhaps it was the original sarcophagus; or, perhaps it had recently been placed there to give tourists a feel for where the pharaoh had been interred. She intended to

The author playing tourist in front of the pyramids, Giza, Egypt

conjure up the spirit of the king, and she could only do so if I believed, deeply enough, that it was possible. She was serious about what she was attempting to accomplish, and I didn't want to do or say anything that would break the spell.

I stood in a dark corner near the only entrance to the burial chamber while she went to the far end and stood behind the empty sarcophagus. She was standing in the only light in the chamber—what appeared to be a small spotlight that was meant to be focused on the stone casket but missed the casket and was shining directly on her. She had chosen the spot and her clothing carefully. She glowed in her white galabiah. She had already told me about the research she had done on conjuring spirits, and it primarily consisted of chanting Om. When she began it was eerie, and if I were a believer, I could have been led into a different dimension.

She began by wailing, "Aaaaahooooohmmmmm," her voice harmonizing with the echo bouncing off the stone walls. As she varied the volume and tone, she waved her arms in rhythm with her a cappella, monosyllable chant, "aAAHOOOooohm." The loose material of her sleeves, slowly moving up and down, looked like wings. She looked and sounded like a ghost in a third-rate horror movie.

I heard hesitant footsteps coming up the tunnel to the chamber we were in. She was in her own trance, with her eyes closed; and I don't believe she was having any success getting the pharaoh's spirit to appear. She never heard or saw the two little kids who stuck their heads into the chamber to see what was making the noise. I didn't move or dare to breathe, and the kids didn't see me in the darkness, though I was standing right next to them. They peeked into the chamber. They appeared to be dark-skinned and might have been Egyptians, but they were dressed like a young American boy and girl. I couldn't tell for sure, because ten-year-olds from all over the world scream in terror the same way. They took one look at the singing ghost and were out of there in an instant, running and screaming their way back down the tunnel. I'll bet their parents, waiting outside, didn't believe a word the kids told them.

Flying to Europe from New York, we almost always arrived early in the morning after working through the night. Our layovers were in downtown hotels, and usually the crew had to go through Customs and Immigration before boarding the bus. But in some countries the bus would meet us at the plane, and we'd get our clearance to enter the country while on the bus. The bus ride to the hotel was sometimes the toughest part of the entire trip for me. The ride took an hour or more, and if we were stuck in the morning rush hour traffic, it could take even longer. Most of the crewmembers would be sound asleep by the time we were off the airport property. I was usually one of the sleepers, but I was exhausted and felt abused that I was getting a restless sleep on a bus instead of in bed in a comfortable hotel.

We had just arrived at Heathrow, in London. The bus driver was taking an unusual route off the airport property, so I was looking out the window and enjoying the scenery. Some of the crewmembers were already dozing when a funny and attractive black flight attendant, in an excited tone of voice, announced that around the next bend in the road we'd see a monument dedicated to her new boyfriend. Everyone was awake and looking out the windows on the right side, wondering what in the world she was talking about.

When she began squealing, "There it is, there it is!" I saw a monument dedicated to the first aviators to fly across the Atlantic. Their flight, from Newfoundland to Ireland preceded Charles Lindbergh's first solo flight. I still didn't understand why she was saying that it was a monument to her boyfriend until I looked a second time at the names of the two men who'd made the historic flight. Their last names were prominently inscribed: ALCOCK AND BROWN.

I loved my layovers in Paris, and over the years the TWA crews stayed in a few different hotels, in different parts of the city. The typical layover was more than twenty-four hours, so I had time to do some of the things that make Paris one of the most popular tourist destinations in the world. The underground subway system, the Metro, goes all over the city; it is fast and user friendly. But when I was laying over at the Hotel Concorde la Fayette, I was close enough to walk to the Arc de Triomphe and then down the Champs-Élysées toward the Louvre. I always walked on the left side of the street, because that was the side with the sidewalk cafés; I enjoyed watching the people watchers seated at the outside café tables.

One beautiful Sunday afternoon, I decided to people watch, along with the thousands of Parisians doing the same thing. When I had walked for several blocks and was coming to the end of the sidewalk cafés, I saw a large group of people across the boulevard. This was unusual, because there were no cafés in that usually quiet area, so I crossed the street to investigate. There were dozens of people of all ages, men and women, milling around and having a grand time, laughing and frolicking in the sun. I noticed that all of them were keeping their eyes on the women walking down the boulevard.

The center of interest was a large open grating across the entire width of the broad sidewalk. The grating was the outlet for the warm air exhausted from the Metro station under the boulevard. The quantity and velocity of air exiting the grate suggested the presence of large exhaust fans; it was sufficient to blow the skirts of any unsuspecting women over their heads; to the great amusement of the crowd. Unlike Marilyn Monroe, famously photographed standing on a similar grate, the women strolling down the Champs-Élysées were not posing for a photographer.

Any woman strolling down the boulevard wearing a skirt could see it was dangerous for her to step onto the grate. Very few actually stepped on it, and those who did immediately backed off and continued their stroll on the side of the grating.

A group of about twenty well rehearsed Parisians picked out attractive women who were wearing the proper clothing, especially pleated skirts, as they approached the grate. They gradually surrounded her with various couples holding hands, a man and woman pushing a baby carriage, and a few teenagers doing their thing. As she got closer to the grating, more of these Sunday afternoon strollers gathered, until she was on a crowded sidewalk, everyone traveling in her direction, and she was in the center of the good-natured crowd. They were blocking her view of the grating while herding her directly over its center.

When she took her first step onto the grate, the crowd around her rapidly moved away, leaving her standing alone and fighting to keep her skirt in place. All of this was accompanied by the hoots and cheers of the crowd, including some who were photographing the event. Some women were greatly upset by the nasty prank, but some were amused and laughed off the crowd, understanding that they had been duped.

One woman drew an extended applause from the crowd. She was wearing a white pleated summer skirt made of light cotton; it immediately flew above her head, displaying her beautiful legs up to her belly button. She initially attempted to force her skirt down but eventually quit trying to be modest. She raised her hands and pirouetted to the far end of the grate, where she curtsied to the crowd, then danced away. She was beautiful, graceful, and wearing exactly the right clothing for pleasing the crowd. The photographers loved her, the crowd loved her, and I fell in love with her, even though I never saw her face. I have always wondered if she showed up every Sunday and was just another actor, putting on her own show; she was too perfect.

I was on the Champs-Élysées a few months later; the sidewalk was redesigned and the grate was gone.

I had flown many flights to Greece, Turkey, Cypress, and Crete, supporting the remote military outposts in the eastern Mediterranean. I usually flew out of Athens, where I stayed in one of the tourist hotels on the beach near the airport. A nice room with a balcony overlooking the Mediterranean was one dollar and twenty-five cents a night and a grilled half-chicken dinner with salad, french fries, and a glass of retsina was seventy-five cents in an outdoor café. The price was about twenty percent of what it would have cost me in the states.

In Turkey we used to get to seven locations all over the country, on a mission we called the Turkey Trot; and I complained to the scheduling officer that in Greece I only saw Athens. He assigned me to a NATO exercise in the northern part of Greece, near Thessaloniki.

I flew airdrop missions every day for three days, slept in a tent, and ate mess hall food before I finally got a day off. Bob Pargin and I couldn't wait to get to town and get some real Greek food. When we got off the bus it was lunch time.

Thessaloniki was a fairly large city; the bus terminal was in an area with many restaurants. We looked in a few and decided on one that was more upscale than the others and had many diners. Our philosophy was the more people eating, the better the food; price was not an issue. We got a small table and immediately had a problem: there was no English menu and no one spoke any English.

I was accustomed to this situation. I began searching the other nearby tables for something I recognized, and I would then point it out to the waiter. It always worked. This time nothing looked familiar and I was worried that I might get something too sour for my taste; they use a lot of vinegar and lemon juice in Greece. I left my table and began walking around the restaurant, observing the various dishes. When the waiter realized what I was doing he took me by the arm to the rear room to select from the seafood display case. Bob followed.

Thessaloniki is on the water, and their primary source of protein is from the Mediterranean. But that doesn't mean fish—at least as we know it. The seafood case was filled with many varieties of shellfish, squid, cuttlefish, and all types of funny-looking fish I didn't recognize. They had only one very large whole fish. It was the only thing in the case that looked like a fish, and we both decided we would try it. We tried to ask how they would prepare our portion with no success.

We waited at the table for a long time, but were kept amused by a few of the other patrons who visited our table and tried to make us feel welcome in their city. They chatted with us, but it was all Greek to me. Finally, our lunch arrived. It was wheeled out on a cart containing the largest platter I have ever seen. Hanging over both ends of the oval platter was the twenty-pound fish. When we finished eating, we only had a three-inch-diameter hole in the side of the monster and we didn't even dig down to the bone. That was one expensive lunch, even at 1967 prices in Greece.

When I was a flight engineer on the Boeing 727, I flew domestic flights and had many layovers in airport hotels or the typical full-service motels located at exits on the interstate. Not very glamorous! If I had a long layover, one of more than sixteen hours, my pilot's contract specified that TWA had to provide a room in a downtown hotel.

One layover in Columbus, Ohio, was in an attractive downtown hotel with an indoor swimming pool just inside the main entrance door. Surrounding the pool were the hotel front desk on one side, and seating for the casual restaurant and cocktail lounge on the other side.

I got to the hotel about nine in the evening. Since I wouldn't be leaving until the next afternoon, I decided to go downstairs and get a sandwich and a beer instead of getting room service and watching TV. When I got down to the pool area, a few of the other crewmembers were there, so I joined them. We pushed two wire tables together in the corner of the bar area, about ten feet from the edge of the pool, and I ordered a sandwich from the cocktail waitress. On the other side of the bar was a group of young men that I assumed were not staying in the hotel but probably were locals, from the Columbus area. It was a Saturday night, and they were downing a large quantity of beer.

At about eleven o'clock there were just three of us left at my table—one flight attendant, the first officer, and me. I was getting ready to leave and go to bed. There were still many tables occupied with hotel guests.

The local beer drinkers were getting rowdy, and they threw the cocktail waitress into the swimming pool. A well dressed, middle-aged couple sitting next to them were obviously distressed with their boorish behavior and got up to leave the lounge. The man, who was dressed in a suit, said something to the ringleader of the group and was promptly thrown into the pool with the waitress. When the woman went to the assistance of her husband, she was also shoved into the water.

I had a decision to make about intervening. I made a comment to my table mate about doing something. We decided it would be a mistake. As pilots on a layover, we were extremely vulnerable to criticism for our actions; and we were, of course, in a bar. I was fearful the press would make the most of a story about two TWA pilots in a scuffle in a cocktail lounge: the newspaper readers love drunken pilot stories. I was always cognizant that I had to protect myself and my company from undesirable publicity.

There were about half a dozen beer drinkers, but just two of them were the aggressors. They were both standing up, challenging the seated patrons, to see if anyone else had any comments about their behavior. Two guys got up to leave the pool area without making any comment to the beer drinkers; but after a minor scuffle, they both went for a swim. We were captives, and it appeared that anyone who attempted to leave was going to get a bath. Next, the two locals walked around the tables, selecting their next targets at random; together they pulled their victims to the edge of the pool and threw them in. It reminded me of the plains of Africa where the lions would select the weakest animal in the herd for their evening meal.

I was lucky during the selection process. The first officer I was sitting with was a huge, powerfully built man and was not easily intimidated. I was sitting on one side of him and the flight attendant was on the other side. We pulled our chairs close to him, and he placed his arms on the backs of each of our chairs, giving the bullies the impression that we were under his wing. Twice during the selection process, as they pranced around the pool looking for their next victim, they started for me but backed away because of the size of my flying partner. We were sitting in a corner with planters at our backs, which gave us added protection, and there were a few other people still dry. No one in the bar surrounding the pool was safe, and anyone who attempted to get away was the next victim.

As I mentioned before, the pool was at the entrance to the hotel, and to get to the front desk you had to walk around the pool, right through the danger area. The first outside guests to enter the hotel after the incident began were two men dressed in tuxedoes who, I assumed, were returning to the hotel after attending a wedding. Before they knew what hit them, they became the center of interest, and in ten seconds they were in the pool. I was correct when I assumed that they'd been at a wedding; following them, the bride entered the lobby wearing her white gown. Her hands were full with the long train, which she was trying to keep off the floor. When she saw part of her wedding party in the pool and the two aggressors heading for her, she began pleading with them to be reasonable – it was, after all, probably the biggest day of her life, and she was still wearing her beautiful wedding dress and had her hair piled high on her head. I was amazed that they had the gall to throw her into the pool along with the groom, who was right behind her. It appeared that there was no limit to their lust for carnage.

I felt extremely sorry for the new bride. When she went for her swim, she was in water over her head, and either she could not swim or the weight of the multiple layers of material pulled her under. For whatever reason, she was not capable of staying on the surface, and was assisted by her new husband and the two members of the wedding party in the tuxedoes, who jumped back in to help her. Without assistance, she would not have survived. The two jerks never paid any attention to the fact that they almost caused someone to drown, and that it took three men to finally get her out of the pool.

Their next-to-last confrontation was with the slight, female hotel manager, who stood nose-to-nose with the ringleader, reading him the riot act. He seemed to be intimidated by her, but when his assistant grabbed her from behind, he readily helped in throwing her into the pool over the wedding party, who were still trying to get the crying, almost incapacitated, bride out of the pool. The final confrontation was the two beer drinkers versus the Columbus Police Department, and the beer drinkers lost. I think the hotel manager called the police before her attempt to stop the carnage. My group was the only one of the occupied tables that did not have someone who got wet that evening. My guess would be that fifteen people went for a swim before the cops came.

19

LANDING GEAR PROBLEMS

HAVE HAD A number of landing gear problems and
they are always very interesting because of the critical
function provided by that massive and complex piece
of equipment. The first emergency occurred while I was a
TWA first officer on the Lockheed 1011, during a flight from
St. Louis to New York. I was in the right seat, and flying in
the left seat was a TWA flight manager, Ed Duenes. He had
just been transferred to JFK. I had never seen nor heard of
him before, and soon I learned that he was not only new to
the New York base but also new to the airplane. Ed told me
that he had fewer than one hundred hours in the L-1011 and
was required, therefore, to make all of the takeoffs and landings; he was a "restricted pilot." Normally, the captain would
fly one leg and I would fly the next one, which was my only
fun in a somewhat boring job, so I was not very happy. I was
soon to find out that he had far fewer than a hundred hours:
he was just out of L-1011 school.

We were on the end of the eastbound runway waiting for
takeoff clearance, and I was thinking about the thousands
of times I had done exactly the same thing in the many dif-

ferent types of aircraft I had flown, for practically all of my adult life. Takeoffs and landings became routine while I was flying for TWA, because all of the equipment was so reliable; emergencies were a rare occurrence, especially compared to my experiences in the Air Force.

When we received our takeoff clearance from the tower and completed the pre-takeoff checklist, Ed pushed up the three throttles, and I could feel the acceleration as the engines spun up to the pre-computed power we would use to get off the ground. I made the mandatory airspeed calls as we kept gaining speed; when I called "rotate," indicating that we were at minimum flying speed and it was time to lift off, he slowly pulled the nose of the plane up to seventeen degrees, and we were flying. The rotation takes a few seconds to complete and is what provides the lift to allow the plane to fly up and off the ground. If it is done too rapidly, the lower aft portion of the plane may strike the runway, and if it is at too great an angle, you lose efficiency and it scares the passengers because the nose is so high.

His rotation was perfect, and a few seconds after lifting off, about a hundred feet in the air, he called for "gear up." I reached forward and slightly to my left to the landing gear lever, and raised it to the up position, as I had done thousands of times before. This time, though, there was the loudest explosion and shock to the structure of the aircraft that I have ever experienced. My initial thought was that we had a midair collision with another plane. It felt as if we'd hit something with the part of our plane that was directly under the cockpit, right under my feet. The shock to our huge aircraft was so violent that I immediately looked out of the window to see what we had hit, but I saw nothing unusual.

The three of us in the cockpit each said something expressing our fear and surprise at so violent a jolt to one of the largest aircraft. Our maximum takeoff weight was close to half a million pounds, and, occasionally, violent things would occur in the rear of the aircraft which we had no knowledge of because we couldn't feel it in the cockpit. This time it was different, and after the "holy shit, what was that?" which reflexively came from each of us, I immediately asked the tower if we'd hit something on takeoff. They said they did not see anything unusual, but no one in the tower had been directly watching the L-1011 as we took off.

I checked the annunciator panel for any warning lights indicating failed systems, and I got my first clue to the extent of our problem; we had numerous failures. I checked the engine instruments and was happy to see that they were all operating and that we didn't have an engine problem. I then checked our flight conditions and was greatly relieved to see that we were still climbing normally. My entire scan of our situation took less than five seconds, and I deduced that we were flying okay but that some sort of explosion or other violent action had taken place that had caused a number of systems to fail. It was very early into my observation when a flight attendant called from the rear of the aircraft; I could tell by her voice that she was scared. She told me that she was in the rear of the cabin and was putting a deadheading pilot on the interphone. He was sitting near her jump seat, in the last row of seats, and was more capable than she was of providing a technical description of what they had experienced. I knew him and had been chatting with him before the flight. He said that he thought we'd hit something right after rotation, and that it struck right under his seat. This new piece of information was confusing to me since I thought it was under my seat in the front of the plane.

All three of us in the cockpit admitted that we had no idea what had occurred. In situations like this, your first thoughts are to get back on the ground as soon as possible, but we all agreed that it would be a mistake in this situation. The plane was flying normally, so we decided to climb to a few thousand feet, declare an emergency with the control tower, and analyze our conditions before making any rash decisions. Ed, in the left seat acknowledged that he was the inexperienced pilot in the cockpit, and he gave me job of solving the problem. We used the TWA procedure of isolating the two pilots; one flies and one handles the emergency. Rick Carlson, the flight engineer, was a buddy of mine, and we had flown together many times. It was now up to the two of us to devise a plan for getting us safely on the ground.

Everyone now had a job to do. The flight attendants were calming the passengers and preparing them for an emergency landing. The deadheading pilot was assisting the flight attendants and staying in touch with me, to provide any assistance I requested. The airplane was being flown from the left seat by Ed, and I was exactly in the position where I could do the most good: solving the puzzle. I had flown for two years as an L-1011 flight engineer, the same as Rick; also, I had a type rating in the aircraft, meaning that I was trained in the left seat and had taken an FAA check ride certifying my qualification, the same as the captain. Rick and I began discussing every warning light illuminated on the annunciator panel, trying to figure out how they were interrelated and what had to be done first. We were doing triage—determining what required immediate action, what we had to accomplish at some point before landing, and what we could defer until after we landed.

Our major concerns were that we had lost our most important hydraulic system, because of a loss of fluid, and would not be able to get it back; we had the left main landing gear down, but the right main gear and the nose gear were both retracted. What concerned me the most was the indication of a bleed air leak on the aft left side of the aircraft, which could cause a fire, if we didn't already have one, and could be very hazardous to the passengers. Bleed air is hot pressurized air from the engines used as a power supply to operate equipment; it can be very dangerous if not contained. The three of us all agreed that the problem was on the left side of the plane, and we decided to make a low, slow pass near the control tower with the hope that maybe they could see any damage by viewing the plane through binoculars. They confirmed that the left main landing gear was down, when it should have been up, and there was hydraulic fluid flowing back from the area. They also told us that we were missing a landing gear door for the left main gear. We concluded that some violent event had blown the door off and had caused the failure of many of our components and systems.

My greatest and most immediate concern was for the safety of the passengers, so I had the deadheading pilot search the rear portion of the passenger compartment for indications of a fire under the floor, aft of the wing; this was where we had the overheat indications. I advised him to feel the floor for indications of heat and to look for smoke that might be seeping from the lower portions of the plane into the passenger compartment. He reported back that he'd found nothing except scared passengers. It was slowly becoming obvious to us that what had occurred was an explosion somewhere near where I was asking him to search for an indication of a fire. The passengers sitting in that location might have been only a few feet away from the explosion, so they must have received a much greater shock wave than I did in the cockpit, and some of them were terrified.

Next, Rick and I ran the checklist for the loss of the hydraulic system and reviewed what additional systems had been affected. We had dual hydraulic systems for our flight controls, to provide redundancy in just such a situation; and we still had one operating. So our flight controls would not cause a problem for landing. Our leading edge and trailing edge flaps were still in the takeoff position, and this was also okay for landing. It appeared that we would have to lower the right main and the nose landing gears with the alternate—mechanical—system, because the hydraulic system for lowering them was the one that had failed. The three of us then spent a few minutes reviewing the condition of our brakes and the nose wheel steering, which were necessary once we were on the ground. Next, we discussed how we would handle the situation if the left main gear collapsed when we landed, which was a possibility. We were all still very much concerned about the continuing overheat condition and the chance that we may have a fire. We then decided it was time to land. We still had no idea what had caused the problem.

I had never actually lowered the landing gear on an L-1011 using the alternate procedure, but I had done it in the flight simulator. Rick, also. The gear had to be lowered using a hand crank, which was inserted into a fitting located in the cockpit floor. Rick moved his seat away from the location, giving himself room to work, and opened the cover over the emergency gear extension mechanism. We slowed to our landing gear extension speed, and I began reading the procedure aloud from the manual. As I read a step, including all of the caution and warning notes, Rick would perform the step, with me checking his actions. The system worked perfectly, and we finally had the landing gear in the down position; however, there was still one additional step: we had to verify that the landing gear was not only extended, but was also locked in the down position. Rick, assisted by the deadheading pilot, had to view each landing gear through a viewing lens to verify that it was really safe to land and that the gear wouldn't collapse.

Once we had the landing gear down and had completed about ten checklists, we made an uneventful landing. We'd been in the air for over an hour. When I finally made it out of the jetway and into the gate area, I was surprised to see television crews and reporters, all attempting to get to a crewmember for a story. Most probably a passenger, using a cell phone, had contacted someone on the ground; and the word spread to the local news media. They heard there might be a juicy story brewing a few thousand feet above the airport and they had time to get there before we landed. I guess they were disappointed that we were able to get the landing gear down before landing, but they were still going to try to make it newsworthy. I politely refused to be interviewed, following the guidance I had previously been given by both the Air Line Pilots Association (the pilots' union) and TWA.

Then I went onto the ramp to look at the left side of the plane, under the wing, where a dozen maintenance personnel and supervisors were gathered. I was shocked to see the great amount of damage that we'd had to the wheel well, the landing gear doors, and the hydraulic mechanism that lowers the left main gear. The landing gear on a heavyweight aircraft is a massive piece of equipment, designed to support hundreds of thousands of pounds without failing, even during an occasional bone-jarringly bad landing. In flight, the landing gear is raised into the wheel well and is then covered by doors, to reduce the aerodynamic drag. The raising and lowering of the gear, and the opening and closing of the doors, is accomplished hydraulically. Also in the wheel well are many other pieces of equipment that are not related to the landing gear; it serves as an accessible storage area for the other systems. At first glance, it looked as if a bomb had exploded in the wheel well.

When I had placed the landing gear handle to the up position a few seconds after takeoff, the three-thousand-pound-per-square-inch hydraulic system went to work, sending high pressure fluid to the largest hydraulic cylinder on the aircraft, the one that raises the landing gear. The steel hydraulic cylinder failed under the enormous pressure and exploded. I'd never heard of this type of failure before, but it is possible for any piece of equipment to fail. The landing gear is secured to the main structure of the aircraft, and when the cylinder exploded it sent a shock wave throughout the airframe, making it feel to me that the problem was right under the cockpit, and to the pilot in the last row of passenger seats that it was right under his seat. It was an extremely violent explosion, and did a lot of damage within the wheel well. The hydraulic fluid for the system was lost almost immediately, making that system unusable and coating the entire wheel well with the blood-red fluid. The explosion blew off one of the landing gear doors and damaged the system that might have indicated an overheat condition in that part of the airplane. The fire that I was so concerned about when we were in flight never existed; it was the result of the false indications from the damaged system.

I was flying with Danny (not his real name) on a Boeing 707, in my early days with TWA. I was an instructor flight engineer; my job was to train other engineers in the 707 flight simulators at JFK. As an instructor, I would fly just once a month in order to maintain my own proficiency; I had selected a flight from JFK to Shannon, Ireland, where we'd spend one hour on the ground, then work a short leg to Dublin.

Danny was a big, rough-looking man, and he played the part well. He was the type of man who would get into bar fights after having a few beers, and because of his overbearing personality, he frequently had verbal clashes with the other crewmembers. The first time I ever flew with him, on the first day of a five-day European trip, he had an argument with the flight attendants; as a result, they refused to set foot in the cockpit. Every time one of the three of us in the cockpit wanted a cup of coffee or a meal, the flight attendants would prepare it and then call me on the interphone to come out and pick it up. Since I was the junior man and closest to the door, I had to get out of my seat, pick it up from the galley, and take it to the cockpit. This was a pain in the butt and made it a pretty miserable five-day trip for me. In later years, after the company had sent Danny for psychological help, he carried with him a copy of a letter that the psychiatrist had sent to TWA, certifying that he was, in fact, sane. At the beginning of every flight, while holding the letter in his hand, he would announce to us that he was not insane and the letter was his proof. Then he would challenge the rest of us: "Can anyone else prove they are not crazy?"

I'd always managed to maintain a working relationship with Danny, but on this flight, he and the first officer were not talking. We had just landed at Shannon, and the two of them had not said one word, other than what was absolutely necessary, during the all-night Atlantic crossing. The first officer just sat with his arms crossed and his lips closed, never assisting or volunteering information. At Shannon, we received our routine servicing, which consisted of fuel and engine oil; in addition, I requested that maintenance service our hydraulic system.

Shortly after the takeoff from Shannon, I had the first indication that we had a problem. We slowly began to lose pressure on one of our hydraulic systems, and I began going through the checklist by myself, since neither one of the pilots seemed to be interested in our problem. Before I had completed the checklist procedure, the same thing occurred on a second hydraulic system! I never had two hydraulic systems fail, one right after the other, and I attempted to get assistance from Danny. I wanted to know if he had any knowledge about what was happening, as it was very unusual. He told me that he was the pilot and would fly the airplane, and he didn't want to be bothered with my problems. The first officer was just an observer.

What was occurring in the hydraulic systems was the mixing of the two different types of hydraulic fluid and heating the mixture from their normal use. This caused the mixed fluid to thicken and the systems to fail. All of the hydraulic reservoirs had been serviced with the wrong type of fluid at

Shannon, I later learned. By the time we were in the air for about thirty minutes, we had total failure of all of the hydraulics on the 707. On each of the systems operated by hydraulics, there were backup methods to operate the equipment. The first backup was a different hydraulic system. With no hydraulic power at all on the aircraft, we had to go to the last backup, which was to be used only as a last resort, when all else failed. The systems without hydraulic power were: all of the flight controls, the leading edge and trailing edge flaps, the spoilers, the landing gear, the brakes, and the nose wheel steering. If it was necessary for flight, it was operating on the backup to the backup. We had a serious situation, and I had a captain in the left seat who was enraged that this could be happening to him.

Danny cursed, shouted, and threatened. At one point I thought he was going to slap me with the back of his hand. I was attempting to run numerous checklists and procedures, and I desperately needed assistance. I was a simulator instructor and was familiar with each individual problem; but with a dozen things occurring at the same time, I was overloaded; I needed the assistance of at least one of the pilots. Anytime I attempted to coordinate an action with Danny he became more agitated with me and would not allow the first officer to interact with me. I do not recall the first officer doing or saying anything during the entire short flight. I have never been in a cockpit where the crew did not work together to solve a problem, other than this time. Not only did we not work together but Danny was placing roadblocks in the way of my solving the problem.

Two things occurred that were very distressing to me: the first was in flight, after I'd manually lowered the landing gear with the hand crank system. One of the things that had to be checked was whether or not the nose gear was in the down and locked position. There was no indication within the cockpit that would guarantee that the nose gear would not collapse when we landed. I informed Danny that I had to open a hatch in the floor of the cockpit and go down into the bowels of the aircraft, the area immediately under the cockpit, which was loaded with high-voltage electrical equipment, thousands of wires, and dozens of motors. It was a cramped, dirty place, and no one would be happy to go there, but, as the flight engineer, it was my responsibility to check that the gear was safely down. Danny did not respond when I told him that I was going to leave the seat and make the check. I put on my leather gloves, took my flashlight and a small tool kit that I carried with me, opened the floor hatch, and climbed down the ladder to get under the cockpit floor. There was a light in the compartment, but I had to squeeze to the very front of the aircraft to make the gear check, and it was too dark to see; I had to rely on my flashlight. It was a fairly dangerous, uncomfortable, dirty place to be, because of all the operating equipment, but I managed to get myself into a position where I could see that the nose landing gear was, in fact, safely extended. As I was working my way back to the open hatch, around the wire bundles and relays, and trying not to touch anything, the open hatch was slammed closed. I'm not certain, and I never commented about it to the other pilots, but I suspect that Danny, in his rage, reached around from his position in the captain's seat and shut the hatch.

When I climbed back into my seat, I got a tongue lashing from Danny because I'd left my seat when we were going to land. I couldn't believe it! He was about five miles out, on final approach, and we would be landing in two minutes. I told him that I needed more time to finish the checklists, but he was insistent on landing the airplane, and that's what he did. Luckily, I had accomplished the absolute minimum that was necessary to have a successful landing. When we completed our landing roll, he did the second thing that greatly bothered me.

He turned off the runway and began to taxi to the gate, about a half-mile away. I informed him that with no hydraulic power, we had neither nose wheel steering nor brakes. He immediately replied that they were working, that he had done okay so far, and he was going to complete the flight by taxiing to the gate. I told him that there were one-way check valves and accumulators in both systems and there may have been some trapped hydraulic pressure allowing them to temporarily operate; however we could not rely on them to continue working. With no hydraulic systems operating, we'd have no brakes and no steering, and I told him that we would taxi into whatever might be in front of us. I then continued: "I am advising you not to taxi, and I am making my statement for both you and the voice recorder."

The voice recorder is one of the black boxes that you hear so much about, after an accident. One of the things that it records is all of the voice communication within the cockpit. I was protecting myself in case he decided to continue his attempt to taxi to the gate, just in case it resulted in a taxi accident. When I became so insistent that we not continue to taxi, he finally stopped the aircraft, and we were towed to the gate.

I am not proud of my actions that day, especially because I'd had to battle with the captain of the aircraft. At TWA, especially in the early days, the captain was only one level below God, and his authority and wisdom were not to be questioned. As the aircraft became more complex, though, it became accepted throughout the industry that one person was incapable of doing everything himself; for safety it was necessary to have the entire three-man crew working as a team. At TWA in later years, we even had classes called Crew Resource Management, attended jointly by the pilots and flight attendants, concerning the necessity of working together, especially during an emergency. Every time I attended one of those classes I would think about my emergency with Danny in command; I felt confident that of the thousands of cockpit crewmembers that TWA employed, not one would have agreed with his decision to taxi the aircraft under the conditions that existed. I think that the psychiatrist was fooled when he certified that Danny was sane.

About two years after this incident I was once again scheduled to fly with Danny and was not looking forward to it. The evening before the flight, I got a phone call from him, and he was as friendly as he could possibly be. He told me that he had been having a lot of difficulty with many of the crewmembers he had worked with, and that TWA was threatening to fire him if there was one more person who complained or refused to fly with him. He apologized for his previous confrontations with me and asked me to remind him of this phone call if he was not acting like a gentleman, either with me or any of the other crewmembers. For the next few days he did conduct himself like a gentleman, and we had a routine flight. That was my last flight with Danny, but I did hear of two taxi accidents he had after my horrible experience with him.

A few months before my last flight with TWA, the airline was in a desperate financial situation. I was a first officer on the Boeing 747, and Dick was the captain. We were flying an aircraft from JFK to St. Louis because the plane was needed for the long Honolulu flight, later in the day. We had only about one hundred passengers, and because the flight time was just slightly over two hours, we carried very little fuel. The aircraft was capable of carrying 430 passengers and flying for twelve hours. We weighed only about half of the maximum weight of three-quarters of a million pounds.

Years earlier, the airline established a policy that takeoffs would be made with a reduced power setting, if the conditions were favorable, to have the engines last a longer time between overhauls. Before every takeoff, the crew would calculate the amount of power required for a safe takeoff but had the excess power available to them, if it was required. When the new technique was initially established, Dick was against it, for various reasons. He was vocal in his opposition, and he never followed the newly established procedure. In addition, he was a proponent of adding takeoff power far more rapidly than was generally accepted.

We were taking off on one of the longest runways in the United States, almost three miles long. It was twice as long as was needed, and we were at only half of our maximum weight. There was no way the conditions could have been safer, yet the captain elected to use maximum power on all four of the engines, against TWA policy as well as common sense. He advanced the throttles to about half power; when the brakes were straining to hold the aircraft from leaping forward, he released them and rapidly advanced the throttles toward the full-power takeoff he was so fond of. We immediately had a loud and violent compressor stall on one of the engines.

A compressor stall occurs when there is not enough airflow into the engine, causing the large, rapidly spinning blades of the air compressor, on the very front of the engine, to stall; it sounds like an explosion in the engine. Sometimes it sounds like a machine gun, with numerous and rapid small bangs, but this time there was only one: a shock wave that sounded as if a cannon had been fired. We all identified it as a compressor stall, and Dick decided to continue the takeoff, which I agreed with at that moment. A second or two after the compressor stall, the aircraft immediately behind us, waiting to turn onto the runway and make the next takeoff, called the control tower to say we had blown a ten-foot panel off the engine and it was blocking the runway. We were now accelerating rapidly because Dick had applied so much power and we weighed so little. He said he was going to continue the takeoff, and I objected, as did the flight engineer. We thought we'd had a compressor stall; however, we might have had an engine explosion, and after the radio call, we knew that we had damage to the engine. The safest course of action was to stop the takeoff and have the engine looked at by maintenance. When we both objected, Dick changed his mind and began to abort the takeoff. We were only at eighty knots when he began stopping the aircraft.

An aborted takeoff from eighty knots should be no more hazardous than slowing the 747 from a fast taxi. The brakes on the sixteen main wheels are designed to stop an aircraft weighing twice as much as we weighed and moving at a much faster speed, so there should have been no problem. As with his application of power to begin the takeoff, however, Dick now applied the brakes too aggressively, in an attempt to exit the runway at a convenient taxiway.

Aircraft brakes are similar to the brakes on your car, only they are much larger. Hydraulic power squeezes a brake puck against the disc, which is rotating with the wheel. The friction between the stationary puck and the rotating disc is what slows the wheel and consequently slows the aircraft. The unwanted side effect of stopping with brakes is that the friction causes heat. In this case, on a three-mile-long runway and with a very light aircraft, beginning an abort from only eighty knots should have been a non-event; however, we had a brake overheat.

When we turned off the active runway onto the taxiway, Dick stopped the aircraft and set the parking brakes, which was a mistake. This kept the pucks in contact with the discs on all of the sixteen wheels, and the heat buildup was great enough to cause the brake pucks to melt into the discs, fusing them together and causing major damage. We could not release the parking brake, and it was impossible to taxi or to tow the aircraft. The series of errors was a direct result of the pilot violating a number of published procedures, and this fiasco cost the company a great amount of money to repair the aircraft. But this is not the end of the story.

I do not believe that the TWA captain ever understood that he was the cause of the incident because he'd violated the company's policies and procedures. I was beyond furious, a few weeks later, when I checked my company mailbox and found a copy of the letter of commendation he had received for doing such a great job during the incident.

✪

All modern large aircraft have retractable landing gear that moves into the wing or fuselage after takeoff. You probably have some idea of how the landing gear pivots, rotates, and moves into the wheel well during retraction, but the military C-130s that I flew had a landing gear that moved straight up and down, which is different from any other aircraft I have flown. The biggest problem with moving this very large structure out of the air stream during flight is getting it back down, in preparation for landing. All aircraft have back-up systems for extending the landing gear and making sure it is safe for landing, but the C-130 had a unique last-resort system that I had to use on one occasion. I had to have my crew chain the gear down before landing, using 25,000-pound tie-down chains.

The C-130 landing gear was positioned on the side of the fuselage and moved straight up and down on tracks. The problem that day was that the left main landing gear did not fully extend. Instead, it jammed about five inches from being fully down. During the last few inches of extension, steel pins fit into a receptacle, preventing the gear from pulling away from the fuselage during sideways movement on landing. When I did not get a safe gear-down indication in the cockpit, and my loadmaster had verified that the steel pins were not in the correct position, I was left with no other option than to chain the gear down. The flight engineer was my main techni-cal man, so it was his job to do, but I had the loadmaster and navigator assist him.

The procedure for chaining the landing gear down was explained on a few pages in the aircraft flight manual that we called the dash-one. We had only about two hours of fuel, so we needed to get it done fairly rapidly; it was a long and complicated procedure, and none of us on the crew had ever done it before. The team had to remove the insulation that lined the inside of the cargo compartment and then unscrew part of the side of the fuselage to make a hole exposing the landing gear strut. If there was a portion of the strut that they could not get to, the manual instructed them to use the crash ax and hack a hole in the side of the fuselage. A diagram showed them where to chop.

Once they had a hole in the side of the fuselage large enough to work in and the landing gear was exposed to the inside of the aircraft, they performed the second step of the procedure. Using the diagrams in the dash-one, they placed the chains, capable of supporting a load of twenty-five thousand pounds each, around the main strut of the defective landing gear and secured the chains to the tie-down fittings in the floor of the cargo compartment. The complex pattern of chains was designed to keep the landing gear from moving sideways, away from the fuselage, when I landed the plane.

When they had finished all of the steps in the dash-one, I told the control tower that I was finally ready to land. The control tower had briefed the emergency crew that I was having a landing gear problem, and the entire fleet of specialized vehicles was waiting for me. My crew had done a perfect job of securing the gear, and the C-130 is a very responsive aircraft. So it was easy for me to make a smooth landing. I touched down using the right main gear only, the technique I would use if there were a crosswind from the right. Once the right main gear was on the ground, I kept the aircraft moving straight down the runway and slowly lowered the left side of the aircraft. The gear was holding, so I very gently began slowing down. I planned to use almost the entire runway to stop so as not to overstrain the left gear. The emergency vehicles followed me down the runway and was instantly available if I needed them, but I didn't. I stopped the aircraft on the runway and turned it over to the maintenance men to repair. I thanked my crew for doing a good job and never spoke about the incident again, until now.

I had recently joined the Air Force Reserves because I knew they were looking for experienced C-130 pilots; they were changing aircraft from an old propeller-driven tactical assault plane to the newer turboprop C-130s. As I had previously been a C-130 instructor pilot on active duty, I was offered the job.

I attended the required training at the C-130 school and then returned to my new unit in Pennsylvania. After completing the training, all that I needed to be a fully qualified C-130 aircraft commander was a check ride from one of the squadron's check pilots. I was the new guy in the squadron, and they would consider me to be an outsider until I had proved myself worthy of their respect. It usually takes years for a pilot to become a member of the inner clique in a new squadron.

The pilot giving me the check ride was Lieutenant Colonel "Lefty" Gensler, one of the most senior pilots in the squadron. My flight engineer during the check ride was the chief of the section; between the two of them they didn't have a hundred hours in the C-130. At the time, I had a few thousand hours of flight time in the aircraft, much of it as an instructor. I think it was evident to them, from the beginning of the flight, that I was just what they were looking for when they'd hired me. If not, what occurred near the end of the flight certainly convinced them.

I handled all of the simulated emergency situations they threw at me, made a number of landings with one or two engines at idle power, simulating an engine failure, and was doing a great job on the check ride. Then we had a real hydraulic emergency. It was a complicated failure that required numerous checklists and necessitated using back-up systems for lowering the landing gear and the wing flaps. It also caused many other problems in all of the aircraft systems that used hydraulic power and was probably one the most complicated problems you could encounter on a C-130. It happened to me only two times—once on this flight and another time on one of my last flights before I left active duty, which had been just a short time before this. My recall of the previous emergency allowed me to brief the crew on the intercom of what we had facing us, the order in which I would ask for the necessary checklists, and a few tricks I had learned during my prior emergency. We then began the long process of getting the plane ready for landing, with me acting as the aircraft commander.

I passed the check ride, of course; but at the same time, I accomplished far more. The emergency came at the perfect time to establish me as a competent and knowledgeable pilot within my new squadron. If the check pilot or the flight engineer had been more experienced, they would not have relied on me, the student, to run the show during the emergency. After that flight, I not only joined the clique but I became one of the leaders. In Lefty's eyes, I could do no wrong; and, at his urging, I soon became an instructor pilot and then one of the few flight evaluators within the squadron. Without that emergency on my first check ride, I might never have risen to the level that I did within the unit. I chalk it up to luck; my prior experience was the reason I was so well prepared for that complex problem.

I HAD TWO TOTALLY different flying careers, military and civilian, and different endings to each of them. The end of my military flying came in the early 1980s, after I had given the Air Force over twenty-two years in the pilot's seat. It was my choice to stop flying; and my decision revolved around four incidents, all of which occurred within a short period.

The first reason for my decision to stop flying for the military was Red Flag. The Air Force had established an outstanding school for providing realistic air-to-air combat training for their fighter pilots. The classroom was the airspace above the Nevada desert, north of Las Vegas. The theory behind the development of the school was that a high percentage of American pilots didn't survive their first few combat missions. Once a pilot had a few missions under his belt, his chances of surviving were greatly increased. Red Flag was the name given to the operation, which provided pilots with their first realistic combat sorties in a controlled environment. Instead of dog fighting with an enemy aircraft, a non-combat-experienced pilot received his first five missions in air-to-air combat fighting other American pilots acting as the enemy. The simulated enemy pilots were trained to use the tactics employed by foreign military forces, and they flew US aircraft with performance similar to those used by other countries. The training was highly regarded by the fighter pilots and was later expanded to include other types of combat aircraft.

When Red Flag was opened to C-130 crews, I was the first to attend from my squadron. I was the mission commander of two aircraft and three crews, and each of us would receive our first five combat missions. Four of my flights were airdrop missions. I would fly at low levels, attempting to stay hidden from the enemy radar. When I reached the objective, I would drop my load of supplies, using various types of parachute drops. On each of these missions, I would have to avoid the simulated enemy forces on the ground and evade their missile attacks on my aircraft. I was shot at with simulated surface-to-air missiles (SAMs) that we called Smoky Sams. These were military-designed small rockets similar to what you see in a Fourth of July fireworks celebration. They were shot from the ground and left a smoke trail, in order to give me, in the cockpit, a visual indication that I had been spotted by the enemy and was being fired at. I had to take evasive action to avoid being shot down by the simulated missile.

The last of my five flights was a mission where three C-130s carried ammunition and fuel for a flight of A-10s, an attack aircraft. Our rendezvous point was a dry lake in northern Nevada, and I landed my C-130 on the flat and dry surface of the lake bed. When the A-10s arrived, the specialized crew I had on board my plane refueled them and replenished them with ammunition for the rapid-fire cannon they used in their primary mission, destroying enemy tanks. It was an interesting and unusual type of mission for me.

I initially considered it a routine flight. We were at low altitude and high speed, flying along the desert floor while weaving around the hills and mesas that are common in that part of Nevada. I had my entire crew looking for indications of hostile enemy action that I had to avoid. It was my third flight into the region, and I thought I was getting pretty good at evading the Smoky Sams. Instead of a hostile attack from the ground, as had happened on my previous flights, there was an enemy fighter aircraft waiting for me. He was about three thousand feet, searching for me while I was twisting my way along a dry river bed. I saw him above and right in front of me, about a mile away. My C-130 was painted with camouflage paint, and he was silhouetted against the bright, clear sky; I saw him before he saw me. Once he found me, there was no doubt that he was going to give me a thrill. It took him only a short time to get behind me, the one place where I could not see him and where he could use his guns most efficiently.

When he was behind me, the only way I could determine his location was by using my crewmembers, who were searching for him by looking out the side windows; we didn't have rearward-facing windows. I had two choices that would let my crew see directly behind the plane: I could either turn or swing the tail of the plane to the side by stepping on one of the rudder pedals. When the enemy was in gunnery position behind my C-130, I had to take evasive action to prevent him from shooting me down. As he gained his position behind me, I could tell how I was doing by the pitch of my helpers' voices in the rear, telling me on the intercom where he was.

I was turning as sharply as I could, in my four-engine cargo plane, attempting to evade the gunfire from the sleek fighter aircraft. I tried putting the hills between me and him, but every report I received from the rear about his position was an octave higher than the one before, and he managed to stay right with me, in firing position, most of the time. After about a minute of my not being able to shake him, I decided to use my ability to fly much slower than he was capable of flying; I dropped my landing gear and wing flaps and pulled my nose up to slow down even more. I watched him whiz by me and wiggle his wings in a "goodbye." It was the most thrilling one minute of my entire life. It was a thrill only because I knew it was a training mission and he was a friendly American pilot; I was in no danger.

That evening, during the debriefing, I met the pilot of the simulated enemy aircraft and saw the video he had taken of our encounter. He didn't shoot me down once; he shot me down a dozen times and was playing with me while I was fighting for my life. He was the cat; I was the mouse; and I'd been eaten alive. I realized that in a real combat situation, with my C-130 against a modern fighter plane, I didn't have one chance in a hundred of surviving. Red Flag did for me exactly what it was designed to do: it taught me how to survive. It placed the seed in my brain that if I continued to fly the C-130 and found myself in a real situation similar to what I had encountered during my thrilling one minute at Red Flag, that I would be the loser. I would not survive the encounter. That was the first time I ever considered getting out of Air Force flying.

In the early 1980s, the Air Force began intensive training on surviving an attack with chemical, biological, or radioactive weapons. I received classroom training, and then I had one flight of two hours for which I wore a hazardous materials (hazmat) suit. This is the protective equipment I would need should my aircraft become contaminated by one of these weapons of mass destruction. Hazmat suits were seen being worn by investigators during the anthrax contamination incidents a few years ago.

In the classroom, I was told that one particle from a nerve gas mist, in contact with any part of my body, would be fatal. What they didn't tell me was that it was almost impossible to wear the protective clothing and still fly the aircraft. I was the first one in my squadron to test the clothing in flight. I suited up and flew from the left seat; Jack Chambers climbed into the right seat, not wearing the suit, and we took off. By the time we'd completed the checklists and were off the ground, I was in a pool of sweat. I had almost no visibility and was basically as miserable as I have ever been in an aircraft. I flew for a while, with Jack doing everything I was incapable of accomplishing, and then we changed positions. We landed, and I took off the protective clothing. It was Jack's turn to suit up and get into the left seat. I have never been so glad to give up the aircraft commander's seat to another pilot as I was that day.

For the second time, I found myself making a mental note that I didn't want to be in the position of having to do my job under those conditions. The seed had been planted in the back of my head that my job of being a combat-ready C-130 pilot was maybe a little more hazardous than I was willing to accept; and if the opportunity arose, I would strongly consider giving up military flying.

A short time later, I was promoted from lieutenant colonel to colonel, and my primary position changed from piloting aircraft to that of a desk jockey. Since my new position was an office job, anytime I flew, I was required by regulations to have an instructor pilot in the right seat. The assumption was that I would not be flying enough to maintain full proficiency, so, in the interest of safety, all colonels and generals were required to have the assistance of an instructor pilot. This really turned me off and was the third condition pushing me toward telling the Air Force that I wanted to quit flying.

The final blow to my Air Force flying career occurred at the Sugarbush ski resort in Vermont. I had just gotten off the lift at the top of the mountain on a bitterly cold morning. There was about six inches of new powder on the ground, and practically no one had used the slope before me. It was my first run of the day, and I wanted to carve my own path through the virgin snow, so I began skiing on the side of the trail. I was only thirty seconds into my run when my right ski went into, instead of over, a small ridge of snow, where it hit something solid. I fell directly over the front of my skis and heard the crack of the anterior cruciate ligament, in my right knee, tearing away from the bone to which it had been connected up to that point in my life. That injury resulted in months of wearing a cast on my right leg from the tip of my toes to my hip, then a brace for a few months, and, finally, a great deal of physical therapy.

When I was finally capable of returning to the cockpit, I decided that this would be a good time to say goodbye to my military flying career. I remained on active duty for an additional few years in a non-flying position, and then I was assigned to a job in the Pentagon for one year as a reservist, before I retired from the Air Force. I view the end of my military career the same way that General Douglas MacArthur described his retirement, in his farewell speech to Congress, when he quoted the words from an old Army ballad: "Old soldiers never die; they just fade away." That's how I ended my almost thirty years of Air Force active duty and reserve time: I just faded away.

My last landing came a few days before my sixtieth birthday. In the United States, the law prohibits an airline pilot from working once he is sixty years old. That law may be changed in the near future to extend the age to the sixty-five-years old that many other countries are using. My last landing was from the right seat of a TWA Boeing 747 after an all-night flight to St. Louis from Honolulu. Similar to the end of my Air Force career, I just faded away and never looked back. I consider that I began my aviation career the day that I entered New York University, where I earned my degree as an aeronautical engineer; and it ended when I retired from TWA, almost forty-five years later. I have had my hours of boredom and my moments of terror, but I wouldn't trade my life with anyone's.

A NOTE ON THE TYPE

THE TEXT OF this book is set in Century Old Style. American printer Thomas Low DeVinne designed Century for *The Century* magazine in 1894. Linn Boyd Benton, of American Type Founders, was the inventor of a punchcutting machine that greatly speeded up the production of new typefaces in the Machine Age; he cut the face on his new machine.

L.B. Benton's son, Morris Fuller Benton, became a type designer—and a prolific one. He added several faces to the Century family over the first decade of the twentieth century, culminating in Century Old Style.

The face was a common one in the books Bob Kline read as a boy and young man. The retro feel of the pages in this book depends partly on the choice of typeface and partly on subtly simulating the look of high-quality mechanical typesetting of the first half of the twentieth century.

The display face used for chapter titles and running heads is a specialty font used by model makers. It is based on one of the lettering styles used by the US Air Force for aircraft identification markings.

The chapter initials are based on the old TWA logo and were designed for this book.